Contested Voices

To Rachel Lee
with love from
her grandmother
Marianne Githens

ALSO BY MARIANNE GITHENS

A Portrait of Marginality: The Political Behavior of the American Woman (1977)

Different Roles, Different Voices: Women and Politics in the United States and Europe (1994)

Abortion Politics: Public Policy in Cross-Cultural Perspective (1996)

Contested Voices

Women Immigrants in Today's World

Marianne Githens

CONTESTED VOICES
Copyright © Marianne Githens, 2013

All rights reserved.

First published in 2013 by PALGRAVE MACMILLAN® in the United States—
a division of St. Martin's Press LLC, 175 Fifth Avenue, New York, NY 10010.

Where this book is distributed in the UK, Europe and the rest of the world, this is by Palgrave Macmillan, a division of Macmillan Publishers Limited, registered in England, company number 785998, of Houndmills, Basingstoke, Hampshire RG21 6XS.

Palgrave Macmillan is the global academic imprint of the above companies and has companies and representatives throughout the world.

Palgrave® and Macmillan® are registered trademarks in the United States, the United Kingdom, Europe and other countries.

ISBN-13: 978-0-312-24020-2
ISBN (Paperback): 978-0-312-24041-7

Library of Congress Cataloging-in-Publication Data is available from the Library of Congress.

A catalogue record of the book is available from the British Library.

Design by Scribe Inc.

First edition: May 2013

10 9 8 7 6 5 4 3 2 1

For Anne Marie Noland, who as a young woman from West Meath, Ireland, immigrated to the United States in 1885. Her success in creating a viable social identity in her new homeland has served as an inspiration to succeeding generations of her family.

Contents

Preface	ix
Acknowledgments	xi
1 Introduction: Structure and Agency: The Discourse on Immigration	1
SECTION 1 DEFINING WOMEN IMMIGRANTS AND REFUGEES: THE OFFICIAL VOICE: PROTOCOLS, LAWS, AND POLICIES	19
2 From Laissez-Faire to Regulation: The Emergence of Immigration Policy	21
3 Government Policies and Women Immigrants: Establishing Conditions and Constructing Identities	39
4 Fleeing Calamity, Seeking Asylum: Women and Refugee Policy	63
SECTION 2 MANAGING SOCIAL PRESSURES IN THE WORKPLACE AND COMMUNITY	87
5 Ethnic Communities and the Construction of Identity	89
6 Between Dependence and Independence: Immigrant Women in the Work Force	109
SECTION 3 IMMIGRANT WOMEN SPEAKING FOR THEMSELVES	139
7 Listening to Immigrant Women (Re)Creating Their Own Social Identity	141
Selected Bibliography	159
Index	167

Preface

Current debates about immigration in Europe, the United States, and Canada have tended to focus on issues such as legal and "illegal" immigration. When women immigrants are discussed the conversation often turns to the topic of anchor babies, the potential drain on costly social welfare benefits posed by immigrants—especially women immigrants—or the problems of cultural integration. Two critical issues, the increased feminization of immigration during the latter part of the past century and the dependency on immigrant women in the caring professions related to children and the elderly are rarely mentioned, and their significance for immigration policy is overlooked. However, the feminization of immigration and the need in Europe, the United States, and Canada for female labor in the areas of caregiving and in the service sector clearly suggest a need for immigration policies that are sensitive to these developments. In looking at current immigration policies in several European countries, the United States, and Canada, *Contested Voices* explores the impact of these policies on women and the difficulties that emerge.

Contested Voices focuses on the various pressures confronting current women immigrants. It details the pressures created by current governmental policies that are based on earlier patterns of male immigration and that reinforce notions about appropriate gender roles for women. Using both the concepts of intersectionality and the social construction of identity the book is able to consider a woman's responses to these pressures and what role her social class, race, religion, or ethnicity play in her adjustment to her new environment and her development of a viable social identity.

In using the concepts of intersectionality and the social construction of identity, *Contested Voices* moves away from the traditional case-study approach to women immigrants. The case-study approach has been very useful, but it offers a snapshot of a specific group of women immigrants in a specific country at a particular moment in time. In contrast to the case-study approach taken by many monographs, journal articles, and textbooks, this book uses intersectionality and the social construction of identity to provide a more comparative perspective of women immigrants in several countries. In so doing it affords a more comprehensive picture of women immigrants. It enables the reader to have a clearer understanding of the impact of immigration policies in various receiving countries, the attitudes and role expectations of both the citizens in these country and the members of the women's own immigrant community in the various countries, and the implication of these for the adjustment of women immigrants and their roles in their new environment.

Many years ago *A Portrait of Marginality*, one of the earliest books on women and politics, pointed out that there is no such thing as the generic woman in politics and that race makes a difference. *Contested Voices*, in utilizing the framework of intersectionality, reaches a similar conclusion. It argues that despite the common perception that the experiences of women immigrants in adapting and adjusting to their new environment are essentially the same, there are differences. There is no such thing as the generic woman immigrant. Race, class, religion, and ethnicity influence perceptions of women immigrants in receiving countries as well as the women's perceptions of themselves. These differences shape their experiences in adapting and adjusting.

The idea of the social construction of identity has also been invaluable in allowing us to move beyond the stereotype of women immigrants as victims. Under conditions that on occasion are particularly oppressive women have often been able to exert agency. Their ability to (re)create a viable social identity that is compatible with their new life and permits them to function in very difficult circumstances and survive pressures that would limit them as a person needs to be understood and celebrated. It is also a powerful argument for the need to listen to immigrant women's voices.

Marianne Githens

Acknowledgments

Like most authors I am indebted to many people for their help, insights, advice, and patience in listening to my ongoing monologues about gender and its significance for the current debate about immigration.

In particular I am grateful to my husband, Stanley Mazer, who despite his serious illness encouraged me to persevere with this project and provided me with the support needed during the period when his own needs were so great. I am also profoundly grateful to my son, Jonathan Githens-Mazer, who read countless drafts of the manuscript and made many useful suggestions and comments. I also wish to thank Lois for letting me stay with her when I wrote some of the early chapters of *Contested Voices*.

I am also grateful to several friends in Britain who did their best to get me access to the immigrant detention centers there and also my students at Goucher College, particularly Judy Dritsis and Erica Sackin who helped me in the early stages of my research. Thanks also to my editors at Palgrave Macmillan for their patience with me.

CHAPTER 1

Introduction: Structure and Agency
The Discourse on Immigration

Immigration is a major topic of discussion today. The United States, Canada, Europe, Australia, Africa, Latin America, or Asia—it makes no difference. In the postindustrial states of Europe and North America, which receive many of today's immigrants, the media play an extensive role in publicizing various strands of the current debates. Television, radio, the Internet, blogs, and newspapers continually include stories about immigrants, undocumented "illegal" aliens, refugees, and asylum seekers. Popular magazines as well as serious journals cover the topic. There are photographs and descriptions of overcrowded refugee camps where inhabitants lack the most basic facilities, like running water and sanitation. Television and radio newscasts recount the misery of refugees in Darfur; the victims of earthquakes in Haiti, Pakistan, China, and Turkey; the devastation and dislocation following a tsunami in Indonesia; and Pakistanis and Afghanis fleeing from the Taliban. Articles depicting the plight of refugees seeking to escape from civil wars in Africa and Asia appear regularly, as do stories about immigrants who leave their home country simply to escape starvation or grinding poverty and who are trying to find a decent, stable life for themselves and their families.

Different parties are involved in these discussions. There is, of course, the general public. Their discussions and debates take place in myriad settings ranging from the family, to a church or synagogue, to a political party. Then there are the governments of both receiving and sending countries, which both influence national discussion and establish immigration policies. Immigrant communities in receiving states call attention to "the immigrant perspective" and press for its inclusion in public policy.

Each of these participants in the discussions seeks to frame the issues and influences the (re)construction of the social identity of immigrants. In conceptualizing "the immigrant" they implicitly and sometimes explicitly make certain assumptions about gender and gender roles. Government laws and policies as well as public discussion in many receiving countries are premised on a generic definition of *immigrant*, who is assumed to be a man. Such a presumption obscures the importance of the intersectionality of gender, ethnicity, and class for both immigrants and perceptions of them. This in turn affects the (re)construction of an immigrant's social identity. For women attempting to (re)construct a social identity that allows them to function in a new physical, social, economic, and political environment such an oversight has important consequences for their well-being and adjustment.

Debates about immigration and public policy regulating it reflect a diverse range of views. Some views are sympathetic. Often they highlight the desperate efforts of those trying to escape poverty or oppression in their home country. In the United States, heartbreaking tales are recounted about undocumented aliens from Central America dying from heat prostration in vans in the Arizona desert or of Haitians crowded together on homemade life rafts, and there are even reports claiming that individuals from China and the Far East have attempted to hide in the landing gear of jets in the hope of reaching the United States. Similar stories appear in the European media. In Britain people are told about Asians suffocating in trucks carrying food across the English Channel and about children trafficked into the country for work in the drug trade or prostitution. The Spanish press and television often feature stories about desperate, exploited North Africans in rubber life rafts drowning off the coast. In Europe and North America there are exposés about mail-order brides who end up in a situation amounting to little more than domestic slavery. In the Netherlands one reads about young immigrant women—many of them from Eastern Europe—forced into prostitution. Both in the United States and in Europe there are sickening accounts of sex trafficking. Heart-wrenching descriptions are given of women and young girls brought from Eastern Europe, Africa, Latin America, and Asia, sometimes bought and sold several times before they reach their final destination—a European or North American brothel.

The exploitation of undocumented farm laborers and the terrible working conditions of those employed in sweatshops and food processing plants in the United States are described in detail, as were the practices of some big box stores like Walmart, which locked up foreign workers in the store overnight to make sure that the cleaning and stock replacement was finished before the store opened the following morning. There are touching stories about foreign college-age students recruited to work during the summer months at beach or mountain resorts in the United States and then cheated out of their wages or charged exorbitant fees for their room and board. Both here and in Europe stories of overworked nannies, some on virtually 24-hour-a-day call, of chambermaids who are cynically exploited, and of women working long hours in the garment trade under unhealthy conditions and for abysmally low wages are commonplace.

Sympathetic attitudes about immigrants do not always stress the theme of them as victim, however. Some emphasize the contributions that they make to their new country. In these instances immigrants are portrayed as a breath of fresh air, as courageous, determined individuals who contribute to both the culture and economy of their new homeland. Immigrants arriving in the United States in the nineteenth and early twentieth centuries, for example, were applauded as risk takers who enriched the country through their hard work and determination to succeed. Fiction and nonfiction alike detail the bravery and success of sturdy, hardworking men and women who came and settled. The country's immigrant heritage is frequently recalled and the United States proudly referred to as a nation of immigrants, a land of opportunity where all can prosper and contribute. Similarly Canada and Australia speak of the contributions of immigrants to the growth and prosperity of their country. Refugees displaced by World Wars I and II are applauded. Their survival and resiliency in the face of concentration camps, war, and upheaval are regarded as inspirational and have come to symbolize the ultimate triumph of good over evil. More recent arrivals to the United States from the former Soviet Union, Eastern Europe, and Cuba have also been welcomed and praised for their initiative, perseverance, and desire for freedom.

Positive attitudes about immigrants, however, are counterbalanced by negative ones that underscore the dangers they pose. This is particularly true in the case of those entering illegally or those who are culturally, religiously, ethnically, or racially distinctive. Current debates about women wearing the veil and the ban on the burka provide excellent examples of this. Muslim women in traditional dress are discussed in terms of the danger they pose to Western values and women's rights. Depicted as hapless victims of male domination, they are viewed as an affront to women's efforts to free themselves from oppressive patriarchy. In Western Europe, immigrants, especially those from Islamic countries, are considered a potential threat to national security. In some contexts, such as the United States, the danger is framed in terms of drugs. Cries to close the Mexican border center on drugs coming in from Latin America. In other instances immigrants are simply considered "other"—as people who must be kept out. They are depicted as taking jobs away from citizens and jeopardizing the hard-won rights of native-born workers. Descriptions such as "illegal," "bogus asylum seekers," "global terrorists," and "economic immigrants" who are only interested in taking citizens' jobs away from them are used to conjure up a host of threatening images (Jordan and Duvell 2002). For those holding such views, immigrants are characterized as a threat, a source of disease, literally as well as figuratively, and as a serious burden on the country's financial resources, particularly its social services. Along with descriptions of immigrants as harbingers of disease, they are derided as parasites that come only to take advantage of the generous social services unavailable to them in their home country. In Germany, for example, immigrants and refugees seeking asylum have been labeled a "force that will swamp the boat," a "flood," an "influx"—comparisons that conjure up images of disease, contagion, destruction.

Similar opinions are expressed in the United States. For example, in *State of Emergency* (2006), Buchanan, a well-known political consultant who at one time sought the Republican nomination for president, argued that the United States is facing the greatest invasion in human history. He went on to claim that if immigration is not stopped America is finished as a nation. In an earlier speech he predicted that if the current pattern of immigration continued, young Americans would spend their golden years in a Third World America (2002).

While comments such as these are considered extreme by many Americans, they resonate with some who believe that immigrants constitute a real danger to both the country's cultural values and the continued use of the English language.

In the United States, as in Europe, anti-immigrant attitudes emphasize the burden immigrants place on already-overstretched social services. This is especially the case for women asylum seekers who are perceived as victims, vulnerable and having special needs (Hajdukowski-Ahmed, Khanlou, and Moussa 2008). A number of communities in the United States have proposed legislation that would eliminate social service benefits for all immigrants and in some cases deny schooling for the undocumented and their children. Some localities have even proposed eliminating benefits for legal immigrants and their children (Espenshade and Huber, 1999). Immigrant women are frequently vilified as another version of the "welfare queen" who lives on government subsidies and strains already-overtaxed social service budgets. Like "welfare mothers" they are accused of having babies simply for the sake of gaining welfare benefits for themselves and their families and citizenship for their children.

The growing numbers of asylum seekers in Europe have intensified anti-immigrant attitudes there. Accused of feigning claims of persecution simply to gain admittance and tagged "economic refugees," they are viewed with suspicion and railed against. A recent report issued by the British Department for Communities and Local Government found that some people believed that immigrants were being unfairly advantaged in terms of housing and social benefits and that ethnic minorities were "jumping the queue" to the detriment of the English working class. As a former minister of Communities and Local Government commented, the (English) working-class people living on government housing estates just don't feel that anyone is listening or speaking up for them (Summers 2009). These anti-immigrant feelings have fueled xenophobic organizations like the British National Party (BNP) and the English Defense League (EDL).

Acting on the notion that immigrants drain resources away from the native-born population, skinheads and those loosely affiliated with groups like the BNP and the EDL routinely harass and physically attack immigrants on the streets. Bullying African Caribbean and Asian immigrants has been virtually a daily occurrence in some British neighborhoods, and in some cases immigrants and their children have actually been murdered. Today Muslims are the targets. In France, Denmark, and the Netherlands, Muslims and Asians have been routinely harassed. In Germany immigrant housing has been set on fire with women and children dying in the blaze. In Italy anti-immigrant activities have intensified and serious episodes of anti-immigrant violence in southern Italy have been recently reported.

On occasion, instances of anti-immigrant violence have attracted media attention. In Britain, for example, several high-profile racially motivated murders and instances of police brutality involving African Caribbeans and Asians have received media attention and resulted in official investigations. In France attacks on North African immigrants by youthful supporters of the National Front, although quite frequent, are occasionally reported in the French press. Recent attacks on immigrants in southern Italy have also been covered in both Italian newspapers and the international press. Frequently, though, violence against immigrants is simply ignored by the authorities and goes unnoticed in the media.

Objections to immigrants center not only on the cost of providing social and health care services to them and on allegations that they exploit the welfare system, fail to pay taxes, and take jobs away from native-born citizens but also on the grounds that differences in language, culture, and religion challenge the cultural integrity and identity of the country. These differences are seen as endangering a shared national identity and undermining a common set of traditions and behavior that hold a country together. Diverse styles of dress, life-style, and even food preferences are seen as detrimental to core national values and differences that should not be tolerated. Indeed, interviews of voters in the first electoral district in Britain to cast their ballots for a member of the far right British National Party as local councilor revealed that many did so because the newly arrived immigrants cooked food that "smelled bad." Newspapers and magazine articles have reported that religious differences are often mentioned as a cause for alarm. In France, Italy, the Netherlands, Switzerland, and Denmark, the presence of Muslim immigrants has sparked a great deal of resentment and led to calls for bans on public displays of their religious beliefs, refusals to grant permits to build mosques, and, in Switzerland, to bans on minarets on mosques. In France a heated debate over the issue of Muslim women wearing the head scarf in schools centered on the claim that it violated the principle of secularism on which the state was built, and most recently a law has been passed that prohibits wearing a face veil in public, the justification being that the face veil indicated a refusal to accommodate to French culture. In Italy a bitter dispute erupted over a large, visible cross that was erected in a predominantly Muslim neighborhood. Muslim objections to the presence of such an overtly religious symbol in their community were met with the response that the cross was necessary to ensure the preeminence of Italian, Christian values. In Britain battles have raged over the observance of Sharia Law in Muslim communities, and government ministers have proposed legislation requiring Muslim women to be photographed without the veil, despite the fact that it would violate their religious practices, and have insisted that women go through a full-body scan at airports despite their religious objections to it. Recently there has even been an effort in Britain to require immigrants to pledge allegiance to the monarch, a practice that many of the Irish challenged in the nineteenth and early twentieth centuries and that Sinn Fein party members elected to the British Parliament still refuse to do.

Negative views about immigrants in the United States, particularly about those coming from Central and Latin America have also emphasized not only the cost of welfare benefits but also the problems created by social, cultural, and linguistic differences. Television, newspapers, and films, for example, have highlighted crime, drug trafficking, violent gangs, and a whole plethora of social problems in immigrant communities. These problems have been attributed to an increase in the number of immigrants, particularly undocumented aliens from Central and Latin America. A belief that social problems are a consequence of immigration has led to the growth of vigilante groups along the Mexican border and demands for a wall to be built between the two countries. In Arizona a law was passed permitting the police to pick up anyone who might appear to be an undocumented alien, and recently a draconian law was passed in Alabama. Advocates of such measures have justified them on the grounds that a wall and civilian border surveillance will protect the United States against the entrance of terrorists and drug traffickers, but many have contended that a primary goal is the prevention of culturally diverse immigrants from Central and Latin America coming into the country. The absence of similar measures along the Canadian border would seem to confirm some of these concerns about ethnic profiling.

Fears about the dangers posed by cultural differences have also motivated demands in some local American communities for the exclusive use of English. Although complaints about the difficulties and expense of programs for non-English-speaking people are often mentioned, an underlying issue is the growth of bilingualism in certain areas of the country and a determination to preserve the dominance of Anglo-American culture. The controversy over the use of English has reached such proportions in some communities that local governments have enacted English-language-only ordinances in an effort to curb the use of foreign languages. Other local jurisdictions have refrained from such drastic measures and instead turned to ridicule as a way of forcing the universal use of English.

Public debate and discussion is only one component of the current controversy over immigration. Government laws and regulations are also important, for they determine who is an immigrant, who may enter and under what conditions, who should be excluded, and what rights and privileges immigrants should have. Just as public debate reflects a series of assumptions about the assets and liabilities of immigration, so too do government policies. Generally speaking the policies of Western European countries and the United States and Canada assume that an immigrant is a male head of household who is accompanied by his immediate family. Government policies also assume that more highly skilled, better-educated foreigners are capable of making a contribution to the economy of the country and are therefore desirable. This translates into policies that permit those falling into the category of highly skilled professionals to enter with relative ease and to have the ability to become permanent residents and eventually even citizens. For the less well educated and less skilled the policies are different. Since people falling into this category are not thought of as being able to make a similar contribution, their entrance and right to remain is instead dependent on the fluctuating needs of the labor market and a demand for a low-wage, flexible work force.

Public debates and discussions of immigration policy have tended to focus on widely held assumptions about the high costs involved, and government policy has tended to concentrate on defining who is an immigrant and what his status is. However, several important issues have been largely overlooked. The first is gender. The common conception is that of the immigrant as male. When immigrant women are mentioned they are thought of as nonworking dependent members of the immigrant family or they are associated with welfare dependency, prostitution, the transmission of sexual diseases, or criminal activities such as petty thievery and backwardness (Chattopadhyay 1997). When they are seen as wives or mothers or daughters, the belief is that they are dutifully accompanying a male head of household. Immigrant women are not thought of as individuals with their own aspirations or as persons who have contributed to the decision to immigrate. Such oversights are unfortunate, for today the typical immigrant is a woman. Statistics report that women now constitute a majority of today's immigrants, refugees, and asylum seekers. According to the *UNHCR Statistical Yearbook* (2006), there are 32.9 million refugees and persons of concern. Of this group data on gender is available for only 13.9 million of which 49 percent are female. Many of these women are accompanied only by their children. When women refugees, asylum seekers, those accompanying their male-headed family, those coming on visas as temporary workers, and those entering illegally are combined, the total number of women immigrants is even larger than the United Nations data on refugees indicates. The large number of women immigrants has led to the description of immigration today as feminized.

A variety of statistical studies done by individual countries further confirms this pattern. In 1986 approximately one-half of all the foreign born in the United States were women, but by 2002 the percentage of women had climbed to over 60 percent (US Census Bureau Statistical Abstracts of the United States). This represents approximately a 10 percent increase in 26 years. In Canada the number of foreign-born females has increased by approximately 7 percent. Figures for countries in the European Union show a similar trend.

A second factor that is often overlooked is the status of women immigrants. Today the typical immigrant woman is likely to be married but not accompanied by a husband or an adult male family member. Her children may come with her or have been left behind in her home country in the care of family members there. Some women do come as part of a male-headed family group, but others do not. Some seeking refugee status come with only their children. Some come alone as temporary workers. Still others enter illegally in the hope of finding employment. This phenomenon of feminized immigration represents a significant change from the pattern that prevailed during most of the twentieth century and resembles instead immigration during the nineteenth century, when women arrived in receiving countries on their own. In the United States, for example, although the number of men and women immigrants was virtually equal throughout the nineteenth century, the majority of women came on their own. Unlike women immigrating today, however, those leaving home in the nineteenth century were likely to be young, single, and unaccompanied by children. In the early part of the twentieth century this pattern changed when government policy in the United States and elsewhere adopted the principle of family unification, which made it easier for women to enter as part of a family unit but made the right to residency dependent on family membership. Since the 1980s the trend has reverted to the nineteenth-century prototype. At the same time twentieth-century official family reunification policies have continued to define women as members of an immigrating family unit.

Present government policies continue to be based on the assumption of a male immigrant accompanied by his wife and children. For the most part women are still considered traditional wives—"tagalongs"—who dutifully acquiesce to the wishes of their husbands. On those rare occasions when feminized immigration is acknowledged, women are thought to be motivated by either a desire for Western feminism or the wish to escape patriarchal oppression at home (Andrall 2000). Reality often tells a quite different story. For women reasons to immigrate are wide ranging and complicated. Sometimes they immigrate to earn money, sometimes to escape from a dangerous situation, and sometimes to escape the chaos of civil war. Western women's increased participation in the work force has created a strong demand for child and elder care. Aging populations in Western nations have increased the demand for caregivers. Low-wage female immigrant domestic workers fit this niche perfectly. At the same time economic conditions in Third World countries and Eastern Europe and a decline in demand for male immigrant workers have encouraged women rather than men to immigrate. There are opportunities for women to work abroad, and their families back home need the money. Civil unrest around the globe and the resulting violence and economic upheaval have also prompted women to immigrate to places where they and perhaps their children can be safe.

The feminization of immigration necessitates a reexamination of the current views about immigration and the policies regulating it. There needs to be a careful exploration of women's experiences as immigrants and the conflicting pressures that confront them. Resembling nomads, men as well as women are faced with shifting boundaries, scrambled codes, and deterritorialized space (Doty 2003). In a new environment old roles and identities are no longer functional, and new ones are problematic. Whether women are admitted as wives or individuals or enter illegally, they have to negotiate the changes that accompany immigration. For women these negotiations are quite complex. Public policies, their own ethnic community, their new environment, employment, previous norms about behavior, and their role within the family each advocate a particular role and identity for her (Portes 1999). Confronted with multiple and often conflicting identities, roles, and expectations at the personal, family, governmental, and economic levels, women face serious dilemmas in adjusting to the demands of reframing their identity. The need to adjust and reconcile conflicting roles, expectations, and identities push them to undertake the task of (re)constructing identities that are functional within the family, community, the workplace, and mainstream society. Policies and programs that minimize or ignore the contradictions and conflicting pressures that immigrant women face deny them the opportunity to contribute, flourish, and in some cases survive.

This book examines immigrant women and the pressures they experience as they adapt and adjust to a new environment. Central to this is the relationship of structure and agency to the (re)construction of social identity and the role of intermediate influences such as the media and stereotypes articulated in mainstream society. In particular the book looks at the role that government policies and ethnic immigrant communities play in the (re)creation of women's social identity and their own efforts to develop an identity that is congruent with their experiences. The implications of their struggle for second-generation women, particularly daughters, to (re)construct an identity will also be explored.

Although there are important differences among postindustrial countries, there are some basic similarities in policies regulating admission, programs and assistance offered to recently arrived immigrants, approaches to integration or assimilation, and the mainstream community's responses to those who are racially, ethnically, or culturally different. These similarities suggest that women immigrants may confront some comparable experiences in their adjustment and adaptation (Yuval-Davis 1997). At the same time there are important differences that must be recognized. This is especially true for ethnic immigrant communities, which can also play a significant role in shaping women's experiences of immigration.

Assuming some basic similarities in public policies regulating immigration in Western Europe and North America, the book begins by looking at government institutions and policies that structure immigrant women's lives and social identity. It does not include temporary refugees. Although the issue of temporary women refugees is a matter of grave concern, their situation is quite different from those who immigrate voluntarily, those who intend to settle permanently, those who enter illegal and wish to remain, and those who have obtained a short-term work visa. Among other things, temporary refugee women do not face the same pressures to conform to a new environment, since their situation is not assumed to be permanent or even semipermanent. Regulations defining their residency as well as mainstream society expectations about their roles and behavior are different. The organization of their ethnic community is usually different as well. Given these differences the book does not deal with temporary women refugees but instead focuses on women who are immigrating for an extended period of time, including those obtaining permanent alien status or leave to remain, those with temporary work visas, and the undocumented who wish to stay indefinitely. The book also does not deal with women immigrating to countries other than those in postindustrial Western Europe and North America. Although Australia has been an important receiving country for immigrants in recent times, it has not been included since research for the book, including interviews, has been conducted only in Europe, Canada, and the United States. Female immigration to Middle Eastern and Asian countries is also not covered. The experiences of these women with regard to behavior and social roles differ appreciably from those of women coming to Western Europe and North America. Although the situation of these women deserves serious scholarly attention, including them here seemed inappropriate.

In focusing on women who immigrate voluntarily and who hope to remain either permanently or for a period of time, this book emphasizes three main constituencies or communities—voices if you will—that influence the (re)creation of their social identity. The first of these is government policies and regulations. They establish the basic parameters for a woman's admission, the conditions for remaining, and the opportunities for participating in civil society. The second is ethnic immigrant communities in the receiving countries. They set and reinforce certain standards of behavior for their members, especially for women, who are often seen as the custodians of the culture of the homeland. The third are the women themselves who must adapt to the host of conflicting demands and expectations arising from their early upbringing, their immigrant experience, and attempt to fuse together the old and new ways of life.

Through protocols, laws, and policies, the government of the receiving state—the first of these forces or voices—plays a major role in (re)creating a woman's social identity. Family unification policies in the postindustrial countries of Europe and North America reflect the notion that women are economically dependent and that they not only are part of a patriarchal family structure but also accept those values. They set family membership as the condition for, at least, women's initial residency. When special training programs are provided they embody stereotypic gender roles related to the domestic sphere, which explicitly or implicitly limit employment options. For example, government programs predicated on the assumption of "at home" wives and mothers emphasize homemaking, hygienic food preparation, and baby care rather than skills that might be useful in the marketplace. Thus admission policies and government programs lay out a social identity for women as housewives—persons living exclusively in the domestic sphere, not people who can live or operate outside the home or in a competitive marketplace. Even policies admitting unaccompanied women entering on temporary work visas accentuate the image of the "at home" mother. The vast majority of temporary work visas are issued to women who will be employed in traditional female occupations: caregivers, nannies, elder caregivers, domestics, chamber maids, lower-level health care workers such as nurse's aides, and those in the garment trades.

A second constituency or voice attempting to construct an immigrant woman's social identity is her ethnic immigrant community. Although these communities differ significantly from one another, they, too, help shape a woman's experience of immigration, the extent of her assimilation, and her role in her family, the ethnic community, and mainstream society. Like government policies, some ethnic communities—although not all—emphasize women's domestic role. Using the dual mechanisms of social approval and material support, these communities attempt to set the boundaries of acceptable behavior by providing guidelines and establishing expectations. In stressing the importance of cultural traditions they influence women who are settling permanently as well as those admitted temporarily on work visas. The social identity they encourage involves the obligation to act as the guardian of culture and traditions and as a protector of community boundaries regarding social behavior. It is the woman's duty, role, and responsibility to pass on the culture, traditions, and moral standards of the homeland to her children, especially her daughters if she lives in a family setting or as a role model to other women in the community. In this role she provides continuity with the home country and serves as a bulwark against alien, or what the community may consider the immoral, values of the new country. This notion of a woman's social identity often does not encourage her to (re)create a social identity consistent with the needs and requirements of her new environment. Instead it accentuates the need to preserve an identity consistent with the community's vision of the "old world," despite the fact that this identity fails to reconcile old habits and new demands. The ethnic community also seeks to perpetuate traditional values and behaviors in the second generation. This often proves to be a difficult if not impossible task for first-generation immigrant women, since young women of the next generation may have little knowledge or identification with the "homeland."

Women immigrants' own aspirations are a third force or voice. For them (re)constructing their social identity is highly complicated. First there is their early training, which inculcated certain norms. In a new country there are different demands on their time, energy, and allegiances. The majority of immigrant women find work in the low-paying, low-skill flexible work force that leaves them little spare time for domestic life. Pressures stemming from government policies and the expectations of their community combined with the need to work create serious stress in their everyday lives, in their family relationships, and at work. Since they are constantly adapting to conflicting pressures and expectations, old or imposed identities need to be modified. The third force or voice reflects their attempts to reconcile government policies and practices, the demands of their ethnic community, and their own needs and aspirations. In their daily lives they draw on social norms and traditions and on cultural frameworks from home. They arrive with certain cultural and ideological baggage, but in a new environment they find that they are forced to discard some of these traditions and habits and adopt new ones. They take up new activities, such as working for wages, and if they are married, their salary allows them to acquire new authority within the family. Traditional social relations and cultural resources neither disappear nor continue intact but are reshaped (Hondagneu-Sotelo 1994; Massey 2004). Facing a new environment and finding previous modes of behavior no longer as helpful as they once were, they struggle to imagine themselves in new ways and to adjust and contribute in new and innovative ways on both a personal and public level. Their efforts involve creating a hybrid identity that reflects both their old and new societies. Sometimes the women are successful in achieving this; sometimes not. Either way, there is a personal cost. In some cases the cost is relatively low, but in others it is high. In some extreme cases the conflicting pressures carry a very high price: mental illness and suicide.

These forces or voices are often contradictory and contested. The first two each assign women a distinctive social identity; the third is an evolving and reactive identity that women fashion for themselves. Sometimes women assume the identity advocated by one of these voices at one time and a different identity at another time. Occasionally they embrace contradictory identities simultaneously, although the personal cost of such an action is high. Sometimes their acceptance of a particular identity is a matter of choice; in other cases, a matter of necessity.

Since the intent of this book is to explore the conflicting pressures on women immigrants and the implications for the (re)creation of their social identity the question arises about the best method or approach to use. Although in earlier scholarship on women immigrants a number of different approaches have been used, historiography and ethnographic studies have been the most popular. Using a historical approach, much of the early research focused on European women immigrants and their role within their transposed family (Anker 1988; Harzig 1991; Dublin 1979; Stansell 1986). Perhaps two of the best known of these works are Hasia Diner's book *Erin's Daughter in America* (1986), which looked at Irish women's roles within the confines of both family and their employment, and Donna Gabaccia's book *From Sicily to Elizabeth Street* (1984), which compared family life and work in the women's home villages with their lives in the United States. Using a historical or ethnographic approach or some combination of the two, researchers have frequently concentrated on the role of women as wage earners, and there is now a considerable body of scholarship dealing with working-class immigrant women. Some of this work has looked at women in the garment trade (Grasmuck and Pessar 1991; Green 1997; Haug 1990; Pessar 1987; Lan 1976); others, at women in domestic service (Romero 1992; Andrall 2000). Increased immigration from Third World countries, which began to accelerate in the 1980s, encouraged a movement away from the study of European women exclusively and spurred scholars to focus on postcolonial women. Recently work on women immigrants has expanded to include biographies, autobiographies, and fiction. Hong Kingston, Tam, Kincaid, Danticat, Ali, and Smith are just a few of the writers who have used this mode for exploring the impact of immigration on women.

Studies that treat immigrants as a generic category run the risk of essentialism. In treating them as a generic category, they mask race, social class, and ethnic and religious differences. Research dealing with women immigrants as a category fails to take into account the variety of women's experiences. However, to understand the dynamics of women's adjustment and their efforts to (re)create their social identity, differences must be taken into account. In an attempt to escape the pitfall of essentialism, existing work has been limited to immigrant women belonging to the same ethnic group. Studies of women from Ireland, the Caribbean, Africa, Asia, or a particular European country, for example, examine them within their own particular ethnic context. When comparisons have been made, as in Gabaccia's book, they have been between women in the homeland and those who have immigrated, or they have focused on women coming from a relatively homogeneous region such as the Caribbean.

While all women immigrants face difficulties in adjusting to a new environment not all share the same sort of experiences. There is no universal woman immigrant, refugee, or asylum seeker (Hajdukowski-Ahmed, Khanlou, and Moussa 2008). Race, ethnicity, religion, social class, and level of education privilege some and disadvantage others. As intersectionality points out, differences create varying levels of subjugation and oppression. Even a cursory examination, for example, indicates that some immigrant women confront higher levels of discrimination than others, particularly when they enter the job market. For example, the experiences of women coming from North Africa to France are different from those of women coming from Canada to Britain, and the experiences of Canadian women are in turn different from those of women coming to Britain from Jamaica. Similarly the experiences of Mexican women coming to the United States are different from those of Northern European women. Since experiences affect responses and adjustment, their implications for the (re)creation of social identity must be kept in mind. Intersectionality allows us to do just that. It rejects the temptation to look at all women through the same lens and instead permits us to explore what differences mean and to understand the effects of social and political inequality and the multiple forms of subjugation and levels of intensity that exist.

The problem of selecting the best approach to use is never simple. A wide-scale acceptance of intersectionality in feminist literature attests to its usefulness in understanding and differentiating women's experiences. It certainly permits us to examine the efforts of women immigrants to resist oppression and escape domination as they attempt to carve out a social identity for themselves. However, in the case of women immigrants there is another consideration that must also be taken into account. In addition to the behavioral expectations of their ethnic community and the day-to-day pressures women face in adapting to a new environment, there are imposed government rules and regulations that shape the (re)creating of their social identity. This is particularly the case in policies implementing family reunification, which push women to conform to specific gender roles. The incongruence between these gender roles and the demands of everyday living often has significant consequences for the physical and psychic health of many women. While this book seeks to examine the implications of race, ethnicity, religion, social class, and level of education for the (re)creation of the social identity for women immigrants, it also wishes to examine the implications of government rules and regulations. Therein lies the conundrum. Histories of particular immigrant groups and ethnographic studies are not suitable for exploring shared general patterns and constraints resulting from government laws among women coming from a variety of countries. Intersectionality tends to play down the significance of government. In short, neither of these approaches alone allows for a clear understanding of the conflicting forces trying to (re)shape the social identity of immigrant women.

In some respects the situation of immigrant women seems somewhat analogous to that of the Puerto Rican struggle to form a distinctive national identity in the face of imposed US laws. In *The Legal Construction of Identity* (2000), Rivera Ramos argued that federal laws and governing norms constructed a particular social reality that affected the struggle for Puerto Rican national identity. In his view the law was an arbiter in the self-perception of Puerto Ricans striving to form a distinct national identity. Although the situation of women immigrants is more multifaceted and differs in a number of important respects from the situation Ramos was attempting to examine, there are some similarities in terms of the importance of the conflicting pressures of laws and governing norms, expectations of the community, and efforts by individuals to construct their social identities.

Crucial to Ramos's analysis are the concepts of social constructivism and social identity theory. In their work on the social construction of reality Thomas and Berger (1966) contended that reality is social constructed and that it is defined by groups with which individuals are affiliated. Different groups hold different meanings and values, and agents of socialization, language, and interaction play a role in the acquisition and reinforcement of perceptions of reality. Socially constructed reality is not static, however; it is a dynamic and ongoing process. When there is a change in a group relationship there is a shift in one's definition of reality. Related to this concept is social identity theory, which argues that individuals define their social identity in terms of group membership and identify themselves in terms of collective categories (Tajfel and Turner 1986). Identification with collective categories may lead to a positive self-identity or a negative one dependent on the groups with which one is identified. This presents a challenge for members of stigmatized, negatively valued groups. For these individuals various strategies ranging from attempts to disassociate themselves from such groups to ranking groups differently may be adopted. Life transitions, changes in cultural setting, and changes in socialization can lead to shifts in identity (Howard 2000; Cerulo 1997). Some work on sexual identity, which has used the constructivist model, has suggested that identity entails a process of recognizing, negotiating, and interpreting one's experiences, while some has emphasized social and legal constraints on the process.

Social constructivism and social identity theory seem to be particularly suited to address the situation of immigrants, including refugees and uprooted people who have multilayered identities before their arrival in a new setting (Hajdukowski-Ahmend, Khanlou, and Moussa 2008). They allow an examination of the social context in which these women operate and their efforts to negotiate and renegotiate their identities. Each of the three groups—the government, the ethnic community, and the women themselves—represents a particular set of values and meanings. In their daily lives women are shifting from one group affiliation/identification to another. Shifts in identity are constantly occurring. Working outside the home entails an identity that conflicts with her identity as envisioned by government legislation and perhaps with her role within the family. Social constructivism offers some insight into the dynamics of identity shifts as well as the problems that often arise between mothers and their children. To reconcile the various strands affecting women immigrants, elements of intersectionality have been incorporated into a social constructivist/social identity approach.

Organization of the Book

The first section of the book concentrates on women immigrants and governments in receiving states. It examines the ways in which gendered immigration and asylum policies and their interpretation and implementation have helped shape the social identity of women. It concentrates on legal issues: the grounds on which they can enter, their status as aliens, and government programs providing opportunity for employment and economic self-sufficiency.

It also attempts to explore the impact of laws and public policies on both immigrant women and perceptions of them in both the receiving country and their own immigrant ethnic community. It begins with a brief overview of the patterns of women's immigration in the late nineteenth and early twentieth centuries when many of the present protocols, laws, and policies governing immigration, refugee status, and asylum were established. In particular it looks at the changes in official policies, which previously classified women as individual immigrants, to a policy that defines them as dependent family members—a trend that some scholars attribute to a shift at the end of the nineteenth century from private to public patriarchy. It then looks at the repercussions of public patriarchy for present-day protocols, laws, policies, and practices.

Present policies classify immigrants as family members, temporary visitors, permanent or temporary refugees and asylum seekers, or illegal aliens. The following chapters explore the ramifications of these categories the (re)creation of women's social identity. They highlight the explicit as well as implicit contradictions and stereotypes relating to women's participation in civil society, particularly in the area of employment, and the extent to which gendered laws, policies, and interpretations have reinforced traditional roles for women in the domestic and service sectors; strengthened public perceptions of immigrant women as backward, submissive, and old fashioned; and encouraged their reliance on the state's economic resources.

The role of the ethnic community in constructing a woman's social identity is considered in the next section. Living on the margins of society, both men and women immigrants are in a vulnerable position. Caught between the world that they left and the one they now find themselves in, immigrants are constantly in the process of (re)creating a social identity. The problems stemming from their marginalized position are compounded by the negative images of immigrants in the media and the measures taken in Europe and the United States to limit further immigration. In this hostile setting, feelings of loneliness and nostalgia are intensified, and immigrants often turn to their ethnic community for support and consolation. Since acceptance by the community may be critical to self-esteem, and even to mental health, the ethnic immigrant community plays an important role in preserving a sense of self-confidence and self-worth. Its expectations and approval are, therefore, not easily disregarded. For women the relationship is often crucial for pragmatic reasons as well. Defined as dependent by immigration laws or practices or by prevalent gender norms, women are often limited in terms of employment opportunities. Frequently they have little option other than to turn to their ethnic community for economic and social support. Often it is members of their ethnic community that help them find a job, advise them about negotiating the bureaucracy in mainstream society, help them find housing, or tide them over in financial crises. This reliance on material support coupled with nostalgia for their homeland reinforces a central role for the ethnic community. Even in the case of women immigrants unaccompanied by their families who are admitted on a temporary work visas, the ethnic community is important for the emotional support it offers and the guidance it provides in instances where their employers are exploitative. Thus, even for these employed women who are on their own, the ethnic community often becomes the center of their economic and social life.

Many ethnic immigrant communities have the expectation that women will preserve the culture, traditions, and rituals of the home country. This has taken a variety of forms, including traditional female activities such as cooking, observing holiday celebrations, ensuring the observance of appropriate marriage arrangements, and performing duties surrounding parenting. Women are under pressure to maintain traditional behavior patterns for themselves and their children, especially their daughters. The expectation has been that they will instruct their daughters about how to observe traditional rituals, values, and behaviors in their own families as well. Women entering on temporary work visas or immigrating without their families have also experienced pressures from their ethnic immigrant community. Although their relationship with the community has differed from that of women who are part of a traditional family, they have also been tied to it, since it is often the center of their social life and a source of information about employment opportunities as well.

The second section of the book looks at the various pressures from government policies and community expectations and the impact on the women's perceptions of selves and their ability to cope. It looks at the attempts of women to reconcile these various forces as they (re)create a social identity for themselves. Although balancing home, family, and work has been difficult for all women, for immigrant women it has been especially so in terms of employment and respect. Required to work in order for the family to survive, often inadequately compensated for their work, sometimes denied upward mobility, and often perceived as dependent family members who willingly accept low wages and expect no benefits, women's sense of self-esteem has undermined. Many are clustered in the informal economy with its subsistence wages. The situation of less privileged women entering with temporary work visas has scarcely been better. They have consistently complained about gender discrimination in job opportunities and pay and advancement and have constantly cited these conditions as a source of stress in their lives. Within this context, women nonetheless have attempted to craft a meaningful social identity. Their efforts to survive and, if possible, thrive have often been creative and sometimes successful, but the stress that their situation has posed is examined in this section.

In the final section the implications of conflicting forces or voices on the (re)creation of the social identity of immigrant women are examined. Some women have been able to forge a social identity that has empowered them and allowed them to move into leadership positions in their new country. In some cases they have become politically active, forming neighborhood movements, even running for public office. Immigration has given them an opportunity to fulfill their dreams. In other cases the outcome has not been as positive. For some women it has involved pain, disruption, and a sense of loss. Surviving and adapting, reconciling conflicting messages, have contributed to high levels of stress, anguish, mental illness, and in some case suicide. The book ends with a brief discussion of some changes in current policies that might better reflect the needs of women and alleviate some of the obstacles they presently face.

SECTION 1

Defining Women Immigrants and Refugees

The Official Voice: Immigration Protocols, Laws, and Policies

CHAPTER 2

From Laissez-Faire to Regulation
The Emergence of Immigration Policy

To establish a context for understanding the situation of women immigrants today it might be helpful to begin with a brief overview of past immigration practices. The first point is obvious: immigration for women as well as men is not a recent phenomenon. Throughout history both men and women immigrated, sometimes as a family unit, sometimes independently. Ancient history is replete with stories of immigration: the establishment of Roman settlements in Britain and the Biblical account of the migration of the Jews from Egypt to Israel are just two of the most well-known accounts. These migrations included women. Archeological findings in Roman settlements in northern Europe indicate the presence of women and children, not just soldiers. There is similar evidence confirming the immigration of women elsewhere. After the collapse of the Roman Empire in the West and the creation of the Byzantine Empire, for example, there was extensive immigration in what is now Eastern Europe. Considerable evidence again points to women's participation in these population movements. Throughout the Middle Ages there was substantial immigration throughout Europe, some of it temporary, some of it permanent. There were also massive immigrations of people from Central Asia, with Turkey being one of the major destinations. Here again archeological evidence and historical data indicate that women immigrated along with men.

Recent scholarly work on immigration maintains that in the fifteenth century the nature of immigration changed significantly. First, it became global in character; second, it influenced domestic and international politics; and third, it had political, social, and economic consequences. The scope of immigration taking place during the past five hundred years certainly seems to support this hypothesis. In the 75 years prior to the outbreak of World War I in 1914, 45 to 50 million Europeans and 35 million Asians, principally from China and Japan, immigrated across the globe. Earlier somewhere between 9 and 15 million Africans were forced to immigrate to the Americas involuntarily as slaves. To put these numbers in perspective, the conservative estimate of the total number of Asians and Europeans immigrating within a 75-year period is approximately 2 million less than the total population of present-day Germany (82.5 million) and approximately 20 million more than the population of either France (60.9 million) or Britain (almost 60 million). If the number of African slaves brought earlier to the United States were to be included, the number would be roughly equivalent to the present-day total population of Mexico (106 million). If slaves shipped to the Caribbean and Central and South America are added the number is far greater still.

One way in which immigration conformed to earlier patterns during this period was that it was neither feminized nor masculinized. Women immigrated in more or less equal numbers with men. With the exception of the initial wave of male Asian immigrants recruited to work in the later part of the nineteenth century, there was roughly gender parity. While immigration existed throughout the ages, policies restricting it are a relatively recent innovation. The state had had the right to deport individuals after they had entered, but it was not until the later part of the nineteenth century that states began to exercise the right to decide who could enter and under what conditions. Previously attitudes about immigration generally ranged from positive to neutral, an obvious exception being the invasion of foreign forces. Gender was not a criterion for either admission or deportation. This laissez-faire approach to immigration was motivated by economic considerations. Since both men and women immigrants provided cheap labor, both were welcomed.

This was certainly the case for immigration to the United States. Family membership was not a priority for European women's admission. Single as well as married women could enter. Immigrants, regardless of their gender, were viewed as valuable to economic development. They helped secure control of land for settlement in the West, their farms provided food for emerging cities, and their labor built much of the infrastructure in cities—bridges, roads, railways, and public works projects, including the New York City subway. Women filled a growing demand for household help and cheap labor in the emerging textile and garment industries. In short, immigrants—men and women—provided much needed labor that helped build the United States. Canada's approach to immigration was similar.

The United States and Canada were not the only countries that willingly admitted immigrants. European colonies also encouraged them to come and settle. Immigrants flocked to southern and eastern Africa, Asia, Australia, and New Zealand and to South America. There they played important roles in ensuring European political power and control. Again women as well as men came. In Asia and Africa many of the European women came as governesses or teachers to furnish instruction for the children of settlers. Some also came to work in what is now labeled the sex/entertainment trade and could be found in brothels in locations as diverse as the American West and Colonial India.

As the number of immigrants increased resentment against them grew. The arrival of young, unmarried women eventually became a matter of concern, especially in the United States. Some objected to unmarried women on moral grounds and attributed prostitution to the presence of foreign women, especially Chinese women. Pressures mounted to limit their entrance. As a result, in 1875 Congress passed the Page Act barring criminals and prostitutes from entering the country. Despite the passage of this law, young, unmarried European women encountered few obstacles to being admitted and continued to do so in significant numbers. They were certainly not required to enter as dependent family members. The same was not the case for Chinese women, however.

Asian exclusion in general became an exception to previous laissez-faire policies in North America and European colonies. In an effort to replace the cheap labor previously provided by slaves, Chinese men had been actively recruited in the years following the Civil War to come and work in the United States on the construction of the railroads. The need for a cheap labor source meant that Chinese laborers were also recruited for other construction projects in the United States and in Canada and Australia as well. Around the same time the British recruited Indians to work on tea, coffee, and rubber plantations throughout Asia and East Africa. In short the recruitment of foreign labor was certainly not unique. In the case of the United States, Chinese workers were considered temporary and their families were discouraged from coming to join them. The inflexible enforcement of the Page Law for Chinese women was in marked contrast with the previous policy of welcoming female immigrants and was indicative of the country's opposition to the idea of Chinese immigrants becoming permanent residents and establishing families in this country.

Throughout this period immigration practices in the United States made no distinction between people immigrating for economic reasons and those seeking to escape religious or political persecution. The categories now used to differentiate immigrants such as political refugees, economic refugees, asylum seekers, and the like did not exist. Of course, not all immigrants were warmly welcomed. Recent arrivals usually worked in the most dangerous and poorly paid jobs, often lacked the protections afforded the indigenous population, and were easily exploited. Living in ethnic enclaves, they frequently experienced serious problems in assimilating and being accepted, and as ethnic communities grew in size, negative stereotypes and nativist sentiments intensified. Despite rumblings against "foreigners," however, immigration policies remained essentially open door for all except Asians, although the right to expel undesirables existed.

The experiences of Europeans immigrating to their overseas colonies—sometimes temporarily, sometimes permanently—were, of course, entirely different. Hardly welcomed, often deeply resented by the indigenous population, which saw them as a conquering force, they assumed a privileged position. So while colonizers were immigrants, issues of assimilation were certainly not the same for them as they were for those whom we ordinarily consider immigrants.

Creating the Precedents:
The Introduction of Immigration Controls

In the United States a change in an open-door approach to immigration was prompted by an increase in the number of Asians arriving in the country coupled with a decline in a demand for their labor. As anxiety about the impact of Asian culture on American values intensified, calls for controls on immigration mounted. In response, the United States Congress passed the Chinese Exclusion Act in 1882, and in 1907 the ban was extended in the Gentlemen's Agreement to include the Japanese. Similar uneasiness about Asian immigration emerged in both Canada and Australia and resulted in the passage of Asian exclusion legislation in those countries as well. Around the same time South Africa adopted restrictive laws regarding Asian immigration particularly from the Indian subcontinent. Ironically, though, outside the United States restrictions on immigration became linked to the practice of admitting whole families. For women this meant that it was easier for them to enter as dependents of a male head of household than as individuals.

Although restrictions on immigration were first directed against Asians they soon expanded to include other groups. The increased immigration of Southern and Eastern Europeans raised fears in Britain and Germany about the preservation of national culture and values. In response to a growing alarm about the number of East European Jewish immigrants arriving in Britain, the government passed the 1905 Aliens Act. Although the law retained the concept of granting asylum to those experiencing persecution—a practice dating back to the ancient world—it distinguished between those immigrating for economic reasons and those who were fleeing persecution. Proof of persecution was required. Economic reasons were insufficient grounds for admission. This was difficult for many since documentation was hard to obtain. As a consequence of these entry conditions, the number of Eastern European immigrants declined somewhat, although not entirely. In an effort to restrict further immigration the British Parliament passed additional legislation in 1914 and 1919 that reaffirmed the precedents set in the 1905 legislation. From a policy perspective the British Aliens Act of 1905 is important, for it introduced a distinction between immigrants fleeing persecution and those seeking to improve the material quality of their lives. Previously there was no such criterion for admission. By distinguishing immigrants in terms of either persecution or economic interests, the 1905 Aliens Act set a precedent for national and international immigration policy that has persisted to the present day. Other European countries followed suit by passing laws barring or limiting immigration motivated by economic considerations. In Germany, for example, foreign workers, particularly Poles, were often denied the right to remain when their labor was no longer needed, although restrictions were periodically lifted when cheap labor was required. France also adopted policies that prohibited foreign workers from being employed on state-funded projects.

By the early twentieth century immigration had become a hotly contested issue in the United States. A downturn in the economy coupled with an increase in the number of immigrants from Southern and Eastern Europe at the end of the nineteenth century created a tense environment. Public debate centered on what President Theodore Roosevelt called "good immigrants" and "bad immigrants"—characteristics that seemed to be dependent primarily on where the people came from. Northern European immigrants were generally deemed to be "good" while those coming from Eastern Europe and Mediterranean countries were considered "bad." In an effort to reduce the number of Eastern and Southern European immigrants entering the country, under the assumption that the majority were illiterate, the US Congress enacted the Immigration Act of 1917, which required immigrants to be literate. The hope was that this, along with the continuation of an anti-Asian immigration policy would curtail immigration. The literacy requirement proved to be ineffective, however, and so in an effort to reduce immigration at the end of World War I, the Immigration Act of 1921 introduced a quota system. The Johnson-Reed Act of 1924 expanded this principle and set up a draconian national-origins quota of 2 percent, which effectively eliminated immigration for virtually all but those from Northern Europe and Latin America. The Immigration Acts of 1917 and 1921 and the Johnson-Reed Act of 1924 also adopted the principle of family unification by granting permission to enter to the male head of household along with his dependents: his wife and children. In essence this gave priority to women as family members over those wishing to enter as individuals.

The principles incorporated into Asian exclusion legislation, the British Alien Act of 1905, and the United States Immigration Acts of 1917, 1921, and 1924 set four precedents fundamental to twentieth- and twenty-first-century immigration policy. First, they substituted controls on admission for the older practice of deportation as the primary means for controlling immigration. Second, the 1905 Aliens Act established the distinction between those escaping persecution and those immigrating for economic reasons and made it a criterion for determining eligibility for admission. By tying admission to proof of persecution it created categories of immigrants. Third, US immigration legislation became a blueprint for family unification by tying a wife and children's immigration status and residency to the male head of family. In giving quota preference to relatives of US citizens and permanent resident aliens, the Johnson-Reed Act (1924), and later the McCarran Walter Immigration and Naturalization Act of 1952 and the 1965 Immigration Act, reaffirmed the principle of family unification. Family unification became and remains a key component not only of US immigration policy but also of post–World War II European immigration policies. Fourth, women immigrants were encouraged to enter as dependents, a status that some argue was a euphemism for property (Luibhéid 2002).

Categorizing women immigrants as dependent represents a break with earlier practices. Until the beginning of the twentieth century European women traveling with their families or alone were admitted on the same basis as men. Both married and unmarried women immigrated, and many entered the labor market after their arrival. Although the gender of those coming to the United States before World War I was not systematically recorded, there is considerable evidence that single women came in significant numbers. One study of female immigration to the United States in the nineteenth and early twentieth centuries found that women averaged around 40 percent of all those arriving in the country, although in certain periods, such as the final decade of the nineteenth century, the number of women exceeded that of men (Gabaccia 1994). In some respects women immigrants differed from their male counterparts. They were more likely to migrate between July and December and to settle in urban areas and less likely to return to their homeland. Unlike men who found employment in the construction trades, women were employed in the female-dominated occupations of domestic service and the garment industry. These findings have been reported in a number of studies. For example, Vernez (1999) found that from the mid-1800s to the 1920s women accounted for two-fifths of the immigrants, and in more recent times they have constituted a majority of legal immigrants. Research on Irish immigration to America indicates that many of the women were either unmarried or themselves heads of household (Jones 1988; O'Sullivan 1995). Public discussion in the nineteenth-century American press about the exploitation of foreign young women and the need to protect them from unscrupulous practices, including solicitation for prostitution, would also seem to further confirm the fact that many of the women were not dependent family members.

Similar patterns of immigration by unmarried women within Europe also exist. For example, research on the movement of labor in nineteenth-century Europe reports that there was a significant immigration of women outside the context of family. The practice of young, unmarried women immigrating from rural communities to take up work in domestic service has been widely reported. Large numbers of young Irish women migrated to England in the nineteenth century, and this pattern persisted well into the twentieth century (O'Sullivan 1995). In France and Germany it was not uncommon for women to immigrate on their own in order to work in seasonal agriculture, a practice that still persists in some rural areas. Recent scholarship has pointed out that it was not unusual for unmarried European women to immigrate to India in the early years of the twentieth century. The demand for domestic servants and governesses in overseas colonies is yet another indication of the presence of unmarried women immigrants in the labor market.

In associating women immigrants with dependent status the United States Immigration Acts of 1917, 1921, 1924, 1952, and 1965 and European immigration policies created an important precedent. In earlier periods no distinction was made between single and married female immigrants. All were treated equally. The policy of family unification altered this practice by linking a woman's rights and privileges to family membership. Some have argued that the change amounted to little more than a shift from private patriarchy within the family to public patriarchy in the state. Clearly illustrating the gender hierarchy that this change entailed and that has continued well into the twentieth century is the fact that although women were allowed to enter as their husband's dependent, the same was not the case for husbands. Husbands were not permitted to enter as dependents. Indeed, it was not until the later part of the twentieth century that Caribbean men were allowed to join these wives in Britain or that women were allowed to be joined by family members on the same basis as men in the United States.

Twentieth-Century Immigration Policy

Early twentieth-century efforts to control immigration proved effective, for, despite the chaos resulting from the massive dislocation of people following World War I, it was reduced to a trickle. However, the enormous displacement of people following World War II, the labor shortages the war produced, the need in Europe to rebuild in the immediate postwar period, and the collapse of overseas empires sparked a revamping of immigration policies first in Europe and subsequently in North America. Immediately following the war, three problems required prompt attention. The first involved the resettlement of war refugees, the second, the need in Europe to recruit foreign labor to aid in the task of rebuilding, and the third, the status of nationals living in former colonies who wished to return to the mother country.

Steps were taken to deal with each of these issues. Since the problem of displaced persons was especially acute, the first set of policies concerned the acceptance of an internationally agreed upon definition of who was a refugee and what a nation's responsibility toward them was. The second involved easing restrictions on the immigration of a foreign work force. There the focus was on admitting male workers who were needed for reconstructing a war-torn Europe and subsequently on policies that permitted their family members to join them. The third involved procedures allowing individuals from former colonies to return to the mother country.

The first step taken was the creation of the International Refugee Organization (IRO) to deal with displaced persons. In 1951 it was replaced by the United Nations High Commission for Refugees (UNHCR). That same year the United Nations Convention on the Status of Refugees drew up the 1951 protocol, which established a standard for differentiating between individuals immigrating because of a "well-founded fear" of persecution and those immigrating for other reasons. This distinction was not dissimilar to the principle incorporated into the Aliens Act of 1905. According to the United Nations protocol a refugee was defined as a person who, "owing to a well-founded fear of being persecuted for reasons of race, religion, nationality, membership of a particular social group or political opinion, is outside the country of his nationality and is unable, or owing to such fear, is unwilling to avail himself of the protection of that country; or who, not having a nationality and being outside the country of his former habitual residence as a result of such events, is unable, or owing to such fear, is unwilling to return to it." The 1951 protocol also prohibited the involuntary return of refugees. The Bellagio Accords adopted later extended refugee status to individuals with a well-founded fear of social, religious, or political persecution coming from communist-dominated or Middle Eastern countries. In 1967 a new

United Nations protocol required individuals seeking refugee status to be outside their country of origin. Countries that are signatories to these protocols agree to abide by them; however, determining if an individual meets the criteria of "a well-founded fear of persecution" is a prerogative of the individual state. What constitutes a well-founded fear, therefore, can vary from one country to the next.

A second major concern was the need to rebuild war-torn Europe. To meet this demand, immigration policies were eased to permit foreign male labor to enter and work. Both the government and the private sector were allowed to recruit foreign workers. As a result immigrants from southern Europe, Asia, Africa, and the Caribbean were encouraged to come and work in Western Europe. In France they came principally from southern Europe and North Africa. Germany, cut off from its traditional labor supply in Poland by the advent of the Cold War, established "guest worker" programs that attracted a considerable number of Turks. Switzerland also actively recruited foreign labor. In Britain the labor shortage was met by granting free access to residents of the newly created Commonwealth countries. Following the collapse of the British Empire, immigration was hastened by economic uncertainty in its former colonies in Asia, the Caribbean, and Africa and the lure of employment opportunities. Other European countries with overseas empires, such as the Netherlands and Belgium, also allowed immigrants from their former colonies to enter, as did France, where first North Africans and later French West Africans arrived in considerable numbers. Africans from areas having close connections with Italy immigrated to that country.

Although the United States did not face the same problems of refugees and the need to rebuild as Europe, it, too, modified its immigration policy. A demand for cheap agricultural labor resulted in changes in the restrictions imposed by 1924 national-origins quotas, and legislation establishing the Mexican Bracero program facilitating the immigration of seasonal workers from Latin America and the Caribbean was passed in 1942 and was subsequently extended until 1964.

In the case of both European countries and the United States, the objective of these new immigration policies was to recruit male workers. With the exception of Asian exclusion policies there had previously been, as mentioned earlier, a rough balance in demand for male and female immigrant labor. However, following World War II there was little demand for female workers. Changing social mores regarding family size, the introduction of household appliances such as washing machines, and postwar housing that provided much less space led to a decline in demand for jobs such as domestic servants and child care in which women had been typically employed. Labor needs were instead in areas such as construction, heavy manufacturing, and mining, where men traditionally found employment. Thus, while men were actively recruited for jobs in Western Europe, no efforts were made to attract female workers. There was no need for them. For a brief period following World War II Britain was the sole exception. Foreign women were encouraged to come there to work in the hospitals and care facilities for injured soldiers and civilian victims of bombing raids. Subsequently Caribbean women also arrived and entered the labor market. However, elsewhere in Europe efforts were concentrated on recruiting male labor. In the absence of employment opportunities women no longer immigrated to find work. Instead they came to join their families.

In Europe it was initially assumed that foreign male workers would only be temporary residents. This did not turn out to be the case. Despite government programs and efforts encouraging workers to return home, they remained. Suggestions were made that if male foreign workers were to be effectively integrated into their new homeland, their families should join them. The thought was that families would give the men stability and allow them to function constructively in the community. As a result family unification programs were put in place. When the demand for male immigrant labor declined, however, there was opposition to further immigration and family unification. Anti-immigrant forces contended that family unification should mean the return of male workers to where their families lived rather than their families moving to join them. As Enoch Powell, a member of Parliament and a prominent leader of the British Conservative Party and an outspoken opponent of immigration put it, "Reunite families by returning them to their country of origin." Despite increased resentment to a growth in the size of immigrant communities, however, the idea of family unification continued to be a part of government policies. Some restrictions were imposed, but they were pretty much confined to having a male immigrant demonstrate that he had sufficient income and could provide accommodations for his family.

Family unification policies and the birth of children in immigrant families resulted in the emergence of visibly distinctive, permanent ethnic communities. The development and growth of these communities coupled with a decline in the demand for foreign male workers resulted in an escalation of anti-immigrant feelings and prompted governments to rethink their immigration policies. By the 1960s further restriction began to be imposed. For example, in 1962 the British Parliament passed the Commonwealth Immigration Act, which limited immigration to Commonwealth citizens who had specific jobs and to individuals with recognized skills, qualifications, and vouchers obtained from the British high commissioner in their country of origin. The concept of patrials—that is, a citizen who had a substantial connection to Britain by birth or descent—was adopted in the hope that it would restrict the entrance of those who were not of British origin. As a consequence the number of Asians and Caribbeans being admitted did decline, but the number of non-British settled immigrants grew as a result of childbirth and marriage to individuals from their country of origin. The growth of a North African population in France prompted that country also to pursue restrictive policies, including a quota system, which was adopted in 1968. Elsewhere in Western Europe a variety of measures regulating work and residency were put in place in an effort to discourage the arrival of new immigrants. For example, in Germany foreign workers and their children born there were unable to become citizens, residency permits were tied to family membership, and work permits were denied to wives and children, although subsequently they were denied only to wives.

In contrast to Europe the United States did not experience a rapid growth in distinctively different ethnic groups until much later. Rather than restricting immigration, the United States liberalized its laws. In 1965 the national-origins quota was eliminated and a preference system for relatives of both citizens and lawful permanent resident aliens was put in place. In 1980 the ban on Asian immigration was lifted. However, a ceiling was imposed on immigration from Latin America and the Caribbean. As was the case in Europe, immigration policy emphasized family unification, with women considered dependent family members. At the same time the precedents of early immigration acts that privileged the entrance of family members without "numerical limitation" were retained. While reaffirming the concept of family unification, the 1952 Immigration Act did make one important modification with respect to gender hierarchy: wives as well as husbands were allowed to sponsor alien spouses and family members as "non quota immigrants without limitation." Although the 1952 Immigration Act and subsequent legislation has permitted women to sponsor relatives, the practice of admitting women and children as dependents of the male head of household has continued to be the dominant pattern. The principle of family unification was reaffirmed in the 1964 immigration law, which allotted almost 75 percent of preference visas to family members as opposed to the 50 percent allocated under the 1952 immigration law. The Immigration Reform and Control Act of 1986 (IRCA), which set a theoretical cap of 675,000 immigrants and was to go into effect by 1995, allocated 71 percent of the slots to family members. Further changes in the 1996 immigration legislation, while increasing the total number of immigrants to be admitted, reserved over 60 percent of the slots for family-sponsored immigrants. Thus, given the slots allocated to family members, single women along with single men have continued to be at a disadvantage.

In 2003 the Immigration and Naturalization Service (INS), which served for seventy years as the guardian of America's borders, was merged into the newly created Department of Homeland Security. The functions of the old INS were split in two: the Bureau of Border Security (BBS) and the Bureau of Citizenship and Immigration Services (BCIS). The BBS was made responsible for border patrol, detention and removal, inspections, intelligence, and investigation, while the BCIS was to handle visa petitions, naturalization petitions, and refugee and asylum applications. In terms of changes in immigration policy the most significant is perhaps the provision for the transfer of the care and custody of unaccompanied children from the INS to the Office of Refugee Resettlement. However, no change was made with regard to the principle of family unification. In the overwhelming majority of cases women continue, then, to be treated as dependent family members.

Immigrants at the End of the Twentieth Century

As ubiquitous as debates about immigration are today, their reappearance is relatively recent. After the massive waves of immigration in the eighteenth and nineteenth centuries and the first two decades of the twentieth century, the transnational movement of large numbers of people subsided. So too did discussion about immigration. Published scholarship on the topic waned. The vast numbers of individuals displaced by World War II and the need for foreign guest workers in Western Europe to rebuild did prompt some scholars to look at the issue of immigration again, but by and large, little scholarly attention was given to the subject until the 1980s. Recent renewed interest has been sparked by (1) a dramatic increase in the number of immigrants, especially those requesting asylum, (2) a growth in the number of undocumented aliens, (3) the countries of origin of the new immigrants, and (4) the extent to which immigration has become feminized.

With regard to the growth in the number of immigrants, there are numerous examples of the increase in their numbers and in the size of ethnic immigrant communities. For example, in Germany, where citizenship is tied to the principle of "jus sanguinis"—that is, citizenship by ancestry—13 percent of those living in Germany at the end of the twentieth century were not ethnically German and therefore not citizens, and slightly more than 6 percent of those born in the country had one foreign parent (Koslowski 2000). In France at the time of the most recent immigration reforms in 2006, it was estimated that there were between two hundred thousand and four hundred thousand nonauthorized (undocumented or, as sometimes referred to, illegal) immigrants living in France.

Although the size of the immigrant community is one important factor in current discussions, motives for immigration are another. While in the past economic improvement was usually the principle motive for immigration, escaping persecution is now a major impetus. In Western European countries (Germany, France, Italy, the Netherlands, Sweden, and the United Kingdom) more than a quarter of a million people (274,416) sought asylum in 2000. In the same year there were 40,867 people seeking asylum in the United States and 34252 in Canada. This means that almost 350,000 people applied for asylum in North America and Western Europe in that year alone. Despite efforts to impose stricter rules governing asylum between 2003 and 2007, the United States received applications from 276,000 asylum seekers, France received 228,000, Britain received 188,000, Germany received 155,000, and Sweden received 133,000 (UNHCR March 2008). This means that almost one million people applied for asylum over a five-year period.

Table 2.1 provides some evidence about the extent to which requests for asylum have grown over recent decades. Although there were considerable fluctuations among countries between 1990 and 2004, the growth in the number of asylum requests is astounding. In the United Kingdom, for example, the number rose almost three and a half times between 1990 and 2002. In Italy between 1990 and 2002 there was nearly a fourfold increase in asylum requests. The latest figures published by the UNHCR indicate a 10 percent increase in asylum application in 2007 with a 10.9 percent increase in the number in EU countries, Canada, and the United States, which was the top receiving country

Table 2.1 Annual number of asylum applications for selected countries: 1990–2004

	1990	1992	1994	1996	1998	2000	2002	2004
Australia	12,128	6,054	6,264	9,758	8,156	13,065	5,775	3,098
Canada	36,735	37,748	22,006	26,120	23,838	34,252	39,498	25,499
France	54,813	28,872	26,044	17,405	22,375	39,775	51,087	61,056
Germany	193,063	438,191	127,210	149,157	98,644	78,564	71,127	35,613
Italy	4,827	6,042	1,786	675	11,122	15,564	16,015	—
Netherlands	21,208	20,348	52,573	22,857	45,217	43,895	18,667	9,782
Sweden	29,420	84,018	18,677	5,753	12,844	16,303	33,016	23,161
United Kingdom	26,205	24,625	32,830	29,640	46,020	80,315	84,135	40,202
United States	73,637	103,964	144,577	107,130	35,038	40,867	58,404	41,667

— Indicates figure is not available.

Source: Governments, UNHCR. Compiled by: UNHCR Population Data Unit

in 2007. Indeed, the United States accounted for 14.5 percent of all asylum claims submitted in 51 countries covered in the report (UNHCR, March 2008).

A second change in present-day immigration concerns the number of undocumented aliens that have entered the postindustrial countries of Western Europe and North America. Although there is considerable disagreement about the accuracy of the numbers of undocumented aliens, there is a universal acknowledgement that they are large. In the United States the estimates range from seven to twenty million. Data from the US Census Bureau reported that there were 8.7 million undocumented aliens living in the country in 2000. In 2003 the United States Citizenship and Immigration Service put the figure at seven million. Canadian data shows that more than 150,000 undocumented aliens reside there. Some sources have claimed that more than 400,000 unauthorized aliens enter the European Union each year. While this figure has been challenged, governmental, intergovernmental, and international agencies all report substantial numbers of unauthorized aliens entering EU countries. For example, Interpol reported that 31 thousand undocumented Senegalese had arrived in the Canary Islands in 2006, and Greece claimed that almost 70 thousand undocumented aliens had entered the country between January and August 2007. Amnesty programs in EU countries confirm the extent of the problem. Between 2003 and 2007 Spain granted amnesty to 548,000 unauthorized aliens, Italy to 634,000, and Greece to 228,000. This amounts to close to a million and half unauthorized aliens who received amnesty in these three countries alone within a four-year period.

A third characteristic that differentiates current immigration from earlier patterns is country of origin. Although there were Asian immigrants and involuntary immigrants from Africa in earlier periods of immigration, many were Europeans. Today immigrants and asylum seekers are likely to come from Third World countries, although some come from Eastern Europe as well. In terms of those seeking asylum, approximately 50 percent come from Asia, and 21 percent come from Africa. Approximately 12 percent come from Latin America and the Caribbean (UNHCR March 2008). This means that around eight out of every ten immigrants requesting asylum come from less developed countries. In 2007 the majority of asylum seekers came from Iraq, Pakistan, Syria, Somalia, and Mexico. Between 2000 and 2007 there were asylum seekers coming from China, Serbia, and the Russian Federation with most of those from Russia coming from Chechnya. The top sending countries to the United States were China and Mexico. In Britain, in addition to Pakistan and Afghanistan, top sending countries included Iraq and Eritrea (UNHCR March 2008).

Several reasons are given for the wide-scale immigration from Third to First world countries. First, globalization has tended to strip less developed nations of their assets. The growing impoverishment of Third World countries and a widening income gap between them and First World countries have tempted many to seek a livelihood abroad. No longer able to support themselves or their families and confronted with the impact of globalization on labor markets, millions of people from Asia, Africa, Eastern Europe, and Latin America have sought entrance to First World countries in Western Europe and North America in order to earn a living. Second, immigration has been a response to the proliferation of civil wars in Africa, Asia, Eastern Europe, and Central America and to an escalation in ethnic tensions in Eastern Europe and postcolonial societies. The destabilizing effects of civil wars on political stability, a disruption in the food supply, and a lack of job opportunities have led people to immigrate to more stable and prosperous societies. Finally, the collapse of the former Soviet empire has contributed to increased immigration. Problems arising from economic dislocation, the transition to a free market system, the disappearance of old social safety nets, and the resurgence of ethnic tensions in Eastern Europe have encouraged people to move to more politically and economically stable countries.

The national origins of present-day immigrants have raised a number of issues for receiving countries. In the first place a different cultural background is thought to limit immigrants' ability to assimilate or adapt quickly to a new environment. In the minds of some in the receiving country this raises fear about the implications of parallel cultures for the national unity and identity. Then there is the matter of physical appearance. In the past racially distinctive groups such as Africans and the Chinese encountered more serious problems of integration and acceptance than European immigrants who, once they were able to speak the language and adopt the current styles of dress and behavior, were able to "blend in." Since the physical appearance of many of the immigrants from Third World countries makes blending in more difficult, they and their children can be easily identified as "foreign." Their integration is therefore more difficult.

The increased number of women immigrants is the fourth distinguishing characteristic. Civil wars or political unrest have created environments that are unsafe for women and children. No longer afforded protection by male family members and often responsible for the economic welfare of their children, they find themselves in a difficult situation. Without male protection it is not uncommon for them to be subjected to sexual harassment or to be without legal standing in matters relating to land ownership and finances. Finding themselves vulnerable, many women seek refuge by requesting asylum in First World countries where they think they will be out of harm's way. The result has been a dramatic escalation in the number of women applying for refugee status, which affords them a way to immigrate permanently and to bring their children with them.

Not all women immigrate to escape a dangerous situation, however. In some cases the decision is the product of a family strategy to improve the economic situation of those left behind. During much of the 1950s and early 1960s men immigrated to fill unskilled jobs in fields such as construction. The money they earned they sent home to their extended family. By the 1980s overseas employment opportunities for men had dried up, but jobs in areas such as child and elder care, the hospitality industry, and domestic service became available. Since these occupations are generally considered more suitable for women than men, families began to encourage women to immigrate on the grounds that their income from overseas jobs would compensate for lost male wages. Employment opportunities stemming from an increased demand in the overseas job market in the service sector provided an incentive for them to immigrate. Seeking a cheap, flexible female labor force, foreign recruiters reinforced the idea and benefits of immigrating. Sometimes it was personal or social networks that promoted immigrating. Friends who moved abroad wrote letters home about their new life and available job openings (Pessar 1999). Churches contributed, acting as a labor exchange by publicizing employment opportunities overseas and promising women who accepted these jobs a safe, protected environment. Last, but certainly not least, home governments promoted women's immigration. Remittances have constituted a considerable portion of the GDP of a number of countries, such as the Philippines and Mexico. Since money sent home would help the national economy, governments took an active role in supporting foreign employers to come and recruit workers, particularly in the areas of child and home care and nursing. For women the chance to earn money and send it home was the third most frequently cited reason for immigrating (Glennie 2010).

It would be incorrect, though, to assume that women have immigrated simply out of fear of violence and civil unrest or in response to the financial pressures. Many women who have immigrated have done so on their own volition. For some women the decision has been based on their desire for upward mobility. For nurses and health care professionals, acquiring additional training and skills, enhancing their credentials, and thus obtaining a better-paying job when they return home has been a motivating reason. For other women the hope was to improve their employment opportunities back home by learning another language. For unemployed women, job opportunities abroad have been enticing. For example, recently a number of Eastern European women unable to find suitable work at home came to the United States to take jobs teaching in understaffed inner-city schools in poor neighborhoods. Kinship has also been a consideration. Having a relative in the country has encouraged immigration, although it has also often led to slower rates of assimilation and lower-paying jobs. Interestingly enough, though, single women who come from countries that have discouraged immigration outside the context of family have been likely to earn more and improve their status more rapidly (Huang 1997). At the same time young, unmarried, less educated women have had greater difficulty in immigrating legally. For example, they have had a much harder time entering the United States than older women. Friends living abroad have often been a powerful incentive as well. Studies of women who have immigrated, as well as women's writing about their experiences of immigration, have frequently mentioned female friends who have urged them to come join them, or they have mentioned the importance of gaining a sense of personal freedom. In short, there has been a wide variety of reasons motivating women to immigrate.

The multiplicity of reasons and the extent to which they are intertwined is vividly illustrated in a study of Moroccan women and their decision to come to Italy to work. In the first place there was the practical reason: a demand for their labor. An aging Italian population created the need for young healthy women to work as caregivers. Moroccan women provided an ideal resource. However, the need for their labor or the money they could earn was not the sole motivation.

The women frequently cited several other reasons. Chief among them were an improvement in their life-style, the opportunity to meet immigrant Moroccan men whom they could marry, and the chance to pursue their studies. Then there was the ability to travel between Morocco and Italy easily. Italy's proximity to Morocco meant that the women would have the opportunity to go home to visit their mothers and that their mothers would be able to come and visit them. Maintaining a connection with their mothers was especially important to them and served as a deterrent from entering illegally. The only negative aspect for the women was that if they married and divorced in Italy it was difficult for them to return to Morocco (Salih 2001).

A study of Somali and Filipina women in Rome also reported multiple reasons of immigrating. For several, advanced training and/or a university degree was the primary motive. For the majority of Filipina women, however, economic reasons were the compelling factor. They reported that they sent their earnings back home to supplement their husbands' salaries, to send their children to school, to save for the future, or to build a house. For the Somali women, civil war was a major contributing factor, although earning money and sending money back to their families were also important factors. For both groups the short-term goal was financial. This is obvious in the case of Filipina women where mothers turned over their jobs to their daughters when their work visas expired. Long-term goals, when they were mentioned, centered on achieving personal goals and dreams. For a few there was the additional goal of a cautious movement toward self-determination and autonomy. Ironically, though, their financial contributions to family often threatened their own economic independence (Chell 1997).

For women with children the decision to immigrate has often been complicated by the fact that jobs in the areas of health and child care, domestic service, or the hospitality industry usually involve temporary work permits. Since recipients of this type of visa are neither eligible for permanent settlement nor allowed to bring their families with them, women have often been faced with the unpleasant choice of either taking a job abroad and earning money to support their families and leaving their children behind or foregoing a job to stay with their children. One way around this dilemma has been to obtain refugee status, which permits them to be accompanied by their children and to remain permanently. However, as will be discussed in a later chapter, refugee status has been very difficult for women to obtain.

For some women wishing or needing to immigrate, entering illegally has been the most costly and dangerous option. Wages available to undocumented women workers are usually very low, and there is no protection from abusive employers. As a consequence they have rarely been able to earn enough money to support a family back home, pay off the debt to people smugglers, or have their children join them. Furthermore, their illegal status has made it virtually impossible for them to return home temporarily in cases of a family emergency or to visit their children.

Immigrants, Refugees, Asylum Seekers: Deciding Their Status

Before turning to the implications of current policies for the social (re)construction of women immigrants' identity it might be useful to take note of some of the key terms currently used in discussing immigrants. They are *immigrant, refugee, asylum seeker,* and *undocumented alien,* sometimes referred to as an *unauthorized* or *illegal alien. Immigrant* is an umbrella term that may be used to include everyone, although it is usually used to describe someone who is granted permission to enter a country and to live and work there. The term *economic refugee* is sometimes used to describe an individual who, although applying for refugee status, is primarily motivated by a desire to improve her or his material well-being. In "Refugees and Migrants, Migrants and Refugees," the author has suggested that economic refugee is the "creation of the Western mind within the particular context of World War II" (Bertrand 1998). Immigration authorities tend to view economic refugees as traditional immigrants subject to national immigration policies. Others have defined them as individuals who are moved more by an instinct to survive or material preoccupations than for direct political persecution. *Refugee* is the term used for individuals who demonstrate a "well-founded fear of persecution" as defined in international protocols. In contrast to an economic refugee, the basis for the claim for refugee status is defined in terms of religious, political, or social group persecution. Individuals who fail to meet the standards established in the various UN protocols but have met national standards defining persecution may also be called refugees, although they are frequently categorized as asylum seekers. Here again there has been some criticism of the understanding of who and what a refugee is. The argument made is that like *economic refugee, refugee* is a Western construct that obscures and obfuscates what is involved. The trauma, the shock of being displaced, and the psychological impact are lost in the present understanding of what it means to be a refugee and that perhaps Southeast Asians have more fully understood the meaning of refugee when they have described a refugee as a person physically fleeing from their country but psychologically remaining there (Bertrand 1998, 109). Individuals who have entered the country or remained there without permission are defined as undocumented or unauthorized aliens; in popular parlance they are often referred to as *illegal aliens,* or simply *illegals.*

As we shall see in the following chapters the criteria for distinguishing between immigrants and refugees are vague and vary considerably from one country to the next. As a result some scholars have substituted the terms *voluntary* and *involuntary immigrant.* These terms perhaps offer a clearer notion about the motives for immigrating, but the criteria for deciding when immigration is voluntary and when it is not are ambiguous. Furthermore, the use of the term *refugee* in international protocols makes it unrealistic to use a different taxonomy.

Conclusion

Although immigration is a phenomenon that goes back to the ancient world, over the last five hundred years it has changed in character, becoming global and impacting domestic economies. In the later half of the nineteenth century and the first two decades of the twentieth century, concerns surfaced over the impact of immigration on the culture of receiving countries and resulted in the passage of restrictive policies. Initially the restrictions targeted Asians, particularly Chinese and Japanese, but subsequently they were directed toward additional groups of immigrants. The new policies not only attempted to limit immigration and included the requirement of demonstrating that they were victims of persecution but also institutionalized the principle of admitting family members as dependents. Despite the fact that the demand for low-wage female workers in areas such as hospitality, service, and caregiving sectors in recent years conflicts with the assumptions about female dependency, perceptions of immigrant women as a dependent family member persist. This association of women with family membership and dependency has continued to be a leitmotif of present day immigration policy.

Present debates over immigration have been sparked by a substantial growth in the number of people seeking refugee status, the national origins of the bulk of present-day immigrants, and the number of women immigrants, many of whom are not accompanied by a male family member but are accompanied by children. Receiving countries, for their part, have shaped their policies on the notion that (1) women immigrants are dependent and therefore potentially an economic burden and (2) immigrant culture poses an intrinsic threat to national unity.

CHAPTER 3

Government Policies and Women Immigrants
Establishing Conditions and Constructing Identities

Three types of people seek legal admittance to a country other than their own: (1) temporary visitors who are sometimes referred to as nonimmigrants, (2) individuals designated as lawful permanent residents who have the right to work and remain indefinitely, and (3) refugees seeking asylum. Temporary visitors or nonimmigrants are legally entitled to remain for a specified period of time, although they may apply for and receive permission to extend their stay. Examples of temporary visitors include tourists, students, skilled workers (usually professionals), and low-wage flexible workers. Ordinarily the right to work does not extend to tourists and students except on a limited basis. Nonimmigrants issued temporary work visas are allowed to work for a specified period—usually between one and three years. This type of visa is ordinarily not renewed, although individuals with special skills are usually granted a work visa for a longer initial period and are more likely to have their visas extended. Individuals wishing to enter and remain indefinitely are classified as immigrants and constitute the second type. In cases where family members immigrate, they do so under the provisions for family unification. This permits the head of the family to enter and remain indefinitely; other "dependent" family members—a spouse and children—are also given permission to enter and legally remain provided that they continue to be part of the family for a specific length of time. If "dependent" family members do not meet this condition, they risk deportation. Refugees who are able to demonstrate a well-founded fear of persecution that precludes them from returning to their home country constitute the third type. Individuals granted refugee status under the terms of the United Nations protocols have a right to permanent residency and are entitled to certain rights and privileges available to citizens, such as employment, social services, and education. They also possess legal recourse under the law to address violations of their rights. Some countries also grant refugee status on humanitarian grounds.

In such cases residency may be either temporary or permanent depending on national law and the particulars of the case. Not all rights and privileges extend to those granted temporary refugee status or temporary asylum. Both temporary visitors and immigrants can be deported in cases of criminal activity. In addition to temporary visitors, immigrants, and refugees, there are individuals who want to enter and stay but who, for a variety of reasons, fear they will be refused admission or are actually refused it. Individuals falling into this category are referred to as undocumented or unauthorized aliens, and unless amnesty is granted to them they are ineligible for a broad variety of rights enjoyed by citizens, legal immigrants, and refugees.

The crucial questions to be explored in this chapter are, what is the impact of present immigration policies on the social (re)construction of immigrant women's identity and how do these policies affect their opportunities? The chapter looks at immigration policies and practices applied to women entering under family unification programs, as well as to women entering independently as immigrants, and to women entering with temporary work visas. It also takes up the topic of undocumented women and the implications for their status. Discussion of refugee and asylum policies as they are applied to women will be considered in the next chapter.

Permanent Residency and Women: The Predominance of Family Unification Policy

Since the early part of the twentieth century the customary policy for admitting women immigrants to postindustrial countries in Western Europe and North America has been family unification. Therefore, it seems most appropriate to begin with this policy and to examine the conditions and repercussions it imposes on women. Before proceeding, however, a caveat is in order. The prevalence of the pattern of women entering under family unification programs is, at least in part, the result of existing laws and practices. The substantial percentage of women entering under programs of family unification is often not a matter of choice. Immigration laws and practices make it easier for them be admitted as a dependent family member than as either an immigrant or a refugee. Even in those instances where women are qualified to enter independently as immigrants or refugees, countries in Western Europe, the United States, and Canada have instead admitted them as dependent family members. Indeed, it is a common practice for immigration officials to encourage women applying for refugee status to enter under the auspices of family unification, and since women admitted as refugees are more likely to be given temporary status than male refugees, they often consider the option preferable (Boyd 1985).

Recently there has been a drop in the number of women admitted under the rubric of family unification. The explanation for this is pretty straightforward. A decline in the need for foreign male labor and an increase in the demand for temporary workers to fill stereotypic female occupations such as child and elder care have resulted in women rather than men being recruited as temporary workers.

However, unlike previous programs recruiting foreign male workers, workers today are not admitted under family unification programs. They are issued temporary work visas that preclude family members from joining them: spouses and children are not automatically allowed to enter as dependents.

Despite the gender change in the demands of the present-day labor market, immigration policy has nevertheless continued to reflect the idea of the immigrant as a male worker accompanied by a wife and children who are dependents. Thus the admission of spouses and family members of individuals granted refugee status continues to be dominated by the principles of family unification. Even in those cases where a wife could qualify for refugee status in her own right, it is the husband who is granted refugee status; the wife is admitted as a dependent. Even when a country has tried to discourage the practice of second- or third-generation immigrants marrying someone from their original home country, the practice of admitting foreign spouses or immediate relatives under the provisions of family unification has persisted.

As discussed in the preceding chapter, family unification policies first introduced in the early twentieth century have become a staple of North American and Western European immigration policy. Although there are some differences in the policies among countries, they share some basic assumptions. The first is that immigrants are men who come to work in countries where employment opportunities and economic rewards are greatest. The second is that these male workers are not likely to return home. In Europe at the end of World War II the initial belief was that male immigrant workers were there temporarily and that after they earned a sufficient amount of money they would return home. The reality was that the majority remained. The third assumption is that the man's family is economically dependent on his income. The belief was that either a woman is unlikely to be employed or her earnings will be insufficient to support herself or her family. Taking for granted the idea that men are the breadwinners and the heads of the households, policy makers pushed for provisions that would allow family members to come and join the men (Hansard 1969).

To some extent the notion of family immigration was consistent with the pattern of families moving from the countryside to newly emerging cities in eighteenth- and nineteenth-century Europe. For example, enclosure laws in Britain forced whole families to leave the land and come to the industrial centers that were springing up. The pattern of immigration from Southern and Eastern Europe in the later part of the nineteenth and early years of the twentieth century also often involved families with a wife, children, and sometimes parents joining a husband who fled to escape the crushing burden of poverty or prolonged, forced military service or religious persecution. Unlike temporary seasonal workers, these immigrants did not intend to return to their original homeland but instead wished to become permanent residents. In such circumstances admitting whole families seemed a reasonable and enlightened position to take.

It should be noted, however, that although a family immigration pattern existed, legislation enacted in the twentieth century actively promoted it. Why? This is a difficult question to answer. It might have been simply a response to the kind of family immigration that was occurring at the time, or perhaps it was the belief that a stable family life would promote integration and responsible behavior. It might also have been based on a preconceived notion of the patriarchal family and the acceptance of the idea of man as breadwinner. Perhaps it was some combination of all these things. Some have argued that it reflected a growing awareness of and sensitivity to the concept of human rights. As appealing as this explanation might be, however, the fact is that concerns about human rights with regard to family integrity did not emerge until after family unification had been widely adopted. Furthermore, despite the importance of human rights in current discourse, there is a growing criticism today of family unification on the grounds that it has encouraged chain family migration. A more controversial explanation has been that patriarchal culture was being weakened by various strands of modernism in the early decades of the twentieth century. Certainly by the end of World War II the concept of a family headed by an all-powerful father had begun to erode. This was the beginning of the heyday of the "new" independent woman who could "do her own thing." In endorsing the notion of the traditional patriarchal family and the dependent woman, the emphasis on family unification was perhaps an early effort in the culture wars to restore the old order. Of course a much more pragmatic—and plausible—explanation has been that an intact immigrant family would best facilitate integration and social adjustment. Regardless of the underlying motivations, however, family unification did become a fundamental dogma of immigration policy in the twentieth century and has continued to remain so.

While the principle of family unification was endorsed in US immigration policy in the early twentieth century, its official recognition did not appear until 1965 when it was formally proclaimed a basic principal of immigration policy. While in Western Europe the arrival of foreign male workers unaccompanied by their families at the end of World War II had caused social adjustment problems and prompted the adoption of family unification, in the two decades following the war a majority of the foreign work force in the United States were temporary, seasonal agricultural workers. The explanation that the formal legal recognition of family unification was motivated by the importance Americans placed on family is therefore somewhat problematic. Preoccupation with family had begun to dissipate by the late 1950s; and by the 1960s the women's movement with its emphasis on equality had begun to assert itself. Why then was family unification declared the centerpiece of immigration policy after the quota system was eliminated in 1965? Perhaps again it had something to do with a growing commitment to human rights spurred on by the recent civil rights battle or with an increasing attack on the patriarchal family structure. Regardless of the reasons, legal primacy of family unification was established.

Family unification policies in North America and Western Europe reflect the archetype of the male immigrant and his dependent family. There are, however, some differences, such as conditional residency and financial obligations of the sponsor. In the United States family unification has required that the sponsoring family member must (1) have lived in the country for a specific number of years,

(2) be able to demonstrate the ability to support immigrating family member(s), and (3) provide adequate housing. The spouse entering as a dependent must remain a part of the family for a given period of time—presently two years in the United States. Some of the additional restrictions on family unification adopted in the early 1970s and subsequently have included (1) changes in the screening process, which has been extended to a provision barring those who might become a public charge, (2) limiting social security benefits to citizens and legal residents, and (3) banning unauthorized aliens from receiving food stamps, unemployment benefits, student loans, and until 2012 in-state school tuition fees. An attempt to bar Medicaid coverage to nonresidents was overturned by the New York Federal District Court in the case *Lewis v. Gross*. A tightening up of financial requirements has been attributed to an increase in the number of women entering as illegal aliens and to the rising costs of immigration control. These changes in policy have not been viewed as an attack on the principle of family unification, however (Simcox 1988).

The Immigration Marriage Fraud Amendments of 1986 have also placed a limitation on family unification: an immigrant entering under the auspices of family unification who has been married less than two years is granted only conditional residency and must reapply for permanent residence status within ninety days after two years of conditional status had been met. Although the purpose of this legislation was to prevent individuals from contracting marriages of convenience in order to enter the country legally and then immediately divorce, there have been serious negative consequences. Conditional residency can imperil legal protection in cases of domestic abuse. Under the best of circumstances immigration is a traumatic experience, and adjustment to a new environment is sometimes difficult. This can cause stress in family relationships and create an environment conducive to domestic abuse. As will be discussed later, the existence of domestic abuse is often mentioned in studies of immigrant women and by social service workers in immigrant communities. However, efforts to combat it are often impeded by the fear of being deported. Conditional residency makes it difficult for dependent family members to leave an abusive family relationship, since leaving the family can result in deportation. Indeed even those who report abuse to the authorities run the risk of being deported. As a consequence, in instances of domestic abuse conditional residency places a dependent family member in a vulnerable position.

Canada's family unification policies differ somewhat from those of the United States. Under the Immigration and Refugee Protection Act of 2002 preferential treatment is given to three categories of immigrants: family class, which is roughly the equivalent of family unification, independent immigrants, and refugees. Family class covers closely related persons including spouses, partners, children, parents, and grandparents of sponsors. Described as important principles of Canadian immigration policy, family class and refugees are given priority, and 28 percent of all those admitted fall into the category of family class. In Canada the explicit rationale for emphasizing family is clearer than in the United States. It is the "belief that people who immigrate to Canada will tend to establish themselves more easily if they are supported by their families"—a sentiment also echoed in a number of European countries endorsing family unification. Critics of Canadian policy have challenged this assertion, arguing instead that the preference for family admission is based on the assumption that a family will take less time to become economically self-sufficient than a woman accompanied only by her children (Boyd 2004).

The policies of family unification in Western European countries reflect the special demand after World War II in those societies for labor in traditional male fields, such as heavy manufacturing and the building trades, and the virtual absence in demand for foreign female labor in areas such as domestic service. Men were actively recruited to come and work, but women were not with the result that immigrant labor was overwhelmingly male. The most noteworthy exceptions to this were Caribbean women immigrating to Britain and Turkish women who came to Germany. Otherwise recruited immigrants were men. When it became obvious that male laborers would not be returning home, the thought was that men would establish a stable life-style and adjust more easily if their families joined them. The leader of the British Labour Party, James Callaghan, speaking in the House of Commons during a debate on immigration, expressed it best when he argued that preventing a man's wife and children from joining him would lead to social problems in the community and the only way to prevent this was to allow families to be reunited (Hansard 1969).

With the exception of a brief period immediately following World War II in Britain, no effort was made to recruit foreign women to come and work or to encourage them to immigrate. Employment for women was virtually nonexistent at this time; their labor was simply not needed. Furthermore, European norms at this time did not include the idea of married women working; hence the belief was that women were unable to support themselves. Given these attitudes it made sense that a woman's right to remain should be tied to her husband's and that her residency was conditional. Building on this assumption, it was felt that if her husband died or was deported, she and her children should also be deported, for unless she could support herself and her children they would be a financial burden on the state.

Initially family unification appeared to be the solution to the problem of social adjustment of male workers in Europe and conditional status for dependents the means for protecting the state against financial liability, but a number of problems quickly surfaced. First, when the recruitment of male immigrants began to decline and the number of women immigrating on their own increased, issues of gender inequities arose. Family unification did not apply to the family of women immigrants. In Britain, for example, immigrant women were not permitted to be joined by their husband and children until 1985 (Bhabha and Shutter 1994). This clearly disadvantaged Caribbean women and soon became a bone of contention. There were also problems with conditional residency status. In Britain, under the 1981 immigration law, a wife's right to remain in the country was dependent on her husband. Until she had lived in the country for the required number of years, she had to remain a member of her husband's family. If she was widowed or abandoned or her marriage collapsed before her right to permanent residency (right of settlement) was established, she could be deported. If her husband was deported, she could also be deported even though she had broken no law. Widows, abandoned wives, or wives whose husbands were subject to deportation were also vulnerable to deportation, although they did have the right to request permission to remain. However, since they had to demonstrate their ability to support themselves and their children, their legally defined dependent status made this a difficult task. Some subsequent modifications to the 1981 act made it easier for wives to remain, but the rules governing conditional residency remained basically unchanged.

In cases where the male head of household was granted asylum the situation has been more complicated, for asylum dependents are not permitted to work. For the dependent spouse, the possibility of getting official permission to work has been next to impossible. Even in those instances where permission to work has been granted, it has been hard to get a national insurance number, which is required for employment. This has meant that if problems arise in the marriage, if the husband dies, or if he violates the law and is subject to deportation, the wife has virtually no opportunity to demonstrate her ability to support herself and her family and is therefore liable to deportation as well.

The problems of linking residency to family membership have become increasingly obvious. Government authorities have frequently viewed complaints of domestic abuse as an indication of a marriage breakup. In cases where a woman has conditional residency status, a failing marriage can threaten her right to remain. Wives or other dependent family members have therefore been reticent about reporting abuse. As a consequence there has been little likelihood of any legal intervention, and even social workers have reported feeling uneasy about reporting domestic abuse because of the possibility of deportation.

In some cases women have attempted to take matters into their own hands by forming grassroots community groups. Perhaps the best known is the Sari Brigade in Britain. Organized to protect widows from deportation, the group successfully engaged in protest actions and demonstrations against the deportation of widows. In some communities other informal groups have sprung up to offer support to abused women. Similar groups and organizations have emerged on the continent of Europe, especially in France. Despite these efforts, however, women with conditional status are less likely to report domestic violence for fear of deportation and possible exile from their children.

Today questions are being raised about the wisdom of family unification—not so much by those concerned with gender bias or the difficulties posed by conditional residency on dependent family members but by those opposing immigration. Questioning the need for family unification and citing the phenomenon of chain family migration, objections have focused on two things: (1) the legitimacy of marriages to foreigners, which are seen by many as a simple ploy to gain legal admission to the country, and (2) the belief that marriage to a foreign spouse reinforces the distinctive identity of ethnic communities and thus interferes with the process of integration. In Britain and elsewhere in Europe criticisms of family unification have usually centered on the allegation that the marriage of a citizen to a foreigner is nothing more than a charade that allows individuals to enter who would otherwise be denied admission. In an attempt to address this issue of "sham marriages," legislation was passed in Britain that provided for special scrutiny of marriages of citizens to foreigners when the ceremony was not performed by the Church of England. Objections were immediately raised on the grounds that the law unfairly disadvantaged members of other Christian sects as well as Jews, Muslims, Hindus, and other religious faiths. When the High Court struck the law down as discriminatory, new legislation was introduced in 2005 that required immigrants wishing to marry a citizen to obtain a certificate from the government and to pay a fee amounting approximately to $270. In cases where a couple was refused a certificate, the law stipulated, they would have to go abroad to marry and then the partner requiring proper immigration status would have to reapply to enter Britain. Although the court also struck this law down on the grounds that it interfered with a "fundamental right" to marry, there have continued to be pressures to restrict, if not eliminate, marriages in which a foreign spouse can gain residency under the provisions of family unification. In an effort to sidestep the objections to previous attempts to restrict family unification marriages, a proposal requiring the foreign spouse to speak English was recently put forward. It is important to remember, though, that present opposition to family unification largely reflects negative feelings about immigration rather than concerns about gender inequities.

Present concerns about immigration in the United States have also focused on the issue of sham marriages. A new emphasis has been placed on interviews of couples when one of them is petitioning for a green card application. In these interviews the United States Citizenship and Immigration Service scrutinizes and then approves spousal green card petitions before the application process for a green card can proceed. In the fiscal year 2008–9 over 241,000 spousal applications were filed. Just over 7 percent (16,810) were approved, but only 4 percent (506) of the applications were rejected on the grounds that the marriage was fraudulent. The remainder was disallowed for other reasons. Despite the fact that few marriages have been found to be shams, all couples petitioning for a spousal green card must be interviewed. In addition to documents showing a shared residence, a shared bank account, and so on, approval or rejection often depends on each of the spouses giving the same responses to a variety of questions, such as "What color is your spouse's toothbrush?," "What did you do on your spouse's birthday?," or "What is your wife's favorite piece of jewelry?" In some cases each has been asked about intimate relations, birth control practices, and sexual activities. If the husband and wife who are interviewed separately give different answers to more than a certain number of the questions, the conclusion is that no spousal relationship exists, and the petition is likely to be rejected. In a recent expose in *The New York Times*, one women interviewed claimed that questions were asked about the couple's sex life, including frequency of intercourse. Another woman claimed that she had been asked about condom use. Another reported being quizzed about who cooked dinner (Bernstein 2010).

Family unification policies in a number of Western European countries have incorporated regulations regarding residency and work. For years Germany was considered to have one of the best and most liberal family unification programs of all. Following the war large numbers of foreign male workers, many of them of Turkish origin, were recruited to come and work. The expectation was that once they had made enough money they would return home. Many Southern Europeans did in fact do just that, but others, particularly the Turks, opted to remain. When the demand for foreign labor declined, the government instituted programs encouraging them to leave. These proved largely ineffective. A family unification policy was adopted as a solution to social issues stemming from the existence of a substantial foreign male population. In the beginning no restrictions were placed on the entrance of family members other than proof of a relationship, sufficient income to support family members, and adequate accommodations for the family when they arrived. Families quickly took advantage of the new program. A decline in the demand for labor coupled with the growth in the number of foreign families prompted the government to modify its policies and take action to protect employment opportunities for Germans. Residency and work permits were linked and granted only to the male head of the family. Since only those possessing a residency permit were eligible to work, only the male head of household could be employed. A wife and children who continued to live as part of the family could be residents, but they were not permitted to work, with the result that there was low labor-force participation among Turkish women. Subsequently a requirement that linked employment with the ability to speak German also disadvantaged Turkish women, since language instruction was largely restricted to male immigrants and their children (Liebig 2007).

The demands of the German labor market soon rendered these restrictive measures impractical. Although there was unemployment, native Germans were unwilling to accept low-paying, dead-end jobs. Immigrants, on the other hand, were willing to take them. Turkish women were an obvious source of low-wage, flexible workers. Then there was the issue of immigrant family income. Male immigrant wages were not sufficient to support a family. Other family members' incomes were needed if a family was to be economically self-sufficient. A solution was to grant immigrant women permission to work. When the ban on women working was lifted the only major qualification was that there had to be a severe labor shortage in the field in which they were employed. Wives were, therefore, most likely to be granted work permits in those employment sectors where there was a strong demand for cheap, flexible labor such as hotels, restaurants, and dangerous, low-skill-level electronics assembly. The rules for children were different, however. If they took vocational courses for at least six months they were exempted from the requirements that restricted their access to employment and were issued their own work permits.

Since temporary work visas have now replaced the older programs for recruiting foreign workers, family unification is no longer considered useful, and further restrictions have been imposed. For example, individuals who immigrated to Germany as children, or who were born in the German Federal Republic, are no longer permitted to marry a foreign wife and bring her into the country under the provisions for family unification. Unlike the situation in other European countries the issue of conditional status as a route to acquiring citizenship has not been an issue in Germany, since foreign workers and their families were not eligible for citizenship under German law.

Immigration policies in France and Italy have also endorsed the concept of family unification. Although France stopped recruiting foreign workers in 1974, immigration continued through family unification. By 2006 family unification accounted for nearly 65 percent of the immigration to France (OECD 2006, Chart 1.2). Initially French work permits were granted to the male head of household, and wives and children were ineligible to work. A demand for a low-paid, flexible work force in catering, hospitality, and domestic service resulted in an easing of these restrictions, and work permits are now issued to dependents except in those occupations where French workers are underemployed. Similar policies exist in Italy.

In France and recently in Italy public attention has been concerned with the cultural integration of immigrants. Legislation requires foreign spouses of French citizens to wait three rather than two years before applying for a ten-year residency permit, and foreign spouses must be married for four years before they are eligible to apply for French citizenship. Any immigrant found to be practicing polygamy can be immediately deported, and the procedures for deporting unauthorized immigrants have been simplified. An additional condition for family unification–sanctioned residency and eligibility for citizenship is a "welcome and integration" contract to respect the basic principles of family life in France. This entails abiding by the principle of secularism (*la laicite*), equality between husband and wife, and monogamy. It also requires taking French language and civic courses. Families with school-age children must enroll them in the French school system and demonstrate a "real will" to integrate. While the purpose of the legislation is to ensure the integration of North African and West African Muslim immigrants into mainstream French culture, the increased length of time of a dependent spouse's conditional status and the obligation to report to the authorities any breach in the equality in the relationship between husband and wife have simply increased the vulnerability of the spouse, since both reporting abuse and failing to abide by the conditions in the new law can result in deportation. In Italy conditional residency for a dependent family member has also adversely affected women. The last Italian election triggered a high level of xenophobia and increased demands for more stringent restrictions including a longer conditional status waiting period and tough enforcement of those laws already on the books.

The matter of conditional residency and employment that dependent family members, and particularly spouses, confront has been a subject of discussion throughout Western Europe. The European Union as well as its member states has endorsed the principle in the Schengen Convention of free movement of spouses and children on humanitarian grounds. However, free movement is dependent on an employed spouse, and so the basic problem of a dependent spouse remains. In implementing the provisions of the Schengen Convention, the Council of Ministers of the European Union adopted a directive in 2003 that sought to address the issue of conditional status. Initially the thought was to establish one year as the length of time required for conditional status; however, the final draft suggested a period of one to three years and a period of five years before independent residence status could be obtained. Such a lengthy period has clearly failed to address the problems that some wives face. The Council of Europe proposed an alternative that, while preserving the principle of family unification, also addressed the liabilities of dependent status. Its plan called for the establishment of training programs that would extend employment opportunities to women rather than just the traditional programs devoted to child care and community involvement in matters affecting their children's schooling.

Recently a group of multinational corporations in Europe and the United States created a foundation to lobby governments to relax work permit regulations for spouses accompanying highly skilled immigrants. Established in the Netherlands, the Permits Foundation has sought to foster international employee mobility and dual-career families. Although the rules vary somewhat from one country to the next, the program is designed to allow both spouses to work (Permits Foundation). As a result of its efforts, the United States, the United Kingdom, and France have taken steps that allow the spouses of intracompany employees and traders/investors who would otherwise be ineligible for employment to obtain employment permits. So far the Permits Foundation has been successful in getting legislation allowing spouses of intracompany transferees and investors/traders or employees to obtain work authorization enacted in the United States (2002), the Netherlands (2005), and France (2006). A similar policy was adopted in Britain in April 2008. In the United States spouses of individuals entering as investors and traders or entering the country as a result of an intracompany transfer may obtain work authorization by providing a marriage certification and paying a $120 filing fee. After a 90-day waiting period required for processing the application Homeland Security can issue a temporary work authorization for a period of 240 days. However, authorization may not exceed two years. One drawback to this program is that it authorizes a shorter employment period than the one ordinarily granted to skilled and professional spouses. Thus the dependent spouse who wishes to work continues to remain at a disadvantage.

It must also be remembered that the Permit Foundation program is applicable only to the spouses of a small, highly trained international staff transferred for a limited time period by the corporate sector and investment traders. Despite its benefits to some it is a clear example of the importance of privilege. It does not apply to the spouses of those employed in other types of occupations—both skilled and unskilled—and especially to those women who are part of the low-wage flexible labor force. In an effort to address the more fundamental problems faced by the vast majority of immigrant women, the European Human Dignity and Social Exclusion Project (HDSE) has called for a drastic restructuring of existing laws and policies that marginalize women by describing them as dependent on their husbands or fathers and leave them legally vulnerable by linking their residency to the head of the family.

Although the notion of family unification has been widely accepted and endorsed, some Western leaders like Sarkozy in France recently began to raise questions about its usefulness, after immigration shifted from being worker dominated to family dominated in the 1970s. Others have based their criticisms on issues such as sham marriages (Meyers 2006). As immigration has become more controversial, there has emerged a growing distrust of foreign spouses or fiancées seeking to enter a country. As we have seen in the discussion of Britain and Germany and the United States, foreign spouses have come to be regarded by some as nothing more than a pretense designed to get around legal restrictions on immigration. Strategies such as denying access to social welfare benefits and citizenship have been devised to thwart foreign spouses or fiancées from immigrating. When such measures have proved to be ineffective, more drastic actions have been taken, such as longer conditional residency periods, compulsory language courses, cultural immersion programs, and time-consuming, costly investigations into the backgrounds of the couples.

While some see family unification as a ploy to bypass restrictions on immigration, others, particularly immigrant ethnic communities, have defended it on humanitarian grounds as necessary for cultural identity and self-esteem. Young men are often urged to marry women from the home country on the grounds that such marriages help preserve cultural traditions, and arranged marriages for daughters with men back home are encouraged for the same reasons. Moreover, as mentioned earlier, marriage to someone from the home country has also allowed some families to fulfill financial or personal obligations.

Unfortunately neither the proponents nor critics of family unification have really considered the needs and interests of women or implications for the (re)construction of their social identity. In classifying women as dependents, family unification policies have infantilized women. Furthermore, in ignoring social, class, ethnic, racial, or educational differences among immigrant women, they have diminished women's agency and promoted dependency (Hajdukowski-Ahmed 2008). The situation of the privileged spouse covered by the Permit Foundation program is quite different from that of the wife of a North African laborer in France or a Hispanic wife in the United States. Unless the varying circumstances of women immigrants are taken into account, conditional residency will remain problematic for women. Moreover, women's contributions to both their ethnic community and the broader society will be diminished or ignored as long as they are viewed as dependent. In short the principle of family integrity should be respected and so too should women's equality before the law.

The concept of family unification rightly acknowledges the integrity of the family. However, it has raised additional problems. First there is the matter of consistency. By privileging traditional, patriarchic families—that is, families embodying the notion of men functioning in the public marketplace and women in the private domain of home—it has tended until recently not to recognize the female-headed families. Furthermore it has failed to grant the right of family integrity to temporary workers, most of whom are women and who as a result have had to leave their children behind. Coupled with these problems is the flawed assumption that in an immigrant family a single wage earner is an economically viable option. This does not correspond with the facts. Most immigrants have tended to have lower earning than anticipated and usually do not earn enough to support a family (Duleep and Regets 1996). Even at the height of male immigration following World War II the financial needs of the family, coupled with a demand for cheap, flexible female labor, led to an increasing number of wives moving into the employment market. The failure of family unification programs to recognize the need for multiple family wage earners has resulted in an absence of programs that would allow many married women immigrants to develop marketable skills. As a result they are precluded from getting decent paying work or even the opportunity of working legally. Under such circumstances they find employment in the informal economy where the pay is poor and working conditions unregulated. As will be discussed in a later chapter, the upshot is that immigrant women entering under family unification programs are often frozen in low-paying, dead-end jobs and severely limited in their interactions with the world outside their home or immediate ethnic community.

There also is the issue of social adjustment. If integration into mainstream society is a desired outcome, mothers who stay at home or who work illegally, often in ethnically segregated jobs, will only be peripherally engaged in the broader community. Discouraging them from entering the formal economy is not the optimal means for achieving their integration into a new environment. Here again there are conflicting messages, contradictory voices. One demands integration while the other fosters exclusion.

In the end family unification constructs a social identity for women that not only attempts to restrict them to a role within the family but also reinforces an image of them as dependent in mainstream society. A good example of this is German legislation, which until recently imposed restrictions on immigrant women working and at the same time made immigrant families immediately eligible for social service benefits (Liebig 2007). Policies such as this makes it easy to label women as individuals who cannot and do not make a contribution outside the domain of the home and reinforce the idea that given their dependent status they can only be a potential drain on the country's financial resources. This description of the women as dependent is at odds with the multifaceted roles many Third World women play in both their country of origin and their new country. Indeed, in many Third World countries women frequently perform the major share of the work in the agricultural sector and operate small-scale retail enterprises, which we in the West prize and refer to as small entrepreneurial business ventures. Family unification policies pose contradictory constructions of self for all married women immigrants and largely ignore the fact that some women are more privileged and others less. Equally important, they feed into anti-immigrant feeling and encourage xenophobia.

Entering Solo

In contrast to family unification policies there is now little formal gender discrimination in the procedures regulating the admission of short-term or nonimmigrant women visitors and students and those who have a special relationship to the receiving country. When anti-immigrant sentiments are prevalent, however, there tends to be some wariness. Women immigrating independently are sometimes thought to be thieves, potential welfare mothers, transmitters of sexual diseases, and prostitutes. Such suspicions may affect the review of their visa application (Martin 2000).

The absence of formal gender discrimination in the immigration process is relatively recent. For the greater part of the twentieth century a child's citizenship was determined by the father, and a married woman automatically acquired the nationality of her husband. Today patriarchy no longer governs citizenship or determines special connection by birth or descent in Western Europe, Canada, or the United States. For example, the right to enter the United States or Britain as permanent residents and to work may be conferred by either mother or father. All that is required is proof of a direct line of descent to an American in the case of the United States or to a British citizen in the case of the United Kingdom. There are some restrictions in the case of some European countries, such as France and Germany, which will be discussed later, and in a recent case, *Tuan Anh Nguyen et al. v INS* (2001) the US Supreme Court ruled in a 5–4 decision that a father does not necessarily establish a claim for the right of return for a child born out of wedlock overseas. In that case the Supreme Court decided that childbirth was a more involved process for women than for men and that women were more likely to form a loving, nurturing relationship with a child than men. Therefore, a father's claim of citizenship for his out-of-wedlock child born to a Vietnamese woman was not upheld.

Despite some anomalies, though, gender neutrality in establishing a right of return is presently the norm. In Britain today, once a special relationship is acknowledged men and women enjoy the same benefits, although this was not the case during most of the twentieth century. In the United States children born abroad may claim citizenship, if its mother or father is a citizen, the only restriction being that the child claiming citizenship must be registered. As American citizens these children have the full right of return to the United States, including the right to take up permanent residency and work. Indeed, an American president, John Quincy Adams, was born in France. Policies and regulations permitting entrance to those with close ties of descent exist in other countries as well. In some countries the right of return is not restricted to immediate offspring but is available to grandchildren as well. Gender of the grandparent is not relevant if citizenship is being claimed through this relationship. For example, Germany, Ireland, and Italy grant individuals full citizenship rights if the individual can document descent by virtue of a grandparent—male or female—although in Germany birth there does not automatically confer citizenship.

However, gender is often implicitly a consideration in cases where individuals are admitted on the basis of a particular skill or area of expertise. A strong demand in today's globalized world for well-educated individuals possessing highly developed skills and abilities, especially in the fields of information technology, engineering, and business, has led international corporations to actively recruit highly trained foreign professionals and encourage them to immigrate (Campbell 1995). Since these individuals are considered an asset, permission for them to take up permanent residency and work is rarely denied. Furthermore, extensions of their visas are commonplace. Of course, it should be noted that post-9/11 attitudes have changed somewhat about who should be admitted even in the case of highly skilled professionals. Country of origin is now sometimes an issue in the United States and to some extent in Western European countries as well. Men of Middle Eastern background, for example, are often scrutinized more closely and are now less actively recruited than trained professionals from elsewhere.

Legislation has been enacted in several countries to meet the demand for both skilled and unskilled labor. The United States included such a provision in the Immigration and Naturalization Act of 1952 for admitting both highly skilled temporary workers and those who could fill low-wage jobs where there was a labor shortage. A similar provision establishing a special classification, H-1B, for skilled and unskilled workers was incorporated into the Immigration Act of 1990. Although H-1B applies to both high- and low-skilled workers, it clearly favors those who are skilled professionals. Seventy percent of those admitted under H-1B are either in the field of IT (58 percent) or in architecture, engineering, and surveying (12 percent). Skilled workers admitted under this program receive an initial visa of three years, renewable for another three years. They are not required to demonstrate an intention of returning to their country of origin, and most remain permanently in the United States. Furthermore, the H-1B program incorporates the principle of family unification. Family members, including a spouse, are eligible to be admitted as dependents. However, they cannot be employed unless they are also themselves qualified to receive a work permit or their spouse meets the requirements established under the Permit Foundation program. Since the fields from which skilled workers entering under H-1B are predominantly male dominated, men are more likely to be granted H-1B visas than their wives, who are more likely to be designated dependent family member. Thus, like family unification programs in general, the H-1B program implicitly accepts the notion of dependent women who have the potential to be a burden on government-provided social services. German policies differ somewhat from those of the United States. For example, German legislation that went into effect in 2005 also included a provision for admitting highly skilled and well-educated professionals. Although it also incorporated the principle of family unification, it differs from the American H-1B program in that it provides for work permits for spouses. A similar program permitting highly skilled professionals to remain in France and work was proposed by the French president Sarkozy, although the provision for the dependent spouse to obtain a work permit was less clearly spelled out.

The situation for less skilled workers is quite different. In contrast to skilled workers, only about 10 percent of those admitted under the H-1B program to the United States are unskilled. Their visas are issued for one year, not three. Although renewable for up to three years they are rarely extended beyond a year. Moreover, while skilled workers may bring their spouses and unmarried minor dependent children with them, unskilled workers may not. The need in the countries of Western Europe and North America for low-wage workers in the service areas—particularly child and elder care, which are usually female dominated—means that the bulk of those entering as low-wage, unskilled workers under the H-1B type program are likely to be women, since with the exception of some Middle Eastern countries men are rarely recruited or admitted to fill low-skill and low-paying jobs in the caring or domestic professions.

Although gender does not appear to be a factor in gaining permission for well-educated professionals to enter a country and work, there are a couple of important caveats. First, women employed in IT consultancy firms are expected to be highly mobile—to live "hypermobile" lives. Although they may adopt this life-style it conflicts with the universal cultural expectation that women are responsible for running a geographically fixed household (Raghuram 2004). Second, as just discussed, the US visa program clearly favors a single family wage earner and discourages the "dependent" spouse from working unless he or she can also obtain an H-1B visa. Obtaining a work visa for those employed in less skilled occupations is not really a viable option for the dependent spouse since H-1B visas for unskilled workers are granted for only one year. As a consequence the H-1B visa program makes a dependent spouse's participation in the labor force difficult if the visa holder is highly skilled and next to impossible if the visa holder is unskilled. Third, although immigration restrictions are not imposed on talented women recruited by international companies, gender discrepancies in types of jobs, pay, and advancement tend to discourage them from immigrating.

Implicit gender bias also exists for skilled women immigrating on their own and without a family. Several studies have shown that although initially the employment opportunities for new immigrants—both men and women—are at a lower level than their training and expertise would warrant, men are more likely to advance rapidly in terms of pay and promotions than women. For example, a study of male and female Russian immigrants to Israel found that within a two-year period, men's earnings and job opportunities had improved substantially and were on a par with native Israelis, whereas women continued to lag behind. Moreover, the gender gap grew over time (Raijman and Semyonov 1997). As will be discussed in a later chapter, there is also a gender gap in pay and advancement for professionally trained immigrant women in the area of health care in both Western Europe and North America. These women rarely achieve the advancement commensurate with their training and job performance. Moreover, there is a growing tendency to admit them under the auspices of restricted, temporary work permits, particularly if they have not received advanced training.

In short, immigration policies predicated on the notion of women as dependent members of a male-headed family group have not only produced gendered results in cases where women enter through family unification but also influenced perceptions of them when they enter independently.

Temporary Work Visas

With a decline in the number of unskilled jobs in traditionally male jobs, few men are now admitted on temporary work visas, whereas women are increasingly recruited to work in service-sector jobs. In Britain, for example—with the exception of jobs in traditional female employment fields such as domestic work, the hospitality profession, and health care and of some categories of agricultural workers—there is virtually no possibility of obtaining a temporary work visa. In fact in recent years, with the exception of skilled professionals, only domestics have tended to be issued work permits. In France temporary work permits, which are issued primarily to female low-wage, unskilled workers, are difficult to renew. The same is true for Italy where the demand for child-care and domestic workers has led to a considerable increase in the number of women entering with temporary work visas. Regulations regarding renewal of these permits in Italy are made by regional authorities and reflect the demands of the local labor market. Typically an extension of this type of visa is denied. Germany routinely rejects all requests for extensions even for those employed in child care, domestic service, and hospitality. In Austria visa renewal is rare, although it is a little less draconian than in Germany. Some countries have gone further by barring the entrance of all low-skill workers. For example, Ireland will now only issue work permits to highly trained, skilled professionals. In short throughout Western Europe, when temporary work visas are granted to unskilled workers, there is very little possibility of extending visas for low-wage workers beyond the originally specified period. As mentioned earlier similar strictures on temporary work visas also exist in the United States with requests for extensions of H-1B visas for low-wage, flexible workers routinely rejected.

Although temporary work visas resemble earlier guest worker programs insofar as they are used to recruit workers for special niche areas, they differ in the type of workers being recruited and the privileges extended to them. In sharp contrast to the situation of skilled, professional workers, the regulations governing work visas for low-skilled workers are much more restrictive. Presently they prohibit family members from accompanying the visa holder. This poses serious problems since those granted these visas are women with children. The NAFTA Implementation Act of 1993, for example, prohibits Mexican women employed in occupations such as child and elder care and hospitality to be accompanied by their spouse and children. Furthermore the women are not automatically eligible for citizenship after the normal period of residency required for a green card.

Today the demand for labor is in stereotypic female occupations such as child care, health care, elder care, domestic service, and hospitality. Since employers tend to prefer younger women who are likely to have children of their own, restrictions on bringing in family members mean that many of them are forced to leave their own children in the care of others back home. This situation often creates serious psychological stress for the women. Feelings of guilt are intensified by studies attributing the emergence of juvenile gangs and delinquent behavior to separation of mother from her family. Certainly maintaining close, emotional attachments with their children, the members of their extended family, and their partners back home is difficult and painful for women on temporary work visas and poses serious problems of readjustment when they do return.

Some programs have sought to address both the need for low-wage workers in the service areas and the issues confronting women coming to take up these jobs. In the United States an acute shortage of health-care workers during the 1980s led to take a moderate position on temporary work visas. The Immigration Nursing Relief Act of 1989 created a special nonimmigrant category for admitting qualified registered nurses. Its provisions allowed nurses to remain permanently, to work, and to obtain citizenship after a specified period of time. For women immigrating to the United States under this program, a temporary work permit represented a means of obtaining permanent residency, citizenship, and ultimately the possibility of being joined by their families.

The situation for low-skilled workers in the caring professions is somewhat different in Canada. Not only are highly trained professionals welcomed, but there is also a special program for low-skill workers in the area of caregiving. Called Live-In Caregivers, it lets qualified caregivers come to Canada on a temporary basis when there are no Canadians or permanent residents available to take the positions. These live-in caregivers must work in private households and provide care for children, the sick, the elderly, or persons with a disability. After working for a two-year period they are eligible to apply for permanent residency. Interestingly enough the opportunity for permanent residency does not apply to other categories of unskilled workers. Women who enter the country as domestic workers, for example, do not qualify under the government's point system as independent immigrants (Bakan and Stasiulis 1997).

Programs that provide opportunities for women immigrants, such as the caregivers program in Canada and programs involving the recruitment of health-care workers in the United States, have raised concerns about gender stereotyping. In pigeonholing women in a limited number of jobs associated with the domestic sphere, such as homemaker and caregiver, these programs have given credence to the idea that foreign women are incapable of handling jobs in the public sphere. In addition to undermining the efforts of women's movements in Western Europe, Canada, and the United States to wage war against gender stereotypes they have also frustrated women's opportunity to upgrade their skills and qualifications. In many cases a woman's decision to immigrate has been influenced by the expectation that her experience abroad will enhance her chances for securing a better job when she returns home. Employment as a caregiver or lowest-level health-care worker hardly permits such a goal to be achieved.

There is also the question of compensation. Like men, women, particularly those entering with temporary work visas, immigrate for economic reasons. Their salary is often crucial to the economic survival of their families back home and provides the money necessary for schooling, which they hope will improve their children's chances for a better life. Their ability to contribute financially to their families also boosts their status back home. Temporary work visas channeling women into caregiving and low-status domestic-type work have instead limited them to low-paying jobs and lessened their opportunity to contribute financially to their families back home. The end result has often been a sense of personal failure.

Illegal Aliens

Fearing that they will be denied permission to enter, some women, as well as some men, do so illegally. Others admitted as nonimmigrants or on temporary work visas simply decide not to return home and instead remain illegally. This is also the case for some who have been denied refugee or asylum status. Called undocumented, illegal, irregular, unauthorized, or black labor these individuals go "underground" or "disappear." According to 2003 estimates of the Immigration and Naturalization Service, which has been subsequently subsumed under the Department of Homeland Security, the number of unauthorized aliens in the United States grew during the 1990s by about 350,000 a year. About 69 percent of the unauthorized aliens were Mexican, followed by immigrants from El Salvador, Guatemala, Haiti, the Philippines, and Honduras, and about one in twenty were Canadian. The problem of undocumented aliens is still more acute in Western Europe. For example, in France it is estimated that the number of undocumented immigrants ranges between two hundred thousand and four hundred thousand (OECD 2006). In Europe immigrants come primarily from Africa, Asia, and non-EU-member states in Eastern Europe.

The number of undocumented aliens in countries of North America and Western Europe cited by individual governments or by NGOs has been consistently challenged as being either too high or too low. In addition to the problem of getting reliable data about how many undocumented aliens there actually are, there is little information available about the gender breakdown. One study estimated that in 1990 between one-third and one-half of all the undocumented aliens from Central America in Los Angeles were women, with the largest percentage coming from El Salvador (47 percent) and the smallest from Mexico (34 percent; Marcelli 1999). Recent conjectures about gender breakdown have been similar.

Ordinarily the undocumented use one of several strategies to gain permanent residency. The first involves initially using some ruse to obtain a visa—typically a student or tourist visa—and then overstaying permission to remain. The second entails overstaying a temporary work permit. A third involves entering without the knowledge of border controls. In each of these instances the individuals disappear into the informal economy, sometimes referred to as the shadow or black economy. The absence of data dealing with gender prevents us from determining if women are more likely to choose one of these strategies over the other, although conventional wisdom suggests that they might be more likely to overstay a work visa.

The third strategy, bypassing border controls, often involves paying people smugglers. This is the most expensive of all the options. For example, recently in an upscale New York suburb a couple and their daughter were arrested and charged with smuggling and harboring 69 illegal Peruvian immigrants, including 13 children who paid upwards of six thousand dollars each for forged visas. Asians using people smugglers often must pay fees that run in excess of twenty or thirty thousand dollars. To repay this debt plus interest owed to people smugglers, unauthorized aliens frequently agree to take prearranged jobs in the shadow or black economy, where they work in the equivalent of slave-like conditions until they are able to pay off their debts. Finding themselves in the equivalent of debt peonage and in a tenuous legal situation, they have little choice but to accept exploitative treatment. It is fruitless for them to complain. If they do, the best they can hope for is deportation.

There has been strong pressure to take additional steps to deter illegal immigration and to enforce existing immigration policies. A growing hostility to an increase in the number of illegal women aliens in the United States during the 1980s is cited for the subsequent adoption of stringent reforms in immigration legislation (Simcox 1988). However, the development of increasing hostility in the United States and Western Europe is somewhat incongruous given the fact that tight restrictions on immigration probably encourage it. Illegal immigration has created a vicious circle not only in the United States but also throughout Western Europe. France and the United States provide convincing examples of this. Tight controls on legal immigration, the restrictions attached to work visas, and the inability of immigrants to be joined by family members have all contributed to and perpetuated a growth in illegal immigration. A demand for cheap labor has encouraged the growth in the informal economy, which, in turn, has encouraged a growth in illegal immigration. Hearing about the availability of jobs abroad, people decide to immigrate, but, lacking the necessary paperwork to enter legally, unauthorized aliens find themselves ineligible for jobs that pay well or carry benefits. The upshot is that they find work in the informal economy where they earn low wages in jobs no one else will take.

The problems posed by illegal immigration are well known. To start with, there is little incentive or opportunity for unauthorized aliens to integrate into the mainstream society, since their continued residency is problematic. Uncertainty about their status reduces the incentive to assimilate. What purpose does it serve to become more fully integrated into the life and culture of a country when you are constantly threatened with deportation (Boeri et al. 2002)? Furthermore, the uncertainty of undocumented status restricts social interaction to the safety of one's ethnic immigrant community. Then there is the issue of family integrity, which is particularly critical in the United States. Children born in the United States are automatically entitled to citizenship regardless of whether or not their parents are undocumented. Although children of undocumented aliens may not be denied a public education per *Plyler v. Doe* (1982), under the terms of the US 1996 Immigration Act they may be denied a number of benefits to which they might otherwise be entitled as citizens.

To complicate matters further, when the parent is undocumented, but the children are citizens the parent is still liable for deportation even though their children are not. As a consequence there is a growing pattern of fractured families among undocumented immigrants. This also impedes integration.

Elsewhere the issue of immigrant family integrity is moot. In Germany, for example, citizenship is not automatically conferred on children born there unless a parent has German citizenship. Children of aliens also do not automatically acquire Irish or British citizenship. Consequently in these countries there is not the same possibility of deporting parents but not their children.

The basic dilemmas presently existing in US immigration policy and practices regarding the undocumented in the United States are not easily resolved, as earlier efforts to grant amnesty have indicated. In many cases the failure of the undocumented to apply for amnesty represented a rational choice. Many of the undocumented did not apply for legal status on the grounds that it might jeopardize child welfare benefits offered by several states. Poor women, especially single mothers, simply did not believe they were in a position to risk the potential cut in child and family benefits that legalized status required.

There were other risks involved in applying for amnesty as well. Women wishing to change their status from undocumented to legally settled claimed that employers viewed undocumented workers favorably as a cheap, pliant labor supply and used both positive and negative tactics to encourage them to remain undocumented. This strategy, which has been cynically referred to as the "employable mother rule," has emphasized the message that it is in the women's best interest to remain undocumented. Employed women believed that the risks of seeking amnesty were just too great. Some women also claimed that prior to its absorption into Homeland Security, the Immigration and Naturalization Service was complicit with employers in the effort to limit women's usage of legalization programs. Whether these claims are valid or not, undocumented women seeing themselves under threat from their employers and vulnerable to being fired refrained from applying for legalization. The concerns surrounding amnesty in the United States are similar to those that existed in France where despite anti-immigrant rhetoric employers continued to prefer cheap, undocumented "black labor"(Wihtol 2001).

As is the case for women admitted under family unification, undocumented women have few options for seeking help in cases of sexual harassment or domestic violence, since any effort to contact the authorities about abuse carries with it the possibility of being deported. Concerns about deportation have also affected their access to health care, for many are apprehensive that they will be reported to the authorities if they go to a doctor or a hospital.

As might be expected, there has been a strong backlash against illegal aliens, particularly women, both here in the United States and in Western Europe. Some groups have been especially virulent in their condemnation. Most often complaints have centered on cost. Citing statistics from the Center for Immigration Studies, the claim is that in the United States 44 percent of immigrants and their children live in or near poverty, that almost 31 percent have no health insurance, and that almost 20 percent receive welfare benefits even though unauthorized aliens are ineligible to receive them. The cost of education, health care, and welfare programs used by immigrants, they contend, exceeds the combined budgets of the Departments of State, Justice, and Interior. Furthermore, they point to the expenses entailed in detaining and deporting illegal aliens. The French National Front has voiced similar criticisms of immigrants and has periodically pushed for the expulsion of all those who were *not born there*. Some have gone even further and demanded the expulsion of anyone who is not integrated into French society or who has maintained a close connection with his or her home country. Likewise in Britain and Ireland there have been increasingly bitter denunciations of immigrants and the labeling of all immigrants, regardless of their status, as illegal.

Government agencies in the United States and in Western Europe have reacted to these demands by interpreting immigration policies stringently. Formal regulations may not bar pregnant women from entering the country; however, permission for them to enter is usually denied. Although official reasons cited center on concerns for maternal health, the underlying motive appears to be to stop women from obtaining social service benefits and citizenship for their children. Ireland provides one example of this practice. It has recently adopted a policy prohibiting the entrance of pregnant immigrants. Reflecting the prevalent attitude that pregnant immigrant women will be idle, welfare-dependent mothers, and "breeders," policies in the United States strongly discourage their admittance as well. Similarly, in France the regulations effectively bar the entrance of pregnant women, and priority cards for immigration are routinely denied to women who are pregnant or have small children (Boyd 1999; Tapinos 2000).

Although most immigrant women are looked upon as potential fiscal liabilities, the undocumented experience the most discrimination. Most of them are less affluent and less well educated and lack high skill levels. Almost invariably they come from poor countries that are culturally different from the country in which they now reside. To understand the dynamics of the (re)construction of the social identity of undocumented women, intersectionality must be fully incorporated into the analysis. The obstacles they encounter and their resiliency in overcoming them merit special attention.

Conclusion

As we have seen, official laws and policies play a critical role in defining women immigrants. While the claim is often made that immigration and refugee policies are gender neutral, their effects can hardly be described in that way. When women legally enter a country in North America and Western Europe under any of the procedures discussed in this chapter, they are most likely either to be admitted as a dependent under a program for family unification or to be issued a temporary work permit. As a dependent there are conditions attached to their continued right to residency and sometimes to their right to work. From the 1960s until the mid-1980s, the overwhelming majority of women immigrated to North America and Western Europe under these programs; hence the governmental construction of an identity of dependency had an important impact on their lives. In contrast, few men joined their wives under these programs. Indeed, it was not an option available to them until recently: husbands were not eligible to enter the United States under the auspices of family unification until 1952, and Western European countries did not enact similar policies until much later.

There are several consequences—psychological as well as economic—stemming from the gender differences in the criteria used to admit men and women. Family unification has defined the woman immigrant in her own eyes, in the eyes of her ethnic community, and in the eyes of the receiving country as less able to prevail in the marketplace than men. It has limited her opportunities to work and participate in educational programs designed to help immigrants become economically self-sufficient. Women who wished or needed to work had few options other than to move into the informal or shadow economy where few health, safety, and economic protections are available. As dependent family members, their right to remain was determined by their continued membership in the family. If they left an abusive relationship or were widowed or abandoned or the husband became involved in criminal activity, they could be deported.

The basic assumptions justifying present temporary work permits for women has defined them as best suited for employment in service occupations, particularly child care, domestic service, and health care. These gendered assumptions, which have underpinned policy interpretations and implementation, have limited their opportunities to acquire new skills or earn more money. As a result temporary work permit programs have relegated immigrant women to lower-paying, stereotypic caregiving roles and rarely allowed for skill improvement. In short, whether the laws and policies involved family unification or temporary work visas, they have constructed an identity that has limited opportunities for immigrant women. Even in the case of undocumented women, policies and procedures, including amnesty programs, have been insensitive to the situations of these women and have failed to address issues of concern to them.

Immigration policies have not only constructed an identity for all women immigrants, but they have also failed to take into consideration social, educational, racial, ethnic, and economic differences. The problems confronted by highly skilled professional women are quite different from those of less skilled women entering on temporary work visas or women admitted under family unification programs. The various problems faced by each of these groups are also different from those of undocumented women. All groups share some similar forces affecting the (re)construction of their social identity, but at the same time each group has to deal with a particular set of factors that affect that (re)construction. As we shall see in a later chapter, failure to differentiate among immigrant women compounds their problem of (re)constructing a functional social identity.

CHAPTER 4

Fleeing Calamity, Seeking Asylum
Women and Refugee Policy

Although women are more likely to immigrate legally under programs for family unification or with temporary work visas, refugee status or asylum based on humanitarian considerations are other widely used options. Beginning in the 1980s, women began increasingly to request admittance to Western European countries and to a lesser extent the United States and Canada on the grounds of asylum. This development reflected unstable conditions in many parts of the world as well as the fact that opportunities for traditional immigration were largely closed off in the West. The dimensions of the refugee situation and the ramification for women are amply illustrated by the statistics. As mentioned earlier, women constitute almost half the more than 32 million refugees and persons of concern listed by the United Nations High Commission for Refugees (UNHCR) for whom data on sex were available. In 2001 70 percent of the new applications for asylum were filed in the member countries of the European Union, 11 percent in the United States, and 8 percent in Canada. Although there were annual fluctuations in the number of asylum applications filed in individual states, Britain usually received the largest number, followed by Germany and the United States, where refugees are approximately 10 percent of the total annual immigration. In 2001 53 percent of those requesting asylum were admitted to EU countries under the provisions of the United Nations refugee conventions, while the remaining 47 percent applied for asylum on humanitarian grounds as defined by individual countries.

The number of asylum applications filed by women has been due in part to their forcible expulsion from their homes by war, civil unrest, famine, or persecution. Seeking safety, women have immigrated. When the journey necessitated leaving their home country they have attempted to immigrate to a more peaceful and stable society where they could raise their children. However, the ability to do so has largely depended on being admitted as a refugee, since restrictions on immigration have afforded them virtually no other option.

Refugee status may be granted on one of two grounds: the criteria set forth in the United Nations protocols or the United Nations Convention against Torture, or asylum granted on humanitarian grounds. The first has generally been considered preferable to the second, since it provides refugees the same legal protections as those available to citizens. Of particular importance to women refugees is the fact that it guarantees both the right of dependent children to join them and the right to permanent residency. Asylum status granted for humanitarian reasons on the other hand does not necessarily extend to other family members, nor does it necessarily ensure permanent residency. Bosnian women admitted to several Western European countries on humanitarian grounds during that country's civil war, for example, were not always allowed to be accompanied by their children. Their difficulties in securing entrance for their children provide a good example of the shortcoming of asylum based on humanitarian considerations.

The general procedures for reviewing requests for asylum are fairly similar in a number of respects. All requests are heard by immigration officers in the receiving country. These hearings largely determine whether or not an individual's situation meets the criteria of a "well-founded fear of persecution." There is usually the right to appeal an unfavorable decision. However, considerable variation exists among countries in the way in which the hearing is conducted and in interpreting a "well-founded fear." It is not unusual for officials in one country to reject a request for refugee status on the grounds that the criteria has not been met, while hearing officers in another country grant refugee status on the same grounds. For example, not all countries agree that there must be individual persecution for a well-founded fear to exist. While some countries accept the existence of a civil war or internal upheaval as sufficient to establish persecution, others require evidence that the individual applying has personally experienced persecution. Conflicting interpretations of "a well-founded fear" are further exacerbated by cultural differences. For example, overly deferential behavior during an asylum hearing or reticence in discussing the details of the persecution suffered may be interpreted by some hearing officers as an absence of a well-founded fear. Similarly indirect statements of the facts may be taken as an indication or even evidence that there was little threat of persecution. Yet such behaviors may merely represent a form of cultural politeness on the asylum seeker's part or a reluctance to describe a particular type of humiliating torture. As a result there is considerable variation among countries in deciding what constitutes a threat of persecution. Moreover, even within the same country, there are instances where similar evidence of a well-founded fear is accepted by one hearing officer but not by another.

In cases where the basis for a claim for asylum is considered serious but not included in the various UN protocols, the receiving country may decide to grant it on humanitarian considerations. In such instances individual states have the prerogative of defining the conditions under which the individual can enter and remain. For example, many of today's refugees suffer from a generalized anxiety stemming from human rights violations, which is not included in the UN protocols. Falling outside the rubric of the protocols, anxiety may be accepted as grounds for asylum in some countries but rejected as evidence of persecution by others. To complicate matters further, some countries make virtually no distinction between refugee status granted under UN protocols and asylum based on humanitarian consideration, but in others a distinction is made.

There is also the issue of adequate guidelines for determining who is a traditional immigrant and who is a refugee (Loescher 1993). The ambiguity surrounding what constitutes the criteria for "a well-founded fear" of persecution makes it hard to determine who is a refugee and who is an immigrant. The US immigration policy offers a good example of this. Prior to the Cuban Mariel boatlift in the late spring and summer of 1980 there was no distinction between refugee and immigrant. During that spring and summer some 125,000 Cubans fled that country and sought refuge in the United States. Initially the Cubans were freely admitted, but the large numbers entering the country in such a short span of time, along with the fact that Castro had permitted criminals and mental patients to join the Mariel flotilla, caused the government to rethink its policies. The Refugee Act enacted in the fall of the same year drew a distinction between immigrant and refugee. It incorporated the definition of refugee contained in the United Nations protocols and called for it to be applied to anyone seeking asylum. At the same time it set a ceiling on the number of refugees who could be admitted annually and specified a maximum number from any one country. Since its adoption, the Refugee Act has been reauthorized on several occasions, and the ceilings have been periodically adjusted. In 2006 the overall ceiling on refugees was seventy thousand, and no more than twenty thousand could come from a single country.

The intention of the Morrison-Lautenberg Amendment passed in 1989 was to provide some additional clarification about who could qualify as a refugee. It called for the US attorney general to establish categories of people from the Soviet Union, Vietnam, Laos, and Cambodia who shared common characteristics that identified them as targets of persecution. People falling into these categories could then be assumed to fulfill the requirement of a "well-founded fear." What they would have to do is assert such a fear and state a creditable basis for concern about the possibility of persecution. Although its purpose was to spell out the necessary conditions for refugee status, many have argued that instead it blurred the difference between refugee and immigrant by lowering the bar for gaining refugee status for some groups while ignoring the plight of others coming from countries, such as Guatemala and El Salvador, that were going through serious upheavals. The facts seemed to support this criticism. Of those applying for asylum, 97 percent of the Salvadorians and 99 percent of the Guatemalans had been turned down. The growth of the sanctuary movement, which sought to protect the right to asylum for those coming from El Salvador and Guatemala, called attention to the problems inherent in US refugee policy and Extended Voluntary Departure (EVD), which provided an alternative course of action. EVD gave special permission to nonresident aliens from particularly troubled countries to remain in the United States until the situation in their home country eased.

EVD has been used for Afghanis, Iranians, Nicaraguans, Lebanese, Ugandans, and Ethiopians.

Morrison-Lautenberg clearly did lower the bar between refugee and immigrant, at least for some groups. Many of those coming from Southeast Asia at the end of the 1970s and during the 1980s displayed all the characteristics of traditional economic immigrants, while those from Central American countries torn by civil war conformed much more closely to the generally accepted notion of refugee. Yet one group was admitted as refugees but not the other. The resulting disparities have contributed to the attitude among many of immigration hearing officers that those applying for asylum under the Morrison-Lautenberg Amendment were simply "queue jumpers" (Simcox 1988). EVD has turned out to be equally problematic. It has been widely criticized on the grounds that ideological considerations have been a major determining factor in easing entrance for people from certain countries.

Although a distinction has been drawn in Western European countries between refugees meeting the United Nations criteria and those seeking asylum on other grounds, "a well-founded fear" must be demonstrated in both instances. In the 1990s and the first decade of the twenty-first century several Western European countries facing increased applications for asylum also developed lists of countries where adverse conditions might warrant a grant of asylum. Individuals from other countries are considered as probable immigrants, not refugees. Then there is the Schengen Agreement. Incorporated into the European Union's Amsterdam Treaty it prohibits the admission of asylum seekers from "safe" third countries. Regardless of the technical procedures used to review asylum applications in the United States, Canada, or Western Europe, however, problems stemming from differing interpretations about what constitutes a "well-founded fear" of persecution persist and influence the outcome of immigration hearings.

Meeting the Criteria: Gendered or Gender Neutral

Although women are more likely to be refugees than men, only a minority of them request or receive asylum (Boyd 1999). Several explanations are offered for this discrepancy. The first involves legal barriers. In several countries there is no provision for a married woman to apply for asylum separately from her husband. When a husband meets the criteria for refugee, his wife is automatically admitted under the auspices of family unification even though she may herself qualify as a refugee. This has been the case in France, Germany, Italy, and Denmark. A second explanation revolves around cultural norms. Even in those countries where a wife can apply separately patriarchal attitudes discourage it. Hearing officers tend to regard women refugees accompanied by their husbands as dependent spouses. For example, Sweden and the United States customarily admit women as family members even if they request and meet the United Nations requirements for refugee status. In Australia, although the majority of the Vietnamese refugees were women, they were less likely than men to be granted asylum and instead were admitted under family unification. Although in Austria and Britain women are eligible to apply for refugee status independently of their husbands, less than one-third have done so. A third explanation is gender insensitivity. It has been claimed that the practice of questioning the woman in the presence of her husband where she must repeat details of her persecution—particularly rape, sexual abuse, or threats of rape—restrains her from actively seeking separate admission as a refugee. Furthermore there is often a tendency on the part of the hearing officer to turn to the husband for an explanation of the persecution suffered by his wife or female family members rather than to provide an opportunity for the woman to speak on her own behalf (Hajdukowski-Ahmed 2008). A fourth explanation emphasizes the gendered criteria used to evaluate claims of a well-founded fear of persecution.

Given the tendency to ignore a woman's request for refugee status and instead to admit her as a dependent spouse, it is no wonder that only about a third of those admitted to Germany, Sweden, and Finland as refugees and asylum seekers are women. Only in the Netherlands has there been an effort to be sensitive to women's requests to enter as refugees. There wives are permitted to apply for refugee status in their own right and are interviewed separately from their husbands by female interviewers. The notes taken during the interview are kept confidential and are not disclosed to the husband. In addition the government has made an effort to ensure that female asylum seekers suffering trauma due to gender-specific ill treatment, such as rape, have access to appropriate counseling services.

The practice of admitting a refugee woman accompanying her family through family unification is problematic. The adjustment problems and limited opportunities that confront immigrant women admitted under family unification programs are magnified in the case of women refugees and asylum seekers who are already dealing with the traumatic aftermath of persecution. These women experience the same liabilities as immigrant women insofar as their right to remain is dependent on their marital status and they do not enjoy the same legal protection regarding deportation, work, and residency as individuals granted refugee status. The absence of these guarantees poses a serious problem. In all likelihood the family—the husband, the wife, as well as other family members—bear the psychological scars of the events that forced them to flee, and in coping with them they all undergo high levels of stress. Politically active husbands who have in many cases previously enjoyed leadership positions often experience a diminished status, which further erodes their psychological well-being. Often a husband's reaction to his new situation is to play a more intrusive and controlling role within the family, which further increases pressures in the marital relationship. The consequences are increased strains in family life, which can lead to family violence and spousal abuse. In these circumstances a woman admitted as a dependent spouse finds herself in an untenable situation. She is confronted with a veritable "Hobson's Choice": her own well-being may be in jeopardy if she stays in the family relationship, but she risks deportation if she leaves. In either case her life may be in peril. Faced with such a choice she may well conclude that there is no way out, and this feeling of hopelessness may account for the above-average number of suicides among refugee women.

Although refugee status is preferable to asylum granted on humanitarian grounds, the drawback is that it is difficult to obtain. As just mentioned, it involves going before a hearing officer and proving that there is "a well-founded fear of being persecuted for reasons of race, religion, nationality, membership of a particular social group or political opinion"—the requirement laid down in the 1951 UN protocol. Substantiating such a claim is, at best, grueling for all refugees—men as well as women, but the small percentage of women filing for asylum suggests that it is especially challenging for them. The question is why. Is gender discrimination a factor? The widely accepted view has been that the definition of a refugee is gender neutral, applying equally to men and women. The justification offered for this position is that there is no gender dimension to the experience of being a refugee. Furthermore, if there were a problem of gender discrimination, the argument goes, necessary changes would have already been made. Since there has been no effort to change the protocols, gender is not a factor in determining eligibility for refugee status.

Despite these arguments there is evidence suggesting that gender does make a difference. First of all, there is the issue of providing adequate evidence of persecution. Imprisonment, attempted assassination, and documented death threats clearly establish such a claim. In lieu of such documentation, personal testimony may be provided. However, there is a tendency on the part of border control agencies and hearing officers not to view women as political persons; hence their claims are automatically considered suspect (Martin 2000). Women also often find themselves at a disadvantage in providing compelling testimony of their persecution, since their public visibility in political movements or their appearance as speakers on public platforms may not have been encouraged in their country of origin. Certainly the disproportionately large number of males awarded refugee status in comparison to the number of women is in part a function of the fact that the common understanding of what constitutes a bona fide refugee is based largely on the model of a politically active man in the public arena. In the mind of hearing officers there is a linkage of the term *refugee* with men who have actively participated in a political group. Then, too, the association in the protocols of a well-founded fear with race, religion, nationality, ethnicity, a particular social group, and political opinion accentuates the connection between refugee and male forms of political activism. The idea of refugee as male has been further reinforced by the fact that until the 1980s the understanding of "membership in a particular social group" was restricted to race, religion, nationality, or ethnicity—categories that are more often than not related to activities in the public arena. Gender, on the other hand, was not considered to fall within the definition of a "particular social group" until the mid-1990s. Given this mind-set, women's requests for refugee status tend to receive less serious attention or be ignored or rejected altogether. Even in cases where women meet the criteria of visible activism in the public arena, they are more likely to be granted admission as a member of a male refugee's family rather than on the merits of their own case (Joly 1992).

Closer scrutiny of women's claims for refugee status suggests other ways in which gender plays a role. Although women may experience the same type of persecution as men, they also tend to be exposed to a wide range of human rights violations and forms of persecution that are unique to them and that are not universally recognized as falling under the categories included in the UN protocols. Specifically, women are more likely to be targeted for sexual violence than men (Bloch, Galvin, and Harrell-Bond 2000). While typically men may point to threats of death or physical torture to support their claims, fear of persecution for women may instead involve rape or threats of rape. Women's participation in racial, religious, national, or ethnic movements is also less likely to be publicly visible than men's. They are more likely to have served as communication links or nurses or to have provided safe houses than to have addressed public gatherings. Many view these supportive roles, which diverge from male modes of activity, as involving less risk of persecution. Claims based on them are often rejected as not meeting the criteria of a well-founded fear of persecution. Another area in which gender plays a role involves activities in the domestic sphere. Women are more likely to experience persecution in the home and family, a domain in which their country may be reluctant to protect them. Examples of this are the failure of the state to step in and prevent such abuses as dowry murder and genital mutilation (Conors 1997; Boyd 1999). The state may also tolerate or overlook the sale of children into prostitution or gender-discriminatory abortion. In these situations women may feel a well-founded fear of persecution. Until recently, however, these practices were not thought of as persecution falling within the UN protocols, and they are still not universally recognized as a basis for granting asylum. While the United States, Australia, Canada, and the European Union accept them now as covered by UN conventions, some countries still do not. For example, in Finland gender-related persecution is not believed to fall within the definition of a well-founded fear as laid down in the UN protocols, whereas Sweden acknowledges persecution on the basis of sex but views it as separate and different from the protocol requirements for refugee status. Hence women's claim of a "well-founded fear" of gender persecution is not universally accepted as grounds for granting refugee status under the UN protocols.

Forms of Gendered Persecution

Of the various types of gender persecution, rape has received the most media attention. The war in the Balkans following the collapse of Yugoslavia spotlighted the plight of women subjected to rape and sexual violence. Of course, this was not the first time such tactics were used as a strategy of war. A long and documented history of sexual violence against women by enemy forces can be traced back to the ancient world with Greek and Roman histories and epics recounting multiple instances of the rape and enslavement of captured enemy women. Time and again medieval history and literature refer to the use of rape, and rape or threat of rape has continued to be a tactic used up to the present day. There were reports of rape, torture, and sexual enslavement during both World War I and II. Although we are most familiar with Nazi experimentation, torture, and rape, the vivid depiction of women's vulnerability and rape captured in memoirs and films about World War II have suggested that the practice was not confined to Nazi Germany but was much more widespread than that. Nor is rape solely a tradition of Western civilization in war time. In the twentieth century, for example, there were reports of wide-scale rape of Hindu and Muslim women by opposing forces during the time of the Indian partition and similar reports of rape during the recent communal riots that took place in India in the spring of 2002. Rape was also used as a tactic to demoralize the enemy in the war to establish Bangladesh's independence. It was widespread in Africa during the civil wars in Rwanda and Uganda and is presently in the Sudan, where there has been systematic rape of women and children in Darfur and in civil wars in the Congo and Liberia. Thus, although the war in Bosnia and now those in Darfur and the Congo are the most publicized and documented instances of mass rape, they are by no means unprecedented, nor has the twenty-first century brought a halt to the practice.

Notwithstanding the long history of rape as a form of persecution, there is no acknowledgement of it as a basis for establishing a "well-founded fear of persecution" in the UN protocols. The nonrecognition of rape as a criterion for granting refugee status prior to 1993 is demonstrated by the case of raped Bosnian women who were not considered to come under the provisions of the Geneva Convention. Furthermore, several countries in the European Union, including Britain, were unwilling at first to admit Bosnian women on the grounds that they did not meet the definition of *refugee*. Even after members of the European Union adopted a policy for admitting "particularly vulnerable" people from the former Yugoslavia, women were not granted full refugee status or accorded the right to be joined by their children or family members. In fact, the use of rape, ethnic cleansing, forced prostitution, and sexual slavery during the war in Bosnia were not recognized as war crimes until five years later. At the same time, Bosnian men fleeing during the war along with their families were usually granted permanent asylum.

Physical rape constitutes one form of violence against women. Threats of rape constitute another. Threatening to rape girls and women in the presence of their families, including very young children, in order to extract information about the whereabouts of relatives represents an insidious type of gender persecution that has serious psychological consequences as well as physical ones not only for the girl or woman raped or threatened with rape but also for the entire family. As brutal and devastating as rape and threats of rape may be, however, they are not considered to meet the criteria of a bona fide case of persecution in some countries, nor are they universally accepted as a sufficient justification for granting asylum.

Women's modes of participation are another area where gender differences have been ignored. Traditionally men play a visible public role, speaking out publicly, organizing the opposition, and overtly working with dissonant groups. In contrast women tend to engage in work behind the scenes, which is more difficult to document. Constrained by home and child-care responsibilities women have often contributed in less familiar ways, such as carrying messages through informal networks, operating "safe houses" that provide temporary shelter, or nursing the wounded. These activities can be very dangerous, however, and if women are caught carrying them out they may be killed, tortured, or imprisoned. In some cases women may be targets of persecution and subject to human rights violations simply because their relatives are considered dangerous or undesirable. As perilous as these roles may be they are often less obvious than those of activists who operate in the public arena. There has certainly been little acceptance of them as evidence for claims for asylum. Gender discrimination emerges in another area, as well. Women tend to be somewhat anonymous as political activists, since they are involved in less public activities. When the standard of visible public activity is used to decide if there is a "well-founded fear of persecution," hearing officers often conclude that women's forms of protest were not particularly dangerous and therefore do not warrant a grant of asylum.

Patterns of Generalized Gender Persecution

The UN protocols specify that membership in a particular social group may be one of the causes for a well-founded fear of persecution. However, despite the fact that women often do suffer generalized persecution simply because they are members of a particular social group—women—they are not necessarily recognized as a particular social group. For example, many women fled from Afghanistan when it was under the control of the Taliban leaders because of the physical, psychological, social, and governmental limitations that were placed on them. In their eyes the imposition of restrictive dress codes, particularly the burka, the prohibition on appearing outside the home, and the prohibition on schooling for girls amounted to gender persecution based on their membership in a particular social group.

Similarly women emigrating from areas in Africa where genital mutilation is practiced felt that they were victims of gender persecution. However, there have been serious problems in getting these types of claims accepted as legitimate grounds for obtaining refugee status. An excellent illustration is provided by the controversy surrounding a Ghanaian woman who sought to remain in the United States rather than return home where she would be subjected to genital mutilation. She based her request for refugee status on a well-founded fear of persecution because of her membership in a particular social group, women. Although American guidelines announced in 1996 recognized genital mutilation as a form of gender persecution, her request was refused. Only after the United States Court of Appeals heard the case and issued its decision on July 19, 1999, was she finally granted asylum. More recently in *Abay v. Ashcroft* (2004) the Court of Appeals did uphold a decision to grant asylum to an Ethiopian woman who feared that her daughter's return to Ethiopia would result in her genital mutilation. However, there continues to be a difference of opinion over the concept of women as a particular social group in asylum cases involving genital mutilation. While the federal courts tend to uphold these applications for asylum, the Board of Immigration Appeals does not (Kim 2008).

There have also been differences of opinion in other cases involving the concept of women as a social group. A Guatemalan woman's request for asylum based on a claim of spousal abuse was initially rejected on the grounds that since she did not demonstrate that the government of Guatemala encourages its male citizens to abuse its female citizens, she could not claim persecution on the basis of membership in a particular social group. The attorney general, Janet Reno, subsequently overturned the decision, thereby affirming the legitimacy of gender as a particular social group eligible for refugee status (*Federal Register* 2000 76588). Despite the outcome in this case, however, the policy regarding asylum in cases of spousal abuse continues to remain unclear. A spokesperson for the Department of Homeland Security has explained that the issue of whether or not spousal abuse rises to the level of persecution resulting from membership to a group is very complex, since a woman may be beaten simply because her husband is drunk or a bully not because she is a woman (Kotlowitz 2007). Some have suggested that the government's ambiguous interpretations in asylum cases dealing with spousal abuse are really related to a surge in asylum applications. Responding to this concern, it has been pointed out that Canada, which adopted the policy in 1993, has never had a surge of requests for asylum on these grounds.

American policies recognizing gender as a basis for requesting refugee status are undercut, however, by conflicting policies, judicial rulings, and bureaucratic interpretations. According to a study that subsequently has appeared in the *Stanford Law Review*, decisions to grant asylum vary substantially from one jurisdiction to another, within the same jurisdiction, and depending on the gender of the immigration judge. For example, in Miami one judge granted asylum in only 3 percent of the cases he heard, whereas another judge in Miami granted it in 75 percent of the cases. Female judges were more likely to grant asylum than their male peers. A procedure known as expedited removal, which was incorporated into the 1996 Illegal Immigration Reform and Immigrant Responsibility Act, has also contributed to an inconsistent policy. Under its terms expedited removal permits immigration inspectors at airports and borders, rather than immigration judges, to order the immediate deportation of an individual arriving in the United States without the proper travel documents. It also provides for the mandatory detention of asylum seekers who are subject to the expedited process. According to a study of mandatory detention procedure issued by the Lawyers Committee for Human Rights in 2002 these provisions have had particularly adverse consequences for women refugees. It reported that women fleeing forced marriage, rape, severe domestic violence, and other gender-related violence were often targeted and denied an opportunity to challenge their detention before an immigration judge. Furthermore the women were often detained in jail for lengthy periods of time. It also found that women seeking asylum on the basis of honor killing and genital mutilation had their applications routinely rejected on the grounds that they failed to meet the filing deadline.

"A History of Gender Asylum in the United State" published by the Hastings College of Law (2000) mentioned other factors that contributed to the greater likelihood of women being subject to expedited removal. One was the women's perceptions of intimidation on the part of inspectors. Another was the practice of shackling and strip-searching women. Women's intense reaction to such treatment was viewed as abnormal and indicative of mental instability and considered adequate grounds for deportation.

The United States' policies on gender-based claims are not unusual. Other countries indulge in similar practices. Requests for refugee status based on a fear of honor killing and dowry murder and the practice of selling young girls into prostitution are often rejected on the grounds that gender discrimination is not defined as a form of persecution in the UN protocols and that women do not constitute a particular social group. In 1984 the European Parliament made an effort to correct this situation by adopting a resolution calling on member states to recognize women as a "particular social group" eligible for asylum status. Subsequently Canada, Australia, Demark, Germany, and Britain, along with the United States, approved guidelines identifying gender as a basis for a well-founded fear of persecution. However, even where gender persecution is legally recognized, implementation is often lacking or intermittent, as in the case of the United States. Many countries, while rejecting applications for refugee status based on the UN protocols, do so instead on the basis of humanitarian considerations. Perhaps Canada provides the best example of just how ineffective the 1984 guidelines have been: less than 2 percent of the asylum applicants have been granted refugee status on the basis of gender persecution.

Two related issues have surfaced regarding claims of gender-based persecution: exoticism and essentialism, both of which perpetuate gender stereotypes. With regard to exoticism there has been a tendency on the part of those sympathetic to the "plight" of refugees to mythologize the refugee or asylum seeker's country as exotic. The resulting stereotype is a country that is horrifically patriarchal, primitive, and culturally violent. Within this context women are depicted as quintessential victims. These black-and-white stereotypes exacerbate the stress levels of those seeking asylum by subjecting them to imagery that is at odds with their more nuanced memories. The stereotypes also encourage refugees and asylum seekers to give essentialist recitations of persecution such as female genital mutilation or fear of Muslim fundamentalism, which will be more easily accepted than the complex and probably less well known narratives that describe their abuse more accurately (Hajdukowski-Ahmed 2008).

Beyond Refugee Status

Gendered assumptions have continued to play a role in government and NGO's treatment of refugee women in refugee camps, asylum centers where they are held until their case is decided, and the housing they are subsequently assigned. While requests for asylum are being processed in the receiving country, employment is prohibited. In the United States refugees are forbidden to work for the first 180 days after an application has been submitted, although they are permitted to receive cash benefits and medical assistance for 8 months from the day they are admitted. Similar policies exist elsewhere. Great Britain, for example, also prohibits working until the asylum application has been approved. During this period and after asylum has been granted, government policies and the activities of many NGOs to help refugees are predicated on the concept of the patriarchal family. This is reflected in the ways in which services are distributed. Women who are without a male protector either go unnoticed or are viewed as totally dependent. The situation is most extreme in refugee camps. For example, in an account reported by the UNHCR of Angolan refugees who fled to Zaire, food was distributed and plots of land earmarked for their use based on the criteria of being "able-bodied male heads of household." As a result 30 percent of the refugees who were women were ineligible to receive aid. It was only after questions were raised by some of the female aid workers that the women were finally given food and land to grow crops. A similar story is told of efforts to provide emergency relief to Kurds following the 1991 Gulf War. In this instance the food marshals were local men, and very little food reached the women. Reports about problems in food distribution to Afghani refugees echo the same themes. In numerous instances there have been reports that sexual favors were extracted in exchange for food. Although these problems are more extreme in the case of temporary refugees, they also exist in postindustrial countries of Europe and North America. Male dominance and intimidation are not uncommon in facilities where women unaccompanied by a male relative are housed in the United States, Canada, and Western Europe. Young women, elderly women, and those who are disabled are often taken advantage of simply because they are physically vulnerable.

Despite the adjustment and material changes occurring in their lives after they receive refugee status, women tend to be treated as hapless victims, unable to function on their own. The assistance they receive is concentrated on meeting basic material needs such as food and shelter. While these needs are pressing, there are others. It is not unusual for women refugees to lack a range of basic skills required in their new country. They often lack literacy skills. If they come from Third World countries restrictions may have been placed on them, particularly in terms of educational opportunities. Assistance and programs emphasizing their dependency endorse the stereotype of them as "vulnerable," "hapless" women (Bloch, Galvin, and Harrell-Bond 2000). In recent years the UNHCR has attempted to develop and implement a number of empowerment projects providing educational, economic, and leadership skills programs specifically aimed at enhancing women's roles rather than perpetuating their situations as second-class citizens, but little has been done along these lines in the individual countries of Western Europe and North America. Moreover the practice of admitting refugee women as dependent family members has perpetuated negative perceptions about them and contributed to the practice of developing programs geared toward the male head of the household Where there have been efforts to develop and implement programs for refugee women, they have emphasized hygiene, household management, and child care only. Consultation with the women about what skills they feel they need are virtually nonexistent, as are programs that could teach them marketable skills. As a report of the UNHCR put it, there is an ingrained gender bias and a baffling level of resistance to gender equality in the humanitarian community that stems from a lack of understanding of the skills and commitment necessary to challenge gender discrimination. The absence of policies and programs to assist women in participating in the world outside the family has negative consequences for the women, their ethnic community, and society as a whole and fuels anti-immigrant sentiments. By failing to provide women with marketable skills while providing them with welfare benefits, receiving countries feed into a whole host of stereotypes that support popular perceptions of refugees, and especially refugee women, as imposing a permanent economic burden on the country.

Asylum Based on Humanitarian Concerns

As previously mentioned, applications for asylum may be based on persecution coming under the UN protocols or involving humanitarian consideration. A word of caution is in order, however. The data are difficult to evaluate, since several countries do not distinguish between individuals who apply under the UN protocols and those who apply for asylum on humanitarian grounds. As mentioned before, the United States did not have special procedures for admitting refugees seeking asylum until 1980; instead permission to enter was based on the geographical location of individuals who were applying. To complicate matters further, some countries do not keep separate records for those admitted as immigrants and those as refugees. Consequently it is difficult to know how many individuals are granted asylum based on humanitarian consideration. Many countries also do not report separate data for men and women. Furthermore, even when separate data are kept, the information is problematic since a number of receiving countries either do not permit or tend to discourage women from applying for asylum in their own right whether their grounds are the UN protocols or humanitarian considerations.

 The data that are available, however, indicate that about two-thirds of those applying for asylum are admitted under the UN protocols and a third for humanitarian reasons. In 2001, for example, 34 percent of the asylum seekers were admitted on humanitarian grounds whereas 64 percent met the UN criteria (*UN Statistical Yearbook* 2001, 56). The increased number of asylum applications has led countries in Western Europe along with the United States and Canada to take steps to reduce the number admitted on humanitarian grounds. One strategy has been to meticulously scrutinize asylum applications for the purpose of distinguishing between those escaping persecution and those who are "economic refugees." In a further effort to discourage asylum seekers, countries have adopted procedures that subject asylum seekers to a host of conditions, including placing them in detention centers and prohibiting them from working while their applications are pending. Member states of the European Union also automatically reject the application of an asylum seeker who attempts to enter from a safe third country. Some countries, such as Britain, have also drawn up a list of countries whose internal situation would merit a serious threat of persecution. Individuals coming from countries other than those on the list are unlikely to be granted asylum. As the number of applications for asylum has grown in Britain there has been a tendency to reduce the list of dangerous countries. For example, Britain removed Sri Lanka from the list, although at the time a brutal guerilla war was in progress. As a consequence anyone coming from Sri Lanka was not eligible for asylum in Britain. The Dublin Convention, which calls for asylum seekers to possess a valid visa in order to enter a European Union country was another means of deterring asylum seekers. Asylum seekers lacking the required travel documents could be immediately deported. Although the convention has been justified as a means for stopping "asylum shopping," it has been criticized as discriminatory against people coming from Third World countries, since visas are not required of individuals coming from a number of First World countries, and as unreasonable, since individuals fleeing persecution are often unable to obtain the necessary travel documents in their home country. Additional restrictions have also been adopted by individual EU member states. In France, for example, no work permit can be issued until asylum procedures have been completed, a process that can take a considerable period of time. In Britain, priority is given to asylum seekers with relatives who reside there. In Germany strict measures for immediate expedited deportation at ports of entrance have resulted in a marked decline in the number of asylum applications, with only 7 percent approved in 2001. Although the conventional wisdom has been that detention/reception centers, prohibitions on working until the application has been processed, and limits on welfare benefits will reduce the number of asylum seekers, a recent study by the British Home Office reported that these policies have had a minimal effect (Zetter et al. 2003).

Although the criteria for granting asylum varies from one country to another, individuals requesting asylum for humanitarian reasons, like those seeking to be admitted under the UN protocols, must demonstrate a well-founded fear of persecution. If they do not, their claims will be rejected as "manifestly unfounded." As in the case of refugee status, the importance placed on particular types of persecution suffered and a lack of sensitivity to gender differences affect decisions on an asylum request and account to some degree for the higher rejection rate of women's applications. Particularly problematic has been the refusal of Western European countries to recognize a girl or woman's fear of female genital mutilation (FGM) as sufficient to warrant asylum (McVeigh and Sutton 2010). Although the proximity of countries where FGM is a fairly common practice may pose some concerns about immigration for Western European countries, a failure to acknowledge FGM as a form of gender persecution overlooks the danger and health hazards women may suffer as a result.

Human Rights Watch has claimed that the association of women asylum seekers traveling alone or only with their children with welfare dependency reduces their chance of obtaining a successful ruling. Interviews with women asylum seekers in both the United States and Britain seem to confirm this claim. Women, especially those with children, felt that immigration officers were suspicious about their motives for seeking asylum and saw them as a potential public burden. Perhaps this perception of dependency explains why even when women are granted asylum they are more likely than men to be granted only temporary asylum, the assumption being that they will take longer to achieve self-sufficiency (Boyd 1985).

Asylum Policy in the United States

The United States first distinguished between those who entered as refugees and aliens seeking asylum status when it created the category of asylee in The Refugee Act passed in 1980. According to the legislation, individuals were to be considered refugees if they applied for admission to the United States from outside the country. In contrast aliens seeking asylum status were either already in the country or at a port of entry. Although obtaining admission involves a long and complicated process for demonstrating a well-founded fear of persecution, there were some important differences between the two categories in addition to geographical location at the time of application. Unlike aliens seeking asylum status, asylees have to wait a year before requesting lawful permanent residence, and there is a limit placed on the number who can enter each year. In an effort to get around the limitation on the number of asylees who could be admitted, Cubans were given a special status and classified neither as aliens seeking asylum status nor as asylees but as "Cuban Entrants."

American asylum policy requires mandatory detention upon arrival in the country. During the Clinton administration there were a number of reports citing poor conditions existing at these centers. Claims were made that the facilities at which asylum seekers were kept failed to meet international standards including language assistance, medical care, culturally appropriate food, and exercise. Moreover, because of the small number of women being held, they were frequently mixed with incarcerated criminals (Dugger 1996). In the detention center in York, Pennsylvania, the warden was reported as saying, "As far as I'm concerned, when you come through the door, you're all the same . . . When we call this a prison that's exactly what we mean. This isn't a camp" (Young 1997). The T. Don Hutto Residential Center, which went into operation in 2006, along with a former minimum security state prison and another facility in Pennsylvania are authorized to hold non-Mexican immigrant families and children. There are additional centers for Mexicans. Asylum seekers may request release on parole from detention centers once they have passed the screening procedure, but in some areas of the country such requests are routinely denied by the Department of Homeland Security. Furthermore, there are no restrictions placed on the length of time an asylum seeker may be detained. Since the position of Department of Homeland Security (DHS) is that immigration judges are precluded from reviewing the detention of "arriving aliens," there is no legal mechanism available for challenging a decision against parole.

Both the UNHCR and the United States Commission on International Religious Freedom have denounced conditions at the US detention centers as detrimental for men, women, and children, and the centers have frequently been characterized as little more than prisons, inappropriate for a noncriminal population. The lack of private, individual toilets for women, the lack of a trained staff to deal with their special needs and concerns, and the nature of the housing units pose special problems for women. A recent allegation of rape of a woman being held at the Hutto Center by a guard there and complaints about guards' threats to separate children from their families suggest that the environment leaves much to be desired. In addition to the problems posed by the residential facilities, women face other hurdles at these centers. There are no provisions for women's cases to be heard by a female hearing officer. Sometimes the case may be heard by a woman officer, but this is not automatic right. Without a female hearing officer women seeking asylum on the grounds of rape, threats of rape, or female genital mutilation often experience a lack of sensitivity to the seriousness of their situation.

The increasing number of refugees from Central America, Latin America, and the Caribbean during the 1980s created a backlash against immigration even before the merger of the Immigration and Naturalization Service with Homeland Security. The growing anti-immigrant atmosphere has encouraged immigration inspectors and hearing officers to view those seeking asylum with considerable suspicion and to view them as "queue jumpers" who are attempting to bypass the normal procedures for entering the country. The Illegal Immigration Reform and Immigrant Responsibility Act of 1996 gave power to immigration inspectors at airports and borders to deport people under the procedure of expedited removal and provided for mandatory detention of anyone subject to expedited removal. The expedited removal order can be executed immediately and cannot be appealed to an immigration judge or a federal court judge. While deportation is not supposed to occur until after the claim of a credible fear of persecution is heard, asylum seekers have complained that this is often not the case, and given the lack of procedural safeguards there can be no guarantee that claims are always investigated.

The Women's Commission for Refugee Women and Children has reported that interviews of dozens of women revealed that claims of rape and abuse were often not taken seriously and that the women recounted fear, intimidation, and confusion about the process. Women asylum seekers also reported being subject to shackling and strip searches, practices that are extremely traumatic for women who had been subject to rape (Lawyers Committee for Human Rights 2004). The Women's Commission has also reported that detention centers have been insensitive to issues of dress, for example denying Muslim women the right to wear the head scarf (*hajib*).

There is considerable evidence that the use of expedited removal has increased under the Department of Homeland Security, and there are numerous complaints that the decisions are often arbitrary and fail to take into account the conditions that forced individuals to seek asylum. Although both men and women suffer as a result of abuses stemming from current policies, the housing arrangements, the issue of privacy, and prison-like surroundings are especially harmful for women and children and are dangerous to their physical and psychological well-being. More serious charges have involved rape and sexual assault by prison guards while the women were being held in mandatory detention.

Asylum Policy in Western Europe

Like the United States, Western European countries are also experiencing escalating numbers of refugees and asylum seekers. Indeed, the problem is much more severe there. Although there is some agreement on general principles among the members of the European Union about the need to establish a common asylum policy, differences in the number of asylum seekers applying for admission in each of the countries, historical connections with the sending country, and geographical proximity have prevented them from adopting a common policy. The discrepancies among them also extend to their sensitivity to the plight of women seeking asylum.

Despite the fact that a recent British proposal calling for the creation of asylum camps outside the borders of the European Union where asylum seekers' claims could be heard and decided before they would be admitted was flatly rejected as insensitive and reminiscent of practices condemned long ago, Britain is considered to have one of the most liberal asylum policies in Europe, including provisions specifically addressed to the concerns of women. A set of "Gender Guidelines" for asylum claims put together by the Refugee Women's Legal Group, assisted and endorsed by the UNHCR, was referred to in a ruling by the House of Lords, and gender-sensitive rules were adopted in November 2002. However, women arriving as a part of a family unit continue to find that the merits of their own claims are overlooked, or superficially examined.

In France asylum seekers cannot be denied entry solely because they are lacking the proper documents, a situation frequently found among those applying for asylum. At the same time if they have entered the country illegally, their request for asylum is subject to special scrutiny. With regard to female asylum seekers, government policies and practices are often inconsistent. Women's claims for asylum status tend to be ignored; and there is no mention of a married woman's right to seek asylum separately from her husband. However, government rules do provide for separate facilities for men and women while their cases are being considered. There is also provision for a female hearing officer and the right to request a private meeting and a female interpreter in cases where delicate issues such as those involving female modesty, abuse, and sexuality are involved.

There is no specific training regarding gender for those working in reception centers outside the country; however, inside the country, trained staff is provided. Despite this training there are complaints about an inadequate recognition of particular social or cultural gender traits—a deficiency, it is claimed, that places women coming from societies that prize female submission at a special disadvantage in arguing their cases.

Asylum policy in Germany is similar to France's in several respects. Claims for asylum are refused if it is obvious from the circumstances that the applicant is in Germany for economic reasons or simply in order to evade a general emergency situation or armed conflict. Asylum seekers must also comply with the "safe third country" rule. Thus women arriving from a third country where they did not experience persecution are unable to apply for asylum. Although there is no mention of whether or not married female asylum seekers can file claims independently of their husbands, there are guidelines specifically regarding the treatment of women seeking asylum. Hearing officers are instructed to advise female asylum seekers who have suffered gender-based persecution that their case can be heard by a female deciding officer and that they may have a person they trust present at the hearing to provide psychological support. However, German immigration officers did not receive any training on gender-related persecution or the needs of female asylum seekers until 1999. Even today gender-related training is not mandatory. Furthermore, since less than 10 percent of the hearing officers have received special training on gender-related persecution and the special needs of female refugees, there is no guarantee that the provisions in the law will be met. Government rules state that single men and women are to be provided with accommodations separate from those of families, but separate rooms do not mean separate areas. Moreover, single women with children are sometimes accommodated in family rooms adjacent to or close to areas where male-headed families are housed. There are also sometimes no separate bathrooms for men and women, especially in the Frankfurt airport, which is the main port of entry, and there are complaints that women's rooms in reception centers often cannot be locked.

Italy's asylum policy, like Germany's, requires that refugees be refused entrance if they come from a safe third country. The first officials that the asylum seekers come into contact with do not receive any specific training on gender, or gender-based persecution, although the UNHCR does provide some general training to the police, border police, and prefecture's officials. One of the grounds for persecution cited in the legislation is "gender," but there are no specific provisions relating to female asylum seekers. However, in practice, women have been recognized as refugees on the grounds of persecution for reasons of membership of a social group when they have broken religious laws or social norms. Thus claims for asylum based on genital mutilation are recognized. Whenever possible, female officials, with the help of female interpreters who were victims of violence in their country of origin, interview female asylum seekers. In recent years Italy has been a major point of entry for women trafficked to Western Europe for the sex trade. Many of these women have been severely abused and traumatized by their experiences. Often Catholic nuns have been involved in the earliest stages of interviewing these women and providing them immediate relief, including housing. Although their work has been highly praised, the reception procedures for trafficked women have posed serious questions about the extent of the government obligations to abused women. At the same time the Italian government does provide separate accommodations, and sleeping quarters are always separate. As in the case of France and Germany, there is no provision in legislation about whether or not female asylum seekers have the right to file a claim independently of their husbands. At the present moment strong anti-immigrant sentiments dominate Italian politics, and there are strident calls for tougher policies on immigration and deportation of illegal aliens. If Italy is to follow the pattern in other countries were xenophobia has surfaced, one may expect requests for asylum to be scrutinized very carefully with the goal of reducing the number of people allowed to enter the country.

There are some distinctive aspects of Danish policy that distinguish it from the policies discussed so far. In many respects it is more gender sensitive; in others, less so. In the first place there is no specific legislation that gives special protection to female asylum seekers. Although the UNHCR states that special attention should be given to the needs of female asylum seekers, there are no definite practices or any specific guidelines with regard to asylum claims based on gender-related persecution. Furthermore, no woman has ever received asylum on the grounds of gender-related persecution alone, and only a small number of women who have made such claims have been allowed to stay. At the same time, there is an effort to use female case officers and interpreters when the case involves gender-related aspects of persecution. If the persecution is gender related and the asylum seeker is a man, he is entitled to have male caseworkers and interpreters. Female asylum seekers who have been the victim of trauma will normally be identified while under the care of the Danish Red Cross in the reception centers. Once identified, they are provided with counseling and other assistance. In the asylum centers, the Danish Red Cross always uses female interpreters during procedures that involve personal issues, such as a gynecological exam. A female doctor always carries out medical examinations of female asylum seekers. Single men and women are accommodated separately. As is the case in France, Germany, and Italy, there is no mention of whether or not married female asylum seekers can file claims independently of their husbands.

Temporary Asylum

The increased number of women asylum seekers and the fact that their situation sometimes does not to fit the requirements for either refugee status or asylum based on humanitarian considerations has led to the practice of granting temporary asylum. This procedure allows individuals to remain for a specified period of time—usually one to two years. After that time the individual can be returned to her or his country of origin. US immigration law, for example, established a category for refugees called Extended Voluntary Departure (EVD), which has subsequently been replaced by Temporary Protected Status (TPS) and Deferred Enforced Departure (DED). TPS is granted on the basis of any one of three criteria: ongoing armed conflict, environmental disaster, and extraordinary, temporary conditions. It allows foreigners who would be endangered if they returned home to remain temporarily. DED temporarily suspends the removal of specific populations and allows them to work legally while they are protected from removal. The earlier program, EVD, gave special permission for nonresident aliens from "particularly troubled" countries to remain until the situation in their home country had eased.

The secretary of homeland security has the authority to designate TPS countries, and those granted admission under TPS may be able to obtain permanent residency in the United States unless the country is removed from the TPS list. Ordinarily TPS status is given to countries where there is an ongoing internal conflict, an extraordinary natural disaster such as an earthquake or hurricane, or exceptional and temporary conditions. In contrast DED nationals are designated by the president. Implementation, however, has varied considerably, with some groups being admitted with little difficulty, as was the case for refugees from Kosovo and Liberia, while other groups, such as Rwandan and Somalis, are rarely ever granted permission to remain temporarily under DED. As a result of the variations in who is granted TPS and DED and who is denied entrance, there have been persistent charges that decisions are motivated by ideological concerns rather than humanitarian interests. More recently TPS and DED have come under attack on other grounds. The objection is that temporary asylum is unenforceable since once individuals are admitted, it is a virtual impossibility to track them down subsequently and make sure that they return to their home country. From the perspective of women asylum seekers, TPS and DED have proved inadequate to address their problems. TPS and DED are rarely ever granted to women accompanied only by children, who are generally viewed as imposing an ongoing economic burden on the country.

Several European countries also grant temporary residency for a fixed time period ranging from 18 months to 3 years to certain types of asylum seekers. The policy called Exceptional Leave to Remain (ELR) was instituted in Britain in 1993 and was adopted in Germany, Greece, and Spain in 1995. Ireland established a similar procedure in 1997. The basic requirements of ELR involve the renewal of residency permits each year for a period of five years. There are no rights to immediate family unification under ELR. When family unification is permitted on humanitarian grounds, it is dependent on the individual demonstrating that he or she can support the family and has met the required residency requirements. For example, when the policy was first put in place in Denmark there was a five-year requirement that had to be met before the immediate family could join an asylum seeker. In Britain and France, however, only a two-year waiting period was needed. Elsewhere there is no right to family unification, and where it is permitted it is dependent on adequate housing and sufficient income.

While ELR does provide some protection to endangered women, it is far less satisfactory than refugee status. Although in practice in countries such as the

Netherlands extensions to remain have been the norm, the growth of xenophobia and anti-immigrant sentiment coupled in some countries with concerns about terrorist activity have resulted in fewer extensions being granted and more stringent monitoring to ensure that temporary residents leave. Needless to say, the temporary nature of DED and ELR poses a serious worry for those who fear returning to their country of origin. The refugee experience is a traumatic one. At best immigrant adjustment to a new environment is difficult. When the possibility of being returned to a country that was a scene of the original trauma hangs over the individual, the psychological stress is intensified. The prohibition on women to bring family members, including their children, with them or the imposition of a long waiting period makes their situation very difficult.

Temporary asylum status poses additional practical problems. Women granted temporary asylum are assumed to be incapable of supporting themselves and are seen as ill-suited to being trained for employment either because they have dependent children or because of their cultural background or limited education. Whatever programs for these women exist emphasize nonmarketable domestic skills such as nutrition, child care, and family hygiene. British statistics illustrate the magnitude of the problem: only 7 percent women are employed as compared to 20 percent of the men, but only 9 percent of the women are enrolled in a training programs compared to 21 percent of the men. The end result is that government policies foster welfare dependency, which in turn reinforces perceptions of women as a financial burden on the state and discourages decisions to grant them even temporary asylum. There are other concerns as well. Children born in a country such as the United States are automatically eligible for citizenship. However, their parents can be compelled to leave when their temporary asylum expires despite their children's right to continued residency. Temporary asylum also contributes to a growth in illegal aliens. Apprehensive about returning to their country of origin, individuals granted temporary asylum may and sometimes do "disappear" into the population rather than leave. Several recent instances, including the highly publicized case of woman member of the Dutch Parliament, illustrate this aspect of temporary asylum. Moreover, procedures ensuring that temporary asylum residents leave are difficult and costly to enforce. Indeed, just recently the US government announced that it would be futile and too expensive to ensure that everyone entering the country left by the end of their authorized visa stays.

Conclusion

The UN protocols established international criteria for granting refugee status and guaranteeing those eligible to receive it certain rights and protections. However, the ambiguity of the criteria has created confusion and has resulted in considerable variation among countries over what constitutes a well-founded fear of persecution. Changing world conditions have also produced situations in which there is a well-founded fear of persecution that does not conform to the conditions set down in the UN protocols or interpretations of them. In such cases some countries grant asylum based on human rights violations or humanitarian considerations. Refugee status and asylum granted for human rights violations and for humanitarian considerations that do not necessarily convey the same rights and protections are critical issues for women who comprise a large majority of those seeking asylum. The absence of clear criteria, the emergence of new types of persecution not covered under UN protocols, a blurring of the lines between immigrants and refugees that has made the institution of asylum suspect, and insensitive gendered interpretations of what constitutes a well-founded fear have proved detrimental to women. Equally problematic is the fact that many governments discourage or do not allow women accompanying their husbands from applying for asylum status in their own right and instead admit them as a dependent family member.

The present rules, interpretations, and practices disadvantage female refugees many times over. The claim that the definition of a well-founded fear of persecution contained in the UN protocols is gender neutral fails to take into account a range of experiences that women encounter. Women often face different types of persecution than men do; hence their basis for claiming a well-founded fear is different. An emphasis on traditional forms of persecution—imprisonment, torture, and death threats—as fulfilling the criteria of a well-founded fear of persecution means that the kinds of danger women are subject to, such as rape or threats of rape, are often not considered sufficiently menacing to warrant refugee status. There are also gender differences in styles of resistance. Males tend to be highly visible in their actions, while women often operate outside the public eye. Again reliance on male models of behavior results in women's lower-profile but equally dangerous work being discounted, ignored, or overlooked. Finally there is a lack of recognition of the traumatic situations women confront at the substate level of community and family because of their gender. In highlighting political activity, interpretations of the UN protocols have excluded gender as a bona fide social group until recently. As a result, forms of gender discrimination such as dowry murder, genital mutilation, and honor killing are often regarded as insufficient in meeting the requirements for granting asylum. In short, the prevailing understanding of persecution places women at a disadvantage. The upshot is that male applications for refugee status tend to be approved, while those of women are rejected.

Even where gender-sensitive guidelines have been introduced, they have been only sporadically implemented. Some of the problems women encounter when they apply for asylum stem from their lack of education or constraints placed on their social interactions in their country of origin that discourage them from speaking out for themselves. However, the disparity between the number of both women refugees and asylum seekers whose claims are approved and the policies and programs that define them as dependents reveals a deeper problem: an acceptance of gender stereotypes that expose a fundamental insensitivity to women's experiences and needs. These problems are compounded by exotic stereotypes of the different countries from which the women come and the encouragement of women to frame their requests for asylum within the context of these stereotypes.

Some countries do not permit women to apply for asylum in their own right if they are part of a family unit. Family unification as an alternative for women seeking asylum is at best a flawed solution, for among other things many women do not have a husband accompanying them. Furthermore the notion of dependency implicit in family unification contributes to an environment that leaves little chance of success for women outside the domain of the family and limits their opportunities to (re)construct an identity, to improve their lives—and in some cases even to survive. Even if there is an opportunity for women to apply for asylum directly, gender insensitivity of refugee and asylum policies discourages them from doing so; and if they do apply for asylum after they have been admitted as a dependent family member, the delay in applying independently may be considered grounds for denial.

Changing world conditions have led to situations in which there is a well-founded fear of persecution that does not conform to the conditions set down in UN protocols or interpretations of them. In such cases some countries grant asylum on the basis of human rights violations or humanitarian considerations. For women with children who are unaccompanied by a male family member the prospects are grim. Their requests for asylum are often evaluated through the prism of welfare dependency. In the United States they are frequently depicted as seeking to enter the country for the purpose of obtaining citizenship for any children they may have and in order to live off welfare benefits provided by the state. This perception is not unique to the United States but is widely shared in countries of Western Europe. It is, of course, true that women, particularly single parents and widows with lower educational levels and limited language skills combined with a lack of child-care facilities are more likely to require substantial support from social services. At the same time the absence of culturally sensitive programs that allow women to acquire the necessary language skills and job training only perpetuates their continuance on welfare. In ignoring the potential talents and abilities of these women, many of whom worked in their home country, government policies thwart women's ability to construct a new, functional social identity.

Many women entering a country as refugees or asylum seekers suffer the additional burdens of coming with few material assets from areas that are not only culturally different but also considered less developed in the Western sense of that term. In addition to coping with problems stemming from the attempts of governmental structures to define who they are and what they can do they must also struggle with issues related to the intersection of race, ethnicity, and social class.

SECTION 2

Managing Social Pressures in the Workplace and Community

Old fashioned ways which no longer apply to changed conditions are a snare in which the feet of women have always become readily ensnared.
—Jane Addams

CHAPTER 5

Ethnic Communities and the Construction of Identity

Immigration, whether voluntary or involuntary, is a momentous and traumatic experience that requires both material and psychological adaptation. Daily life is no longer the same as it was in the home country. At a bare minimum old rules governing behavior have to be modified and adjustments made in order to survive in new surroundings. The effects of these changes on an individual's way of life and social identity are magnified by official policies that set immigrants, refugees, and asylum seekers apart from members of the main stream community by their precarious occupational status and by a social isolation that encourages ethnic segregation and marginalization.

Confronting the problems posed by a new environment, both men and women turn to their ethnic immigrant community for social interaction and for help and assistance in adjusting to new surroundings. These communities serve an important practical function. They are source of information about employment opportunities and provide informal networks for a broad range of support services, such as tips about available housing, advice about where to get medical treatment, and information about schools and where to go for social and legal services when problems arise with the bureaucracy. In many communities they even act as an alternative to banks by helping individuals obtain credit and advancing loans when they are needed.

Immigrant communities perform another equally important function, however. They serve as a surrogate homeland. To alleviate feelings of confusion, homesickness, and isolation they attempt to recreate an idealized version of the homeland (Kleiner 1977; Shukla 1997). This is accomplished by emphasizing traditional values in a variety of ways, ranging from organizing festivals and celebrating holidays to adhering to certain patterns of personal conduct. Food, styles of dress, and modes of deference take on a symbolic meaning and provide comfort in a strange, foreign, and often intolerant land. Immigrant communities in the nineteenth and early twentieth century offer numerous examples of this phenomenon. In the United States in towns and cities where there was a significant Italian population a "Little Italy" was created. Similarly Irish, Polish, Eastern European Jewish neighborhoods like New York's Lower Eastside, and China Towns appeared. In the later part of the twentieth century Vietnamese, Hispanic, and Caribbean neighborhoods have sprung up. Little Havana in Miami is perhaps the most widely known of these newer ethnic enclaves, but there are also large Caribbean neighborhoods on the East Coast and Little Vietnams on the West Coast. Similarly in Britain there are Indian, Pakistani, Bangladeshi, Somali, Kurdish, and West Indian neighborhoods. In Germany and Denmark there are Turkish and Kurdish enclaves, and North African and West African quarters in France. South Asians have recreated the atmosphere of their homeland in districts in many British cities. Bradford, which is a center for Pakistani immigrants in the north of England, is a perfect example of this, as are Somali neighborhoods in Tower Hamlets in London and in Liverpool, and Bangladeshi neighborhoods scattered throughout London and the West Midlands.

As previous chapters have pointed out, government laws and policies play an important part in (re)constructing the social identity of immigrant and refugee women. So, too, do immigrant communities. Government laws and policies—especially family unification, which makes a woman's right to remain for the first several years, and in some cases her right to work, continent upon being a family member—reflect the traditional Western notion of a nuclear family headed by a male wage earner and place women in the stereotypic gender roles of "at home" housewives and mothers. Immigrant communities also emphasize women's role within the home. Women are expected to play a critical part in recreating the idealized version of the homeland. It is their job to maintain traditional rituals within the home and to teach them to the children. Since these functions center on activities that take place within the home, assigned gender roles have a particular significance in the community.

The social identity that government laws and public policies suggest and the one that immigrant communities propose create difficulties for women in the terms of their (re)construction of a social identity that is congruent at individual and collective levels. The assumptions both make—that the lives of immigrant women are wholly centered on home and family life and that they do not actively participate in the labor market—are at odds with reality. Whether women are admitted as part of a family group or as workers, they are not exclusively stay-at-home wives and mothers. To the contrary, most immigrant women work in either the formal or informal economy. The economic situation facing most immigrant families requires multiple wage earners, and women's salaries are often crucial to the family's survival. Even low-wage-earning women who have been granted temporary work visas for employment in traditional female occupations such as child care, domestic service, and health care are working to support a family back home. However, working requires changes in family relationships, which in turn create tensions. These tensions contribute to marital problems, to strained relationships with children, particularly daughters, and in some cases to domestic violence.

Gender Relationships in the Immigrant Community

Although immigrant communities fill important material and emotional needs, their institutions and leadership accentuate gender distinctions. Invariably men drawn from the elite in the old country or from the dominant religious institution hold positions of leadership. In this capacity they often advocate and reinforce rules for behavior based on rigid conceptions of gender roles. For men these norms partially alleviate the challenges to male identity that accompany changes in their status resulting from immigration. A struggle to (re)assert their identity takes the form of masculine rituals, which are implicitly and irrevocably gendered. Moreover, a nationalist culture guides them toward civic life and ushers women away from it. In contrast, the role for women is culture keeper in the home (Jacobson 1995).

A number of studies of immigrant communities in both the United States and Europe provide evidence of these public/private gender spheres. One study of ethnic Caribbean communities in New York City, for example, suggests that men finding themselves in jobs that are below either the status and class positions they held in their home countries or what they expected to have as a result of immigrating attempt to compensate by creating a social arena where their previous status is acknowledged (Jones-Correa 1998). One means of achieving this is participation in the public life of their immigrant community where their status will be recognized and supportive male networks established. By maintaining bounded ethnic enclaves, immigrant men have minimized the stress they experienced from a loss of previous social networks and have ensured the continuation of their old status and identity. Similarly, Mexican, Dominican, and Cuban male immigrants in the United States finding themselves in unskilled or semiskilled occupations rather than the higher-status or white-collar positions they held prior to immigration have compensated for their loss of importance by immersing themselves in the activities of both their immigrant community and their home country. A study of Chilean refugees in Britain has reported similar findings. For men exile represented a loss of power, a loss of identity, and feelings that their role as head of the family was gone. Their response was involvement in refugee Chilean politics and intensified gender divisions (Kay 1989). Some studies of Somali families in London reported comparable responses among the men there as well (Chell 1997).

The position of women in their ethnic community stands in sharp contrast. As Yuval-Davis put it, women "often symbolize the collective unity," but "they are often excluded from the collective 'we' of the body politic" (1997). The public domain, the marketplace, is viewed as a male domain, whereas home and family—the domestic or private sphere—is considered to be the woman's. Thus, while a man's status is enhanced by his involvement in community affairs, a woman's comes from preserving ethnic values and life-style within the family and not from playing an active role in ethnic community organizations. Furthermore, a loss in status is not a motivating factor for women. In many instances their status may actually have improved since the salary they bring home to the family from working allows them to have a bigger say in household decision making than they had previously. Under these circumstances the impetus to preserve traditional social networks is not particularly helpful to women. Some studies have gone further. They have argued that women tend to be more adaptable to their new surroundings than men, who tend to be disparaging about their new environment and more depressed (Quack 1995).

There are, of course, exceptions. Chilean women in Britain reported that the pressure to work and the removal of familial support systems that had existed in Chile resulted in a loss of their autonomy. This finding indicates that social class affects the immigrant women's perception of their new status. Intersectionality suggests that women who were forced to flee because of political upheaval and had previously enjoyed a privileged position and an extensive support system in their home country experience a loss of prestige, whereas those less privileged see immigration and working as a possibility for improving their position.

There are also practical considerations that may account for the absence of women's participation in community leadership. Family responsibilities in combination with employment leave women little spare time for activities outside the home. However, here again there are exceptions. Hispanic women in the United States sometimes participate actively in local grassroots community groups concerned with issues such as schooling and social welfare (Jones-Correa 1998; Kibria 1990; Hondagneu-Sotelo 1994). In some instances this leads to their greater participation in mainstream local politics, but it is unusual for it to result in female leadership positions in the organizational structure of their ethnic community.

Despite the responsibility for upholding and enforcing ethnic values within the family, a woman's role in the family is limited by its patriarchal structure. She is subordinate to the male head of household, and when she fails to conform to accepted norms or her husband's wishes she may be subjected to a wide range of punishments within both the family and her ethnic community. These may range from shunning to domestic violence and in some instances even to honor killings. The power of the ethnic community to enforce gender-appropriate behavior for women is dependent, however, on a number of factors, such as the circumstances under which a woman entered the country—for example, family unification; a temporary work permit; asylum; illegal status; whether or not she lives in the community; and her ethnicity, social class, and level of education. For instance, among South Asian women in Britain, the importance of patriarchal authority within both the home and the community is affected by the woman's level of education. More highly educated women—that is, those with a university or graduate-level degree—experience a different form of patriarchy than less well educated women and are more "independent," at least with the family and the ethnic community (Bhopal 1997). Women coming from a more privileged background and who are able to blend in physically as well as culturally with mainstream society are less constrained than other immigrant and refugee women, although, as will be pointed out later, they are not entirely free of pressure from their community. Less-privileged women admitted under programs of family unification and those who are in a country illegally are much more likely to be concerned about adhering to community norms than women who either have temporary work visas or work and reside outside their community. Undocumented women along with those who have conditional residency, including widows and women whose husbands either have left them or have been deported are legally liable to deportation. In such cases community support can sometimes make the difference between remaining and being forced to leave. The Sari Brigade in England is one instance where community support prevented widows from being deported. Women admitted on temporary work visas, on the other hand, are dependent on their employers; hence the approval of their ethnic immigrant community is usually less essential. This is especially the case where the employer is not a member of the ethnic community. In short, the material and emotional support provided by the ethnic community allows it to have some measure of influence over women, even those who are more privileged.

Good Wives, Bad Wives

Although ethnic communities depict and emphasize women's role in the home, most women work. They have little option to do otherwise if the family is to survive economically. However, working has a significant impact on husbands, families, and women's role in the community. A woman's salary allows her to have some say in family decision making and undermines the patriarchal family structure. Faced with a loss of his role as breadwinner and his wife's efforts to make decisions, the spouse may resort to domestic violence to maintain control over the family and preserve the status quo (Kelson and Delaet 1999). Although some argue that the rate of intimate partner abuse is about the same in immigrant families as in native families under high levels of stress, the contradictory pressures of a wife's participation in family decision making, the community endorsement of the patriarchal family, and her husband's frustration with a diminished status can produce volatile marital relationships (Anderson 1993).

Although little systematic research has focused directly on immigrant family dynamics and intimate partner violence, several studies have looked at abuse in case studies of particular ethnic immigrant groups (Abraham 1995; Evans 2007; George and Ramkissoon 1998; Menjivar and Salcido 2002). In the United States these studies have concentrated primarily on Asian families—Vietnamese, Cambodia, Laotian, Korean, and South Indian (Camino and Kruefeld 1994). In Britain they have looked at patterns of intimate partner violence among Somali, Indian, Pakistani, Bangladeshi, and Afro Caribbean families. A study of a Somali immigrant community in Britain, for example, found that since men's identities were tied to work, the loss of their role as breadwinner coupled with an erosion of the patriarchal family structure, which they attributed to the British welfare system, and their perceptions of a growing emancipation of women led to high levels of anxiety and intensified feelings of underachievement, particularly among unemployed men. Their response often led to their becoming more resistant to change and more abusive (Griffith 2002; Fawz 1993).

Except in the most extreme cases, intimate spousal abuse is not always easy to determine. Cultural norms vary. Despite this there are some common characteristics. One is women's recognition and willingness to identify it as such. In various studies of many different ethnic groups, a significant percentage of the women respondents reported that they personally knew women who had been victims of intimate partner violence (Bhopal 1997). In a study of South Asian women in Boston, 40 percent of those interviewed reported knowing women who had been abused. Of those women experiencing abuse, 75 percent were married and 50 percent had at least one child (Dasgupta 2000).

A second theme has been a rigid patriarchal family structure. A study of Korean immigrants in the United States, for example, found that while there was a decline in status for men and an increase for women who worked outside the family, the men did not modify their rigidly patriarchal attitudes (Min 2001). Indeed, the more wives worked and earned, the more likely they were to experience marital conflicts. Furthermore, it was not the long hours that husbands and wives worked together in family-owned stores that were responsible for high levels of marital discord, the author claimed, but rather an increasing discrepancy between gender behavior within the family and the traditional gender roles sanctioned by the ethnic community.

Although studies of Turkish women in Germany and Denmark have focused mainly on their participation in the work force, they reported similar findings. The women in these studies consistently complained about the unequal distribution of household responsibilities and mentioned in some detail the problems that traditional roles and patriarchal attitudes created in their lives. They asserted that despite the long days they put in at labor-intensive jobs in factories, their husbands still demanded cooked meals and refused to participate in any jobs around the house on the grounds that it was women's work. The respondents did not mention marital tensions as such but it is quite clear from their comments that they resented the fact that they were forced to work the equivalent of a double shift and distressed that their husbands refused to assume any responsibilities in the household (White 1997).

Although the findings regarding patriarchal control and domestic violence in immigrant communities point to the troubles emerging from an incongruity in gender roles that characterize contemporary immigrant family life, studies of South Asian communities have emphasized the importance of cultural context in understanding the phenomenon of domestic violence (Anderson 1993; Rimote 1991). They contend that the cultural, social, economic, and political experiences that mold women's perceptions of acceptable levels of marital discord and domestic violence complicate the establishment of a universal understanding of what constitutes intimate partner violence. Among other ethnic communities studied, the evidence suggests what amounts to domestic violence in one community is not viewed necessarily the same way in others. For example, although the norms for appropriate behavior between husband and wife may be based on patriarchal principles and contribute to marital conflict, this does not necessarily mean that women reject the concept of patriarchy out of hand or that they wish to restructure their relationships. A study of a Vietnamese community in the United States found that the women accepted the male-dominated family system because it afforded them some economic protection and validated their authority over the younger generation (Kibria 1990). The women saw their capacity to become economically independent as limited and viewed male economic protection as a necessity. As a consequence, women considered the traditional family system to be valuable in terms of its economic benefits as well as the privilege it gave them to wield influence over the lives of their children. Other studies have found that there are differences among ethnic communities about just what constituted physical as well as psychological abuse. In some communities there is a higher level of tolerance toward physical abuse like slapping or hitting than there is in the mainstream community.

High levels of domestic violence, spousal abuse, intimate partner violence, and marital tensions are often attributed to the trauma of immigration, an adjustment to a new life-style, and the ethnic community's endorsement of rigid gender roles. Traditional gender roles are difficult to maintain given the upheaval in daily life resulting from the move. Problems in the marital relationship, particularly in families where the wife has entered the work force, contribute to dysfunctional behavior—in some cases to domestic abuses. Then, too, new opportunities for education and employment are often inconsistent with accepted notions of appropriate gender behavior. There is often stress over issues such as reproduction, birth control, and women's pursuit of work and education (Camino and Kreulfeld 1994).

As in nonimmigrant communities, alcoholism or substance abuse may also contribute to intimate partner violence. In addition, language barriers, isolation from a social support group, as well as the fragile nature of women's legal status when they are admitted under family unification or are illegal increase the likelihood of domestic violence. Groups working with abused immigrant women express grave concerns that many of them are often trapped in violent situations. For example, in New York City more than half the domestic violence homicide victims are foreign born (Evans 2007; Albor 2006), and a study done in Washington, DC, reported that two-thirds of the immigrant women were subject to weekly physical or emotional abuse (Monahan, 2006). Yet women admitted conditionally under family unification are reticent about speaking out about domestic violence, because they fear that they will be deported. Indeed, the most frequent comment from the women suffering from domestic violence is that they have no recourse against the abuse since they may be subject to deportation. An alternative route is for women to seek help from their community. However its leadership structure, with its emphasis on distinct gender roles and acceptance of the patriarchal family authority structure, make this an unlikely source of support for them. Perceiving the leaders of the community as unsympathetic, women are reluctant then to approach them for help in dealing with family violence.

The situation is perhaps even worse for undocumented women whose status makes them liable not only to abuse within the family setting but also to immediate deportation. Government policies are complicit by targeting illegal immigrants—a practice that often makes women more vulnerable to domestic violence. For example, a law passed in Massachusetts and just recently rescinded authorized the police to investigate the immigration status of anyone registering a complaint. As a consequence, women refrained from reporting domestic violence, since to report domestic violence meant risking having one's name sent to the Department of Homeland Security and possibly being sent to a detention center and then deported (Monahan 2006). Then, too, threats by the abusing partner to go to the police if the abuse is reported simply contribute to the vulnerability of a woman who is undocumented.

Of course, patriarchal gender roles endorsed by ethnic immigrant communities are not solely responsible for the problems of domestic abuse in immigrant families. Government policies also contribute. In 2000 a law establishing a program in the United States known as U Visas allowed ten thousand visas a year to be issued to victims of domestic violence, rape, sexual exploitation, involuntary servitude, attempted murder, and assault and authorized the recipients of these visas to apply subsequently for permanent residency on humanitarian grounds. However, as late as 2006 the federal government had not implemented the program, and only one-year work permits and interim protection had been extended to the 5,800 applicants who had passed the first hurdle (Bernstein 2007). A bill to correct the situation, the Immigrant Victims of Violence Protection Act, was introduced in the United States House of Representative in 2005 but was never put on the agenda or voted on (US Fed News 2005).

Indifference in the United States to immigrant victims of domestic violence is in no way unique. Spain has an estimated seven hundred thousand undocumented women. Until 2004 illegal aliens in Spain were subject to immediate deportation, did not qualify for the benefits available to the victims of domestic violence, and were not eligible for shelter in housing for battered women. Women who filed a complaint were often arrested on the basis of their immigration status while the abuser went free. Even today government programs to combat domestic violence rarely target immigrant populations. As Maria Naredo of Amnesty International of Spain observed, the Spanish state has subordinated the human rights of women who are victims of domestic violence to their immigration control policies, which without doubt accentuate the invisibility, lack of protection, and vulnerability of immigrant women. As a result intimate partner violence among immigrants in Spain remains unabated (Fraeman 2005). Ethnic communities' standards for appropriate gender behavior are propped up by the lack of sympathy on the part of the government to the plight of immigrant women.

All women suffer from some of the liabilities of the patriarchal culture that has persisted in the West as well as the Third World. However, those liabilities vary depending on ethnicity, social class, and education. Immigrant and refugee women are no exception. Some of them enjoy privilege; others do not. In the case of some women immigrants the consequences of patriarchal community pressures are less burdensome and gender roles within the family more fluid.

Guardians of the Hearth

In an article on colonialism, nationalism, and colonized women, the Indian anthropologist Partha Chatterjee argued that, confronted with British control in the nineteenth century, Indians, while acknowledging their conquerors' preeminence in the domain of material things such as science, technology, and European statecraft, saw themselves as superior in the spiritual realm. They dealt with these dissonant self-perceptions by dichotomizing the world into an outer world, a place of oppression and daily humiliation where they were forced to adjust, and an inner world where their spiritual selves and identities could be preserved. The outer world was the preserve of men, the environment in which they found themselves daily. In contrast the inner world represented by the home—an inner sanctum—should remain uncontaminated by the material world. Women epitomized the home that embodied the inner self—one's true identity. Regardless of what conditions men might find themselves in the external world, it was women's responsibility to protect and perpetuate this spiritual oasis—the home. According to Chatterjee this dichotomy of outer and inner worlds subjected women to a new form of patriarchy. Feminine virtue—modesty and decorum in manner and conduct expressed through appearance, behavior, and spiritual qualities—characterized this new woman and differentiated her from both her predecessors and modern, Westernized women.

Although Chatterjee developed this paradigm to link nationalism and gender within the context of nineteenth-century colonial India, aspects of it would seem to apply to contemporary ethnic communities and their expectations for immigrant women. In many respects present-day ethnic communities see the home as this oasis where the dignity and respect denied immigrants in the mainstream world can be preserved. It is a woman's obligation to safeguard this sanctuary by preserving ethnic culture and traditions and transmitting them to the next generation. It is especially important to instill these traditions and values in daughters so that the next generation can maintain the home as that oasis of ethnic identity and self-esteem. Some of the duties consist of celebrating ethnic holidays, preparing and cooking ethnic food, and continuing a traditional lifestyle. Just as important, if not more so, however, in some communities is abiding by the norms of modesty and decorum in dress and behavior. These norms are seen as critically important for the second generation as they are for the first. The proper behavior and proper clothing embody the community's boundaries (Yuval-Davis 1997).

Fulfilling these duties and obligations poses a heavy burden on women, particularly if they are employed. Many of the women put in long hours in low-status and low-paying jobs and have very little time for the shopping and cooking necessary for ordinary meal preparation, let alone the time-consuming preparation of ethnic meals or the elaborate activities involved in the celebration of ethnic holidays. Then, too, like men they must adapt to their work environment in terms of their behavior and in some instances their dress. Limited time for doing household chores and observing a different dress code are only part of the problem they confront. The reticence that the family and the ethnic community expect of them is often viewed negatively in the workplace and even associated with "backwardness." Indeed, it reinforces perceptions of immigrant women as "old fashioned" and ill equipped to cope in their new, modern environment. A different set of behaviors is required in the workplace where initiative, not passivity, is valued. Taking orders may be considered a virtue in immigrant women, but employers also want their workers to be self-motivated and to show initiative. As we shall see in the following chapter, German employers often praised Turkish women workers for their willingness to follow orders exactly but grumbled about their lack of initiative (Munchen 1984). Other activities outside the home also call for behavior that is at odds with community norms. For example, women need to be assertive in their dealings with the schools their children attend, obtaining health-care services for themselves and their children, interacting with social service agencies, and even using a public transportation system. Bifurcated patterns of behavior stemming from expectations that women conform to community norms while at home but other norms while working outside the home and interacting with mainstream institutions such as schools create serious stress in women's lives. Contradictory demands drain them of their time and energy and often adversely affect their physical and mental health, as we shall see in a following chapter.

Perhaps one of the most challenging areas for which women are responsible is ensuring that their children observe appropriate behavior with regard to sexuality. Their duty within the confines of both family and the community is to act as the guardian of morality and see to it that their children observe the norms for proper behavior. Sexualized Western societies make this a difficult task to accomplish. For example, in immigrant communities where gender separation is insisted on, the rules requiring girls to shun all mixed-gender social activities clash with the norms of mainstream society. In Turkish communities in Western Europe, although gender separation is not demanded, a daughter's virginity is of paramount importance. Unregulated dating and public displays of affection are therefore unacceptable (White 1997). However, norms such as these are rejected and in some cases denounced outside the boundaries of the ethnic community. The media, schools, and the workplace prompt children daily to consider miniskirts, tight jeans, low-cut T-shirts, and highly suggestive ads and behavior as acceptable. The contradictions between these norms and family expectations often leave children and young adults socially isolated, marginalized, and confused as they struggle to develop a single or dominant identity (Camino and Kruelfeld 1994).

In a terrain of conflicting norms, tensions over appropriate behavior are likely to emerge between mothers and their children and especially with their daughters. From a child's perspective the mother's insistence on community-approved behavior is often interpreted as demonstrating a lack of love, support, and understanding of the world in which they must operate. For the mother, her standing in the community is at stake, for it is she who is held accountable for ensuring the continuation of traditional values and behavior. Mothers are torn between conflicting demands, but so are children, for they must negotiate the rules of both their own community and mainstream society. Urged to hold fast to the community's standards, they also participate in mainstream society where a different set of rules prevails (Foner 1999). For girls this can be particularly problematic. Their peers and the media push them to dress and behave according to the norms of mainstream society. Moreover, these pressures exist not only at a personal but also at an institutional level. For example, gym shorts, school uniforms with short skirts, and certain types of physical education classes and coeducational extracurricular activities are mandatory in some schools, despite the fact that they are taboo in the girl's community. The clothes and behavior of their peers outside their immediate community and their involvement in the dominant culture at school or work challenge their sense of who they are. Self-esteem and the development of a dominant identity suffer as a consequence. The situation is made worse when there is a lack of respect for their cultural background and traditions at school and in the workplace.

Conflicting demands governing a mother's behavior and that of her children can have serious and long-lasting effects on the relationship between them. The issue of female genital mutilation (FGM) offers one illustration. Mothers may feel obliged to see that their daughters undergo this culturally required procedure despite their own misgivings and their daughter's reluctance. For the mother, community pressure may be overwhelming; but from the daughter's perspective the ritual may be seen as a violation of her body and her mother's lack of love and understanding. Less extreme parental and community demands, such as gender separation at social events, arranged marriages, prohibitions on Western-style dating, and type of dress also often produce ongoing strains in the mother-daughter relationship. Quarrels between mothers and daughters are intensified by the importance the community attaches to the mother's duty to preserve its values and traditions. This obligation leaves little leeway for accepting a hybrid identity in her children, particularly her daughters or for allowing her to adopt new norms regarding her role as the guardian of traditional values. In short, community expectations and children's need for understanding and flexibility place women on a collision course in terms of family relationships. Their standing in their families and the community is dependent on preserving traditions.

Needless to say, not all immigrant mothers and children experience conflicting pressures and tensions. Conflict over norms is likely to be minor when immigrants share many of the values and traditions of the receiving country. Western Europeans immigrating to North America or Australians and New Zealanders coming to live in Great Britain, for example, may have some different customs involving particular ways of observing shared holidays or food preferences, but these variations are not likely to be critical. While children may still face some challenges in terms of developing a dominant identity, their adjustment to a new environment will in all likelihood be less difficult for them than for immigrant families—first and second generations (and sometimes third and fourth generations)—that come from Third World countries or belong to non-Judeo-Christian sects or are racially distinctive. For these immigrants adjustment is more complicated. The differences in their background and values probably explain at least in part why the current wave of immigrants and asylum seekers in postindustrial countries in Western Europe and North America has created so much controversy and why well-educated, professionally trained, more affluent immigrants are readily accepted.

Educating the Children

The task of ensuring that children adhere to the proper values is an onerous one, for, like their mother, immigrant children confront multiple problems in their new environment. Research dealing with the adjustment and education of first- and second-generation immigrant children suggests that they face a broad range of obstacles and that they suffer significant strain as they try to accommodate to the demands of both mainstream society and their ethnic community. Ethnicity is a construction for them, particularly if they are adolescents. They have no single or state identity (Camino and Kruelfeld 1994). They must negotiate the Scylla and Charybdis of their cultural values and learn to navigate the institutional cultural obstacles of the host state—often while simultaneously facing hostility and discrimination on all sides. A recent study of Guatemalan children living in the United States reported that they experienced stress and attributed it to the fact that they were living in two worlds and that the situation was exacerbated by an emerging transnationalism that situated them in neither country. Pressures at home emphasized the "old country," while restrictive policies of the state pushed them to focus on the host country (Menjivar 2002). The conflict of a bifurcated identity would seem to be confirmed in a number of other studies. For example, one found that a significant proportion of immigrant children were seen by school mental health workers (Aronowitz 1984). This finding would seem to be in line with earlier work that found an association between psychological disorders and immigrant status among adults (Kleinberg 1979). Although more recent studies have suggested that the connection between mental illness and immigrant status is much more complex than earlier studies indicated, there seems to be agreement that there is a correlation between cultural change and mental health in adults.

The negative stereotypes that have emerged from linking immigrants and mental illness have led researchers to move away from that emphasis and concentrate instead on issues relating to the performance of immigrant children in school. Current research now focuses on behavior. Recent studies have reported that West Indian children in London and immigrant children in Canada are more likely to have social or emotional adjustment problems than nonimmigrant children (Xin Ma 2002; Bagley 1972; Nicol 1971; Goldenberg 1973; Graham and Meadows 1967). Similar findings were reported for South Asian children from

Uganda who came to Canada (Minde and Minde 1976). The results reported in studies of immigrant children in other countries are similar. For example, in Sweden teachers described immigrant children as having higher levels of anxiety, aggression, and an inability to tolerate frustration as well as exhibiting lower self-esteem, greater dependency, and poorer relations with peers than other children (Takac 1976). A similar study looking at immigrant children in Germany, Sweden, and Britain reported behavior problems particularly among West Indian children who tended to express either aggressive opposition or depressive seclusion (Wilke 1975).

This pattern of depressive seclusion among African Caribbeans and Nigerians in Britain is described in Caryl Phillips's recent book, *Foreigners*, which chronicles the deterioration of immigrants as they experience rejection at a personal, societal and governmental, and institutional level. A newly published British government report further confirms the difficulties faced by first- and second-generation immigrant children. It found that children born to black mothers were more likely to be expelled from school, suffer alcoholism, and get into trouble with the police than their peers (Reaching Out: Think Family 2007). Like earlier studies, it mentioned problems at school and in socializing and argued that these adolescents externalize their problems through criminal or antisocial behavior. Identity conflicts and psychiatric disturbance were two conditions frequently cited by teachers who were surveyed.

Although not all immigrant children exhibit behavioral disturbance and a propensity for disorder, those who do are more likely to exhibit adjustment difficulties during adolescence than their peers. The commonly held assumption is that conflict with parents has contributed to behavioral and adjustment problems and is most likely to occur when children are forced to choose between the values and identities of their old and new cultures. Psychiatric dysfunction and adjustment and behavioral problems were not found to be unique to immigrant boys. West Indian girls in Britain also exhibit higher levels of antisocial behavior than their English counterparts. The explanation offered for their behavior is that the difficult and stressful circumstances faced by immigrant girls as they grow up along with racial discrimination and a high student turnover in predominantly immigrant schools create the conditions leading to conduct disorders and antisocial behavior (Rassool 1999).

Studies of immigrant children in the United States have tended to emphasize educational achievement rather than the psychological and behavioral adjustment focus of European research. However, in looking at the relationship of parental expectations and the children's educational accomplishments, the American studies found that when there is a high level of interaction between parents and children there is less disagreement about educational expectations and better school performance (Hao and Bonstead-Burns 1998). By the same token, when the children are not guided by their parents or their parents resist change, educational achievement is adversely affected. In particular, immigrant children were found to do less well in school when the parents were unable to adapt to their new environment at a rate similar to that of their children. This dissonance is seen by some researchers as accounting for the difference in performance between Asian and Mexican immigrant children.

The research dealing with immigrant children in both Western Europe and North America has been interpreted to mean that in their adolescent years both girls and boys are likely to experience problems in adjusting to conflicting values and norms and that this sometimes results in behavioral disturbances and antisocial behavior. In the United States, parents' ability to adapt and assimilate to a new environment was found to affect their children's school performance. Given the assumption in Western society and especially in the United States that the primary responsibility for raising a child rests with the mother, poor school performance is her fault. In many ways mothers face a "no win" situation. Adjustment and performance problems are a product of their ineptitude. If their children, especially their daughters, get into trouble or flout the norms of their ethnic community, the mothers are held accountable. At the same time a mother's effort to make children meet community expectations may actually contribute to their children's behavioral problems. To make matters worse, when children fail to internalize community norms for appropriate behavior the mother is blamed for being too lenient—an accusation that in turn exacerbates existing family tensions and marital stress in her life.

There has been some concern that negative assessments of some immigrant children reflect cultural stereotypes or lack of sensitivity to cultural difference. Children and adolescents' behavior, some have argued, are simply a response to attitudes that are disrespectful. That mothers should be held accountable in such cases is ironic to say the least. Similarly children and adolescents may find negative stereotypes of immigrant mothers in mainstream culture as offensive and deeply disturbing. Under these circumstances the fact that mothers should be held responsible for misbehavior at school amounts to an additional burden that women must confront and that influences the (re)construction of their social identity. There has been another issues raised as well. By and large discussions of the role of mothers and children's adjustments to school are based on a generic notion of "the immigrant." Often this prototype of the immigrant is based on Third World immigrant groups, which are racially or religiously distinctive from the mainstream society. However, not all immigrants have substantially different cultural, educational, or economic backgrounds. Religious or racial differences may be minimal. Generalizations about mothers' or parental roles in children's adjustment to school, when based on observations of and conclusions about particular immigrant groups and applied to all immigrants, are of limited value.

Even in those instances where the burden of enforcing immigrant community creates problems and tensions, it is wrong to see women simply as victims, for despite the myriad liabilities they confront, they are often able to develop creative and life-affirming strategies that allow them to transcend the situation in which they find themselves. It is true that the psychic costs are often very high and probably account for numerous physical and mental health problems observed in many immigrant women. However, they survive and prosper in many instances. In many respects they bear a resemblance to the women described by Chatterjee.

They are not the same as either women in their country of origin or women in the country in which they now reside. They are caught between two worlds: the old and the new. They are subject to intense pressure from their families and their community to maintain ethnic traditions. At the same time employment pressures them to adapt to their new environment. Furthermore, the responsibility for preserving the "old ways" creates significant stress and conflict in terms of their relationship with their children, particularly their daughters. For the next generation contradictory pressures remain. Both mothers and daughters living simultaneously in two separate worlds, exemplify perfectly the condition of marginality.

Women Immigrating Solo and the Role of the Immigrant Community

In terms of their relationship with their ethnic communities, there are some important differences between women admitted on temporary work permits to fill positions in areas such as health care or under special programs and women admitted under family unification. In the first place, the integration of women entering on a temporary work permit or on their own into mainstream culture is shaped from the outset by the jobs they hold, the length of their stay, and the presence or absence of family members and friends who have already immigrated there. For example, if they are employed in domestic service or elder care, their active involvement in the affairs of their immigrant community, with the possible exception of the observance of holidays, will probably be limited. If their job entails "living in," their free time may be extremely limited. Employers often demand that they be on call 24 hours a day, 7 days a week, even though work agreements may include 1 day off a week. In addition some employers feel free to switch days off without consultation or simply ignore the requirement altogether. The situation was perhaps best summed up by Ryan, who, in writing about Irish women immigrants in Britain in the 1930s, observed that their employment provided no differentiation between public and private space (2003). Under these circumstances, regular participation in the activities of the immigrant community is difficult. Women with less demanding jobs may be more involved, although given male dominance in the political structure of the community their activities are more likely to revolve around social events.

A number of factors affect a woman's rapport with her community. If women anticipate returning home within a couple of years, they may be concerned about stories of inappropriate behavior getting back to relatives or children (Foner 2001). For them community approval may be an important consideration. The type of work the women do also affects their involvement in community activities. For example, employment in the sex/entertainment field is usually scorned. Women holding these jobs are looked down on, and their participation in community activities is usually discouraged. Of course there are exceptions. Some Nigerian women have been encouraged by their families to go abroad and earn money as sex workers. Since many are subsequently reintegrated into their families and society with little stigma attached to their past employment, the approval of the immigrant community is not particularly important. Its disapproval counts for little back home.

Where a woman lives also plays a part in determining the amount of influence that the community enjoys. Although living somewhere else poses problems in terms of work load, the potential for sexual exploitation, and the opportunity to enjoy some element of a private life, it also eases some of the pressures to maintain traditional norms and to serve as a moral guardian. Studies of immigrant women in the nineteenth and early twentieth centuries found live-in domestics enjoyed some real degree to freedom and were able to adapt relatively easily to a new environment. At the same time they are still not exempt from the obligation to maintain and foster traditional cultural values and behaviors altogether. All immigrant women tend to rely on their ethnic community for their social activities. This means that there are pressures to conform. Young Irish women who immigrated to Britain to work as domestics during the early years of the twentieth century provide some interesting insights into the role their ethnic community played in their lives. Feeling homesick, they spent their days off in Irish neighborhoods where they felt at home and could reaffirm their sense of ethnic identity. Their acculturation to a new environment in England meant, however, that they were different from the stereotypic rural Irish lass. Diaries and interviews record that while being "among their own kind" reduced feelings of loneliness, the women were also apprehensive that stories about their adjustment to a new life would compromise their reputations and rupture their relationships with their families. This was an issue of particular stress for them since a day away from the house confirmed in the minds of their employers that they were prostitutes (Ryan 2003). The same concerns exist today for women immigrating on their own. Easy and cheap international transportation, the Internet, and cell phones all increase the chances for rumors of misbehavior to reach home. For example, studies of Caribbean women who have come to work in the United States report that although they come to their ethnic neighborhood for social activities, they fear that news about things like their going unescorted to a bar for a drink will get back to their families or hometown and have serious repercussions for their reputation (Pessar and Graham 2001).

Eliminating contact with their immigrant community in order to avoid these pitfalls has not been a feasible option. Many women, particularly those who have left a family or children behind, are subject to homesickness. Socializing with others from their home country lessens a sense of estrangement. However, the social and material support provided by the immigrant community gives it an ability to monitor the women's behavior. In short, women immigrating alone may be less constrained by community norms than women admitted under programs of family unification or than undocumented women, but they are still beholden to them; their independence does not preclude nostalgia for their homeland.

Women Seeking Asylum

In many respects women asylum seekers resemble immigrant women in all aspects except one: they are victims of violence. They experience not only the anxiety and stress resulting from the upheaval of immigration and subsequent adjustment to the host state but also the documented trauma necessary to be granted refugee status. Studies have confirmed high rates of anxiety and stress among refugees in general and women in particular, of posttraumatic stress disorder within refugee families, and the physical and mental turmoil that women refugees go through (Robertson et al. 2006; Agger 1994). At the same time, while the rates of trauma among refugee women are high, programs to address their problems are few and far between. In short, refugee women face additional burdens in terms of adjustment.

International protocols and government laws and policies that determine who qualifies for refugee and asylum status regard women seeking asylum as falling into one of three categories: women accompanying a family headed by a man, women entering on their own, and women accompanied by their children but not by a male relative. In the case of women traveling as part of a family, they are subject to the same legal requirements for conditional residency as women admitted under the auspices of family unification. Given the high levels of stress and posttraumatic stress disorder in refugee families, women's conditional status poses additional risks for their abuse. With few government programs available to help women experiencing volatile family life, they are even more vulnerable to abuse than nonrefugee women.

In this situation the role of the ethnic community on (re)construction of women asylum seekers' social identity is both complex and nuanced. As mentioned earlier, refugees are ordinarily placed in reception centers until the government rules on the merits of their case. In some instances families or individuals from the same country are placed in a particular center, but this is not always the case. The dominant ethnic community in a center may not be the same as that of the particular refugee. As a consequence the importance of the ethnic community in setting norms varies. In some instances it may have considerable influence; in others, little or none. After a determination on the request for refugee status has been issued, the refugee, along with her family if she is accompanied by one, is moved to regular housing, which again may be ethnically diverse. Depending on the ability to speak a common language, diverse housing can afford an opportunity to newcomers to become cultural integrated more easily. It can also limit the power of an ethnic community to impose a uniform set of norms on everyone. However, the pull of the ethnic community in terms of meeting psychological, economic, and social needs along with the tendency for the mainstream community to define all immigrants, including refugees, as "other" encourages refugees to move to their own immigrant community where patterns of male leadership and stringent gender roles exist. Indeed, there is frequently a more prominent emphasis on gender roles in a homogeneous refugee community than in immigrant and mixed ethnic communities as a compensation for men's loss of power and control. As a study cited earlier of Chilean refugees to Britain reported, there was intense pressure on the part of the men to compensate for their diminished status and loss of control by imposing more rigid gender roles than had existed in their home country (Berns and McGown 1999). Their study of Somali refugees in Britain also cited earlier has described similar findings. This research suggests that the ethnic community's enforcement of gender roles results in women refugees having problematic relationships with their children and facing considerable marital stress.

Women seeking asylum either on their own or accompanied only by their children face additional problems. Like all other refugees they are initially housed in reception centers. Many of these centers do not make adequate provisions to protect women and children from abuse. These circumstances increase women's need for a male protector and make the women dependent on men who are most likely to come from the same ethnic community. Whether an ethnic community informally controls the center or a male "protector" is required, there are pressures for women to conform to strict gender roles. Government programs or staff do little to alleviate the situation, and little attention is given to women's vulnerability.

Conclusion

Women who are admitted under a family unification policy or who are undocumented are under serious pressure to conform to the norms of their immigrant community. These range from preserving traditions surrounding food and the celebration of holidays to conforming to dress codes and "appropriate" conduct. Women are expected to conform to rigidly defined gender roles and to accept patriarchic traditions. As guardians of the home, it is their duty to make sure that their children also observe community norms for proper behavior. Moreover, it is their obligation to transmit these values and traditions to the next generation. These requirements in themselves are difficult for the women to implement, for they are also dealing with the problems of adjusting to a new environment. When they work outside the home the burden is even more overwhelming, for at work and in their activities outside their immediate community they are under pressure to adapt to different cultural norms. The tensions and conflict arising from contradictory norms for behavior generate marital discord, which sometimes results in a pattern of domestic violence, as well as problems in the women's relationship with their children, particularly their daughters. They and their daughters epitomize the condition of marginality, for they both live simultaneously in two different worlds. The consequence is high levels of anxiety and stress.

In contrast women immigrating on their own tend to be somewhat less constrained by the norms of their immigrant community. However, feeling nostalgia for family and friends left behind and faced with an often intolerant and sometimes hostile new environment, they turn to their community for social support and interaction. Its importance in their lives gives the community some degree of power over them. The extent to which the pressures on women to conform exist, though, varies, depending in part on whether or not they live in the community and the degree to which the ethnic community offers them economic and social support.

For women seeking asylum the situation is somewhat different. If they are admitted as part of a family they are subject to many of the same pressures as other women entering under a program of family unification. There is one important difference, however. Since refugees are often suffering from posttraumatic stress disorder, family dynamics tend to be volatile, and the chances for strained relationships and domestic violence are increased. In the case of women seeking asylum on their own or accompanied by only their children, a sense of powerlessness and dependency along with the majority community's perception of them as dependent on social welfare increases the importance of the protection of their community for their safety and well-being. For them conformity to the norms of the community is not an option; it is a necessity.

Not all immigrant women suffer from the same liabilities, and some are much more privileged than others on terms of social class background and education. At the same time they are all caught in a vortex of conflicting pressures that leave them hard pressed to construct a coherent and meaningful identity that accommodates their past, present, and aspiring sense of self with the expectations of their community and the restrictions imposed on them by government policies.

CHAPTER 6

Between Dependence and Independence
Immigrant Women in the Work Force

Nowhere do government policies, expectations of the ethnic community, and the efforts of women to (re)construct their social identity collide more powerfully than in the area of employment. Both government laws and policies and attitudes endorsed by immigrant communities visualize women in terms of the home, and each imposes special burdens on their lives that in turn shape their options for (re)constructing their own social identity. Government laws, regulations, and practices identify immigrant women as "stay-at-home moms" or surrogate mother/daughter caregivers. This association with the domestic sphere represents a classic catch-22 for women. In labeling them as dependent family members, governments have contributed to popular impressions in mainstream society of immigrant women as unemployed and have limited their chances for being considered for a broad range of occupations. Many immigrant communities have also tended to view women in terms of home and family. Perceived as guardians of the old country's culture and traditions, women have been expected not only to preserve those values within the home but also to pass them on to the next generation, particularly their daughters. Unlike the official voice articulated in government policies and practices, which reflects a 1950s media version of a Western nuclear family, the immigrant community has tended to emphasize the maintenance of an idealized version of the norms and values of the old country. This has often included clearly prescribed gender roles. Such expectations have also limited women's employment opportunities.

At the same time, for the vast majority of immigrant women the possibility of not working has been nonexistent. They must work. Their ability to find a job has been dependent on several factors, however. These have included the laws regulating conditions for working imposed by government, which were discussed in an earlier chapter; their level of education; their ability to speak, read, and write the new language; their possession of marketable skills that extend beyond homemaking; and social support systems such as child care, which permit them to work outside the home. Research has found that in the

United States, level of education and an ability to speak the language were the most important criteria for employment (Stier and Tienda 1992). These same qualifications have been highly valued in the other postindustrial countries of Western Europe and North America.

Meeting these qualifications has not been a simple matter. Many of today's women immigrants have come from Third World countries and possess only a minimal level of education. In addition their ability to speak the new language has often been minimal. As a consequence, the opportunities for being employed have been restricted. To get a job their credentials must be enhanced. Unfortunately government policies defining women as dependent family members have discouraged publicly and privately funded programs that could provide them with the credentials they need, and the programs that have been funded have emphasized domestic skills such as household management and child care. Instead of teaching women marketable skills, these programs have perpetuated gender stereotypes, which in turn have limited the range of jobs available. The end result has been that women have been less competitive than men in the labor market and less able to advance in terms of wages and promotions. Furthermore, the association of women with dependent status has contributed to perceptions in the broader society that immigrant women are basically unqualified to hold demanding jobs in the public marketplace.

The role played by some immigrant communities has compounded the problems posed by government policies in a number of respects. The expectation that women serve as the embodiment and transmitter of cultural traditions has reduced the amount of time available to them to work, to participate in the activities of the mainstream society, and to adapt to a new environment. As a result, their employment choices have been further constrained, especially in terms of working full time. Even in those cases where women have been fully qualified to move directly into the labor market in terms of their skills and language proficiency, employment, home responsibilities, and pressures to maintain the cultural norms of the old country have competed for their time and attention and entailed obstacles beyond those experienced by native-born, acculturated working women.

Other factors have affected employment as well. As was discussed in a previous chapter, the importance the immigrant community places on traditional values and on the mother's responsibility for transmitting them has been a potential source of tension between a mother, her husband, and her children. Dealing with pressures from their families and their community coupled with the need to work has extracted a high psychic cost, which drains women of the time and energy needed on the job. Since the lives of all immigrant women have been shaped by both government policies and their community's pressures to conform to traditional norms, all women have been affected to some extent regardless of whether they immigrated independently or as part of a family.

The irony of immigrant women's situation is that the idea that they could be fully dependent on a single male wage earner is farfetched. Male immigrant incomes have rarely been sufficient to support a family. Men's salaries, although likely to be higher than women's, have usually not been sufficient to support a household, and opportunities for career advancement have tended to be limited. As a result, women's wages have often been crucial to the financial viability of the family. Their earnings have simply not been used as an "extra" for nonessential spending or for luxuries. Immigrant Mexican families in the United States have provided a number of examples of instances where female wage earners have been critical for the family to survive economically (Greenlees and Saenz 1999). The same has been true for female wage earners in Korean families in New York City (Min 2001). At the same time the concept of at-home wives and mothers articulated in government policies and the expectations of some immigrant communities coupled with the need to augment family income have placed women in the stressful situation of reconciling vastly different demands, with the result that often their health, adjustment, and sense of well-being, as well as their ability to remain employed, have been adversely affected.

There is another employment-related conundrum confronting immigrant women. Throughout the postindustrial countries of Western Europe and North America there has been a widespread belief that women immigrants and asylum seekers will have to rely on government subsidies to support them and their children. Data frequently cited by opponents of immigration have indicated that the initial income earnings of nonprofessional male immigrants are low and that in a country like the United States immigrant men are also likely to have either limited health care insurance coverage or none at all. The conclusion drawn has been that government will have to step in to support immigrant families. The feminization of immigration has intensified anxiety about this issue. In the United States, for example, the number of women immigrants increased from almost 50 percent in 1985 to close to 55 percent in 2004, and by 2004 women outnumbered men by 85,000 (Immigration Policy Center 2006). About 41 percent, or about 3.2 million women, have entered the United States illegally over the past 20 years. If the undocumented were also included, the number of foreign-born women would be much higher. Using these statistics, the argument is made that the cost for the government to support immigrant women has become too large to sustain.

The claim that immigration has become too costly a burden for the state has become a rallying cry in both the United States and Western Europe. In the United States, opponents of immigration have emphasized women's economic dependency and equated it with the negative stereotypes of the "welfare mother" and with welfare abuse regarding their children. Anti-immigrant websites have continually cited the amount of taxpayer dollars that go to pay the cost of providing immigrants, particularly immigrant women, with social services, such as medical care, food stamps, and schooling. One website, for example, claimed that health benefits for immigrant women in the United States amounted to ten billion dollars annually. Other websites have cited even higher costs, one going as far as to claim that the cost was 17 billion dollars a year (Camarota 2004; www.cis.org/article/2004; Caswell Evans 1995). Similar claims have surfaced elsewhere. The recent intensification of anti-immigrant feelings and xenophobia in the Netherlands and Sweden, for example, has played on images of Muslim women in burkas lining up to receive child welfare benefits while citizens have been denied those similar benefits.

The regulations contained in government policies, the expectations of some immigrant communities, assumptions that women require financial assistance from the government in order to survive, and the need to augment immigrant family income are all intertwined in the area of employment. It is here that women are confronted with the immediate task of (re)constructing a functional social identity and creating a space for themselves that somehow weaves together the concepts of a dependent "stay-at-home mom," guardian of the immigrant community's cultural identity, and mainstream society's perceptions of them as a financial burden with the need to earn money. This chapter explores these conflicting demands placed on women as they move into the labor market, the conditions constraining their opportunities to work and be promoted, and the impact of their employment on their attempts to (re)construct a social identity.

To Work or Not to Work: Is There an Option?

Arguments raging around the claim that immigrants threaten the welfare system and increase citizens' tax burdens have failed to take into account the fact that for the most part immigrant women—documented as well as undocumented—work and thus contribute to the economy. According to a recent study of OECD countries, among those legally admitted only 14 percent of foreign-born women described themselves as homemakers. The remainder—86 percent—see themselves as part of the work force. Far from the stereotype of the nonworking dependent wife, unemployment rates for immigrant women have been roughly the same as those for immigrant men. Of course, there are variations among countries. In Ireland, Sweden, Germany, and Norway, for example, women have been less likely than men to be unemployed but have been more likely to be unemployed in Spain, Italy, and Greece (OECD 2006).

The data have indicated that in the United States 42 percent of all immigrant workers—documented as well as undocumented—were women. This percentage compared favorably with native-born women. If only documented women were included, the percentage of immigrant women working increased to 80 percent, though here, too, there were regional variations (Schoeni 1998). For example, in the 1990 census 60 percent of New York City's working-age, foreign-born women were in the labor force. This was only slightly less than the percentage (66 percent) of native-born New York women who worked. Among some immigrant groups the percentage of women who worked was very high. For example, between 80 and 85 percent of Filipina women worked, and the overall employment rates for Caribbean women were about the same (Immigration Policy Center 2006). Among some immigrant groups the percentage was lower, however. For example, despite the overall high percentage of Caribbean women who worked, only 52 percent of women from the Dominican Republic were in the work force (Foner 1999).

According to the Immigration Policy Center's 2006 study, the occupations of women legally admitted ranged from professional and technical fields (32 percent) to service jobs (20 percent) and included office and administrative support positions (16 percent) and work in sales and related areas. The remainder was in production, building and grounds, cleaning and maintenance, food preparation and serving, health practitioners or technicians, fabricators, operators, and laborers. In some urban areas the number of women seeking work as day laborers has increased dramatically. For example, it was been reported that in New York between 100 and 150 women showed up daily at day laborer hiring halls(Immigration Policy Center 2006). It is hard to determine if it was documented or undocumented women who were applying for day laborer jobs. Indeed, whatever data exist about the occupational distribution of the undocumented is unreliable. Although the assumption has been that undocumented women are clustered in caregiving and domestic work, reliable data neither confirms nor denies such a pattern.

As might be expected given the near-universal gendered wage gap, women's salaries have lagged behind those of immigrant men and native-born women. In 2003 62 percent of foreign-born women earned less than $25,000 a year in contrast to 55 percent of native-born women and 47 percent of foreign-born men (Immigration Policy Center 2006). The wage gap did not apply uniformly across the board, however. In the United States, British, Canadian, European, Korean, Japanese, Philippine, and Middle Eastern women's salaries were closer to the median of native-born women, while those of Mexican and Latin American women were much lower (Schoeni 1998). Undoubtedly these differences reflect in part disparities in educational level, although other factors, such as the degree of social acceptance accorded to a particular immigrant group are probably also to blame. Indeed, such variations point to the importance of differentiating among women immigrants in terms of the status and the social acceptance of their immigrant group if we wish to understand their needs and situation.

Given women's level of economic activity, it is strange that they are perceived primarily in terms of their role within the home. Perhaps the distorted perception of their minimal participation in the labor market stems from preeminence of family unification policies throughout the twentieth century in combination with the practice of governments to routinely admit men as principle visa holders. Despite the feminization of immigration, even today only a small number of women are admitted as principle visa holders. For example, in 2004 slightly over 73 percent of the men who entered OECD countries did so as principle visa holders whereas only 27 percent of the women were admitted on this basis.

When women have entered as principle visa holders, they have been well educated, trained professionals. Moreover, they have been more likely to have doctoral or professional degrees than native-born women. Many of these women entered under the auspices of special programs that encouraged nurses and health-care professionals to come and fill shortages in the allied health and medical fields. As mentioned in an earlier chapter, countries like the Philippines and

Sri Lanka contributed to this pattern of immigration by encouraging foreign agencies to recruit trained women health professionals, especially nurses, in the hope that they would send part of their earnings back home and bolster faltering economies.

In terms of pay, working conditions, and status, a higher level of education has proved to be no panacea for immigrant women, however. In the United States professionally trained women holding an H-1B visa or its equivalent have still experienced a gender gap in terms of wages and have been less likely to get high-paying managerial positions than similarly qualified immigrant men (OECD 2006). There have been consistent complaints about these inequities. Women have asserted that employers sponsoring them for a green card have underpaid or overworked them. There have also been allegations that there is little recourse against abusive practices. Since obtaining a green card usually entails a five-year work contract, complaints could jeopardize their immigration status and perhaps result in deportation. Occasionally stories about the exploitation of health-care workers have appeared in the media (*The Washington Post* 2002). Investigations of working conditions for Filipina nurses recruited to work in US hospitals have noted abuses in terms of pay and overtime, and one study concluded that gender and ethnic stereotypes, rather than their skills, were often the standard used to assess the qualifications of immigrant women for pay or promotion (Zulauf 2001). Similar stories about working conditions for professional women in other fields have surfaced as well. Russian and Filipina women recruited to teach in Baltimore City schools, for example, have complained about poor treatment, and their stories have appeared in the local press.

Needless to say, advanced education is not characteristic of all immigrant women. Levels of privilege differentiate them. Unlike women professionals, many have come to fill positions classified as low-wage, flexible labor. These women have tended to have lower levels of education than native-born women. This has been true in the case of undocumented women, although even here the reality is somewhat more complex than it first appears. In the case of the United States, the educational level of many of the undocumented women from Central and South America, although lower than that of native-born women, has been higher than that of the average woman in her home country.

Many of the women immigrants entering Western European countries, the United States, and Canada today have come to fill the need for low-wage, flexible labor. The demand for these workers has been fueled by an aging population, the entrance of large numbers of native-born women into the work force, and the privatization of some government services, especially those involving child and elder care. Globalization has helped meet the demand created by privatization by providing a ready pool of low-wage female workers. Less well educated immigrant women, including the undocumented, have come and taken these jobs, most of which are poorly paid and provide few if any benefits and little chance for upward mobility (Mattingly 2001).

Many of the jobs in the area of domestic work and caregiving are filled through information networks in the immigrant ethnic community that serve as informal labor exchanges. Women write to their friends back home about possible jobs, tell women in the community about jobs that might become available, or pass their own job on to another when they have found something better. In some cases a fee is involved for passing along word about a job or subcontracting work to newcomers (Hondagneu-Sotelo 1994). Working conditions in many of these jobs are poor. In a recent study of hotel workers in the United States published in *The American Journal of Industrial Medicine* (2009), it was reported that the injury rate for women was disproportionately high. Hotel housekeeping staff, the majority of whom were immigrant women, held the most injury-prone jobs, and among the Hispanic women chambermaids the injury rate was the highest of all. Almost 11 percent of the Hispanics as compared to 6 percent for white housekeepers, 6 percent for black housekeepers, and 7 percent for Asians, had experienced on-the-job injuries.

Regardless of whatever health risks may be involved, undocumented women work in the informal economy because it is virtually the only option available to them. A study of the undocumented living in Chicago reported that 91 percent sought work in the informal economy. In Los Angeles, where there have been a relatively high number of undocumented aliens, it is estimated that 15 percent of the entire work force is employed in the informal economy. However, despite the demand for low-wage, flexible labor, there has been a gender gap in unemployment rates. In the Chicago area unemployment rates for Latin American women have been 20 percent higher than they have been for Latin American men. This disparity has been attributed to being undocumented, being female, and being from Latin America (Mehta et al. 2002). There is also an additional plausible explanation: the kind of jobs women hold. Higher unemployment rates are at least in part a function of the jobs available to women in the informal economy. Their jobs are inherently sensitive to economic fluctuations jobs in the informal economy, subject to high turnover rates and likely to dry up during economic downturns. Individuals holding them can be easily fired. After all, during economic hard times domestic help can be easily cut back or eliminated, and an unemployed parent does not need a child minder.

Under normal economic conditions, though, employment in the areas of domestic work and child and elder care has been readily available to women, particularly the undocumented. Unable to afford the high costs of child or elder care, families have sought out the cheapest workers to fill the need. For the most part they have been immigrant women who are paid "under the table." These jobs carry no benefits. Minimum wages are ignored. Social security contributions, paid holidays, sick days, and vacation leave are rarely provided even to documented workers. There is no health insurance or workmen's compensation. Moreover, safe working conditions are not legally enforced. Even in the case of employment at care facilities such as nursing homes or day care centers, workplace inspections are rare if they exist at all. Human Rights Watch and the Institute for Policy Studies Campaign for Migrant Domestic Workers have documented numerous instances where there has routinely been exploitation in terms of an excessive work load and obligatory and uncompensated over time. Various studies have often mentioned other abusive practices, including the practice of some employers to confiscate their workers' passports and visas. In the case of live-in domestics, there have often been complaints about sexual harassment.

Women holding jobs in the fields of domestic service and caregiving have had to confront other problems as well. The unstructured nature of the work and the absence of any group or agency to intervene when problems involving working conditions arise are frequently mentioned. For the most part the women holding domestic and caregiving jobs operate as individual contractors. In some cases they are forced to work several different jobs a week. This means that they must negotiate with several different employers each week in order to earn enough money to make ends meet. Pay and increases in wages and benefits have to be individually negotiated. Even when a woman has been recruited by an agency, there is rarely anyone available to intercede on her behalf when a work agreement is breached. The end result is that women who often have limited language skills and little education must be responsible for enforcing work agreements regarding hours, pay, and conditions of employment and navigate periodic pay increases on their own.

Numerous studies have suggested that the situation of live-in domestics and caregivers is particularly oppressive (Condero-Guzman, Smith, and Grosfoguel 2001; Menjivar 1999; Hondagneu-Sotelo 2001; Anderson 2000). Employers often expect "live-ins" to be available to work around the clock. Days off are frequently changed at the convenience of the employer and at the last minute. To make matters worse, the women—most of whom are in their twenties or thirties—are often discouraged from socializing outside the home or place of employment on the grounds that they ought to be "on-call." In some cases this is motivated by their employer's desire for round-the-clock coverage; in other cases it is motivated by a fear that giving a woman free time will lead to her becoming involved in prostitution or engaging in immoral or criminal activities that can potentially affect the family adversely (Condero-Guzman, Smith, and Grosfoguel 2001). The upshot is that live-in domestics have little opportunity to advance in terms of pay and upward mobility and are also socially isolated.

Undocumented women face especially dismal prospects. Research findings have indicated that they were more than twice as likely to be employed in cleaning, and house and caregiving jobs, with one-fifth employed in private households (Menjivar 1999). Their status as "illegal" aliens has precluded them from objecting to their working conditions, since if they do so they risk being reported to Homeland Security and being subject to deportation. Although individuals may wish to leave an abusive work situation, their status is just not conducive to taking legal action (Hondagneu-Sotelo 2001; Anderson 2000). Seeking help and support from their community is not always a viable solution to their problem. The leadership in some ethnic immigrant communities has not always been sympathetic to their predicament or has pressed the women to take equally oppressive jobs within or controlled by the community, which offer low wages, minimal benefits, and little opportunity for advancement (Anderson 2000). Unlike the Sari Brigades or groups providing support to women experiencing domestic violence, support from other women in the community has not been particularly effective in counteracting abusive labor practices, since economic resources are largely outside women's control. Retreat into employment in a family-owned business has not always provided a solution either. In these settings women have often found themselves to be considered "helping out," and compensation for their work has been minimal or nonexistent (Min 1994).

Descriptions of the working conditions of immigrant domestic workers in Europe indicate comparable conditions there. Studies of domestic workers in Italy, for example, have attributed women's immigration to a similar demand for cheap domestic labor. Although the ideas that women immigrated in search of Western-style feminism or that they were attracted to occupations associated with traditional gender roles have often been proposed, the Italian data do not seem to be supportive of either of these hypotheses (Andrall 2000). Instead the research has attributed immigration to the entrance of Italian women into the job market, attitudes that have endorsed the belief that performance of household tasks is inappropriate for men, and traditionally embedded notions about the importance of child bearing and the central role of the family. These three factors, the research has argued, created a crisis that was resolved largely through the recruitment of foreign women for domestic work. Some research has also suggested that in addition to meeting a demand for cheap household help, foreign-born domestics have also been considered a status symbol in much the same way that they were in the late Victorian period.

In Italy two-thirds of the live-in maids have come from the Philippines. Although fees to recruiting agencies have ranged somewhere between two and three thousand dollars, pay has been low, and the women have been forced to work long hours, often in casual and unstable conditions with little or no job security (Russell and Black 1997). Like studies of foreign domestic caregivers in the United States, descriptions of working conditions in Italy have pointed to abusive practices in terms of hours and opportunities for free time. The findings have also suggested tense relationships with the employer's family, particularly its women members. There have also been complaints about women being harassed by their employers.

Immigration of Caribbean women to Britain has also been attributed to a demand for cheap domestic labor (Phizlackea 2009). Since 1967 a large percentage of the immigrant visas have been issued to private household workers from Barbados, Jamaica, and Trinidad and Tobago, the majority of which have been awarded to women (Dominguez 1975). In Britain, immigrant women have also been employed in the needle trades, where working conditions, wages, and opportunities for advancement are poor (Anthias and Lazaridis 2000).

In Canada a demand for domestics and caregivers resulted in a program that actively encouraged foreign women to come and work there. However, working as a domestic in Canada has posed problems for those women who subsequently wished to qualify for permanent landed status under the country's point system. It has been difficult for women to convert their status to landed immigrant under the point system. Perhaps just as important, though, has been the isolation live-in domestics reported that they have felt. Interviews have frequently revealed the women's problems in coping with the ambiguous situation of living in a family but not being part of it (Bakan and Stasiulis 1997). These feelings of not belonging were accentuated for women of color (Schaeter 1998).

Of course, not all women with less education are employed in the fields of domestic service, caregiving, or the needle trades. Recently there has even been an increase in the number of women day laborers in the United States, although these jobs have been thought of as exclusively male in the post–World War II era. Since these jobs do not provide women with opportunities for upward mobility, they do little to improvement their situation. Again this is especially true in the case of undocumented women. Like domestic service, caregiving, and jobs in the service sector, day labor involves low wages and no chance for advancement and rarely provides the range of benefits available to native-born workers.

All immigrant women tend to be more vulnerable than immigrant men or citizens in terms of employment. However, older women tend to experience higher levels of unemployment and lower wages than younger women. The reasons for this are not as straightforward as some have assumed. Closer inspection has indicated that age discrimination is probably an explanation. Immigrant women tend to be clustered in jobs like child and elder care and domestic work where younger people are preferred. Older women are usually not considered as desirable a choice. The widely accepted notion is that child and elder care and domestic work require some degree of physical stamina and are therefore jobs better suited to younger workers. Young immigrant women are also considered more desirable because they are thought to be more adaptable to new norms and less traditional in their willingness to move beyond limiting notions of appropriate gender roles. In contrast, older women are thought to be less willing to work and more demanding. Ironically, while employers tend to prefer younger women, they are often intolerant of a younger woman's need for an active social life apart from her job. Perhaps this preference by employers for youth and at the same time for workers with a more settled life-style explains the presence of so many young married women immigrants with children back home and reflects a demand for women who are young, have established marital and family attachments in their home country, and are willing to work for low wages.

While being older is an obstacle to immigrant women's employment, youth is not necessarily an asset. Young women are associated in some people's minds with pregnancy, motherhood, and a lower commitment to the workplace. Such attitudes raise questions about their suitability as employees. The possibility that they may have boyfriends is also an issue. These twin concerns would also seem to make married women with children back in their home country most desirable. Since women who fit this model may not always be available, the issue of pregnancy has continued to be a matter of importance to some employers. Despite the prevalence of these worries among employers, childbearing does not appear to have affected women's participation in the labor market (Stier and Tienda 1992). What does seem to have had an effect on their employment is their status as a documented or undocumented worker, the limited range of jobs available to them, and the cost of child care. These factors are more likely to determine women's labor force participation than childbearing.

Although educational level, problems speaking the language, and immigration status account at least in part for the clustering of women in low-wage jobs, they do not fully explain salary inequities. Gender discrimination also appears to be a cause. In 2003 62 percent of the foreign-born women in the United States earned less than $25,000 as compared to 54.4 percent of the native-born women and almost 48 percent (47.8 percent) of foreign-born men. In Los Angeles during this period women were concentrated in janitorial and cleaning services, domestic and personal service, and light manufacturing jobs. Foreign-born men holding janitorial and cleaning jobs earned $13,308 a year, whereas women holding similar jobs earned not quite $7,000 ($6,869)—a difference of close to $6,500 a year. This far exceeded the national wage gap between men and women's earnings. Using the present gender wage gap, immigrant women should have earned on average $10,650, not $6,869. In this same study the overall average earnings for foreign-born women in Los Angeles was $7,630, while for men it was $16,553. In this case, the difference between men and women's salaries amounts to almost $9,000 or 46 percent of what a male immigrant earns. This means that women earned only 46 cents on every dollar earned by their male counterparts. Again using the normal gender gap in salaries in the United States, women should have earned $13,240 annually, not $7630 (Pearce 2006).

These differences cannot be fully accounted for by differences in part-time versus full-time employment. In a study of undocumented workers in Chicago, the findings showed that although overall about 10 percent were paid less than the minimum wage, Latina women faced greater barriers than Latino men in terms of wages and access to better jobs. Although the findings were not broken down along gender lines, they indicated that a disproportionately large number of women were in the subminimum wage earning group (Mehta et al. 2002). In Washington, DC, the situation was pretty much the same, with women earning less overall and more likely to be clustered in domestic service. The belief that the 1996 changes in the immigration law and the opportunity to receive amnesty would correct some of the inequities by making jobs easier to obtain has never materialized. With scant employer regulation, few requests by employers for any documentation of their status until recently, and the impression given by employers that they preferred to hire the undocumented, subminimum wages and the absence of benefits have persisted (Repak 1995). To make the picture even disturbing, the gender gap in wages, benefits, and opportunities for advancement did not narrow following the passage of amnesty (Powers 1998).

A persistent gender wage gap has also characterized the situation of women immigrants in Canada. Women with twenty years of education and at least five years of work have experienced a wage gap ranging from between 2 to 7 percent that over a five-year period doubled to between 5 and 13 percent. Highly educated women have been particularly disadvantaged, with a wage gap ranging between 9 and 17 percent. Although wage differentials have been attributed to language proficiency, over 60 percent of the women have not been eligible for federal language programs, which have been geared more toward men than women (Beach 1993).

It may be argued that government policies with their emphasis on women as dependent family members has dulled the conscience of employers about the need to pay immigrant women wages and benefits more closely resembling those paid to native-born women. Fifty years ago employers felt fully justified in paying native-born women in the United States considerably less than men on the grounds that men were the "breadwinners," while women simply worked for "nonessential extras." By emphasizing the role of immigrant women within the confines of the family, government policies have shaped their employment opportunities, which in turn have channeled them into low-wage and dead-end jobs. Negative perceptions of them in the broader society have also reinforced gender stereotypes now considered politically incorrect to apply to native-born women. The role of guardian of the hearth and preserver of home country traditions assigned to women by immigrant ethnic communities has also buttressed the idea that women's employment is of little consequence. Last, but certainly not least, the absence of affordable child care and social support systems have often obliged women to accept part-time employment, which pays less and rarely provides the same benefits or the chance for advancement that full-time employment does.

Although in several West European nations documented immigrant women are less likely to be unemployed because they are specifically recruited for jobs in the areas of domestic service, health care, and the service sector, data appearing in OECD reports indicate that, as in the case of the United States, it has been harder for immigrant women to find a job than it has been for either immigrant men or native-born women. The occupations of women in the pool of flexible labor resemble those of women in the United States and Canada. In some countries, such as Germany and Denmark, where a flexible work force was needed, women have been employed in low-paying jobs such as electronics manufacturing. In other countries they have been employed in the areas of domestic service, health care, and the service sector. As might have been predicted they have been overrepresented in these fields and have been twice as likely to hold jobs at hotels and restaurants as native-born women. The demand for foreign male labor, on the other hand, has disappeared, and whatever residual need has remained has been met by workers from the recently admitted members of the European Union.

Gendered wage discrepancies exist in Western Europe as they do in the United States. Like in the United States, immigrant women in EU countries are likely to be found in low-paying, dead-end jobs regardless of their qualifications (OECD 2006). For example, a recent study by the Equal Opportunities Commission in Britain reported that Pakistani, Bangladeshi, and African Caribbean women were less likely than their white counterparts to get a job or win a promotion and that the problem could not be attributed to family or cultural resistance to women working (Commission for Racial Equality 2006). Even qualified women have experienced serious discrimination with regard to employment. In general they have held positions for which they were overqualified and have faced larger gaps in both employment and occupational attainment than comparably skilled native-born women and immigrant men. In 2006 this was true in eight of the EU countries (Austria, Denmark, Finland, Germany, Greece, Ireland, Italy, and Spain) and particularly the case for women from non-OECD countries. The picture is even worse when one looks at employment patterns over time. In Austria, the Netherlands, Germany, and Britain the employment situation of immigrant women has deteriorated (OECD 2006). Moreover, despite the educational attainment of the immigrant women the difference in employment levels between them and native-born women has increased. Women with lower levels of educational achievement have higher unemployment rates than native-born women.

At the same time, there are some interesting variations in employment both among European countries and in the United States. In Britain the majority of legal women immigrants have entered under the auspices of family unification to join family members who were already residents or citizens. This has meant that they were required to reside in the country for a specified period before they were eligible to obtain permanent residence status. With residency status dependent on being part of a family and being liable for deportation until they have met the requirements to remain permanently, the ability to work has been largely dependent on family approval. In some ethnic communities this has posed a problem. For example, in some Somali families there has been considerable male resistance to the idea of women working outside the home on the grounds that it undermines the husband's authority.

In Britain 71 percent of all men and 70 percent of all women are employed. For ethnic minorities the figure drops to 68 percent for men and 52 percent for women. There have been several explanations for the lower labor force participation of women immigrants. One has credited it to attitudes in some ethnic immigrant communities about women working. The degree to which the community has emphasized women's role in the home has been seen as important in encouraging or discouraging them from working. Attitudes in the Somali community have provided an illustration of this. Despite the economic pressure on families, there has been considerable resistance to Somali women working, and as a result there are a relatively low percentage of them employed. In other cases lower labor force participation has been attributed to gender and ethnic discrimination. It has been widely claimed that discrimination has contributed to the underrepresentation of Bangladeshi and Pakistani women in the labor force (Commission on Racial Equality 2006). Adaptability to the British job market has been another explanation. Many of the Bangladeshi and Pakistani brides arriving in Britain under the auspices of family unification have come from small rural villages. Such a background has presented significant adjustment problems for them in terms of finding jobs. Patterns of social behavior appropriate to small nonwestern rural communities have made it difficult for them to adjust to the demands of the urban settings in which they live and must work. Then there are the structural constraints imposed on women asylum seekers who, while awaiting a decision on their asylum application, are not legally eligible to work. Some have even gone as far as to assert that government restrictions on working imposed on women asylum seekers in combination with programs emphasizing women's domestic role have promoted feelings of dependency and inadequacy about negotiating the world outside the home.

As in the United States, immigrant women in the European work force have often found themselves in a vulnerable situation that has left them prey to pressures to work in the informal economy for low pay and in poor conditions. Lacking money to support themselves or needing to contribute to their families economically, women often agree to work as subcontractors—sometimes in operations owned by members of their own ethnic immigrant community. Complaints about being subjected to abuse, including sexual exploitation, in these jobs have been commonplace. Policies regarding work permits have been another problem. In Britain the employer, not the employee, must apply for the work permit, and it has been the practice of some unscrupulous employers who wish to avoid the paper work involved to ignore the requirement. While the penalties for employers who fail to obtain work permits for their employees are relatively minor, the consequences can be very serious for an employee. Working without a permit can result in deportation. Even legally admitted workers who have not yet obtained permanent residency status, as well as asylum seekers whose applications have not yet been approved, can be subject to deportation if an employer has failed to obtain their permit. As a consequence of these policies regarding a work permit, not only undocumented workers but also legally admitted workers are highly vulnerable and at risk for exploitation and abusive labor practices.

As in the United States, the situation of skilled and professional immigrants differs from that of individuals falling into the category of low-wage, flexible labor. Immigrants with professional or highly skilled backgrounds usually have longer-term contracts and higher wages than those recruited for the lower-skilled, flexible labor force. Even in the case of skilled professionals there are exceptions, however. Foreign nurses with diplomas, for example, have been paid less by the National Health Service than their British counterparts and offered less desirable shifts and assignments. Those employed in low-wage, flexible labor force occupations usually have short-term, insecure labor contracts and low wages, and there are virtually no opportunities for career advancement. Unlike visas for professionals and those in the highly skilled labor force, work visas for those in the low-wage, flexible labor force are ordinarily not renewed. Furthermore their jobs are frequently subcontracted and imposed overtime is typical. However, since immigrant women have few alternatives, they often feel that they have to agree to whatever conditions are imposed on them.

In Britain as in the United States education has affected immigrant employment. Immigrants compose 10 percent of the total working-age population of the country and almost half of them are members of ethnic minority communities, principally Pakistani, Bangladeshi and African Caribbean, and Indian. The educational level of women immigrants from countries such as Australia,

New Zealand, and Canada roughly resembles that of women immigrants in the United States. Ethnic minority immigrant women, the preponderance of whom are married to men from their own ethnic community, are more likely to have the British equivalent of a high school (O Level) education than either their husbands or native-born British women and were almost as likely to have the same educational background as white women immigrants. However, they were less likely than their male counterparts to have attained the next highest level of education (A Levels) and less likely to have it than either native-born women or white women immigrants.

Although husbands of women immigrants have been less likely to be employed than those of native-born women, there are differences among immigrant groups. Husbands of ethnic minority women immigrants have been less likely than husbands of either white European and Commonwealth immigrants or native-born women. However, the husbands of white women immigrants have been less likely to be employed than the husbands of native-born white women. Seventy-two percent of the husbands of white women immigrants contrasted with 84 percent of the husbands of native-born women were employed. With regard to women immigrants' employment, ethnic minority women have experienced the lowest rate of employment. In comparison to 64 percent of the white women immigrants and 71 percent of women who were native born, 47 percent of ethnic minority women were employed. However, there was considerable discrepancy in unemployment among ethnic minority women. Bangladeshi and Pakistani women had the lowest rate of labor force participation (36.8 percent and 36.9 percent respectively), while Afro Caribbean women had relatively high levels of employment.

Work hours also differed among immigrant women. Ethnic minority women who worked put in longer hours (33 hours a week) than white and native-born women. The average work week for white women immigrants was 31 hours, and it was 29 hours for native-born women. Although ethnic minority women who worked had higher weekly earnings than the other two groups of women, this reflected the fact that they worked longer hours, not that they held better paying positions. Indeed ethnic minority women immigrants were concentrated in jobs at the bottom of wage scale, whereas white immigrant women were at a significant advantage with regard to their wages and earnings. White women immigrants were also likely to move into middle-class status. In short, although all women immigrants have experienced discrimination in terms of wages and promotion, there are significant differences among them. Not all women suffer to the same degree. The importance of ethnic and racial privilege should never be overlooked.

There are some interesting differences in the employment patterns of British immigrant women and those in the United States that should also be noted. In Britain, male immigrants, particularly those of Pakistani and Bangladeshi origin, were more likely to be employed in the fields of hotel service, catering, distribution, transport, and communications, while white immigrant men were more likely to be in production industries. In contrast to white immigrant women, who were more likely to be employed in catering, hotel service, and similar service-sector positions and health-related occupations, ethnic minority women were more likely to work in public-sector jobs. More than half the black Caribbean, black African, and Bangladeshi women worked in public-sector jobs. However, they tended to be concentrated in lower-grade and more poorly paid positions (Commission for Racal Equality 2006).

As was the case in the United States, educational level and higher fertility rates alone did not explain the employment situation of women immigrants satisfactorily. As the British Commission for Racial Equality pointed out, race is partially a reason white women immigrants fare better than ethnic minority women. After controlling for family size, educational level, and English fluency, the commission concluded that ethnic discrimination offered the best explanation for the discrepancy in the employment of ethnic minority and white women immigrants. Certainly it would seem to account for the lower participation rate of Bangladeshi and Pakistani women in the labor market, as well as the variations in terms of pay, upward mobility, and occupational clustering.

Over the past 25 years there has been a sharp upsurge in the number of immigrants throughout Western Europe, and France, like Britain, has been affected. In addition to North Africans who came to live in France during the colonial and immediate postcolonial period, asylum seekers principally from North and West Africa arrived in France throughout the decade of the 1980s. The March 1999 census reported there were over three million foreigners residing in France. This constituted not quite 6 percent (5.6 percent) of the total population. Despite a growth in the number of immigrants elsewhere in Europe throughout the 1990s, France experienced a decline, however. This was due in part to immigration policies that allowed citizenship to be acquired by birth in France and by amnesty programs that regularized the undocumented.

Amnesty adopted in the United States in 1996 did not resolve many of the issues surrounding immigration. The same was also true in France. The French regularization reforms establishing amnesty, which were adopted in 1993, increased the waiting period for family unification from one to two years and denied residency permits to foreign spouses who were in the country illegally prior to marrying. For many, illegal status appeared preferable to the extended waiting periods set up by the reforms. Thus the reforms proved to be no panacea for controlling the flow of immigrants into the country. In fact, the number of undocumented immigrants grew, and in an effort to circumvent the new residency requirements women who wished to be with family members in France entered illegally or opted to remain without papers. To escape deportation these women have assumed a low profile and have tended to avoid participation in any activities outside the ethnic suburban housing estates (*banlieues*) ringing the central cities. For the undocumented, living in these segregated ethnic neighborhoods has retarded integration into French life and limited interactions with those outside their community. As a consequence the chances for the women's integration into French culture and life have significantly decreased, and options to work outside the home have been at the very best limited.

As elsewhere, immigration has become an increasingly contentious issue in French politics. Anti-immigrant sentiment, aroused at least in part by the war with Algeria over independence and the growth in the size of the North African population in the post–World War II period and coupled with the increasing the cultural isolation of ethnic immigrants, the phenomenon of asylum seekers, and periodic weakness in the job market has intensified and become part of the platforms of centrist as well as right-wing parties. Calls for the deportation of all foreigners including those born in France have become commonplace and are a rallying cry of Jean-Marie Le Pen's radical, ultrarightist party, the National Front. They have been echoed by more centrist parties in the last elections. Negative feelings have been further exacerbated by the fact that by 2006 the percentage of foreign born had almost doubled from what it was a decade earlier, with the number of undocumented estimated to be somewhere between two hundred and four hundred thousand. Family unification is credited for the 64 percent growth in the immigrant population. A demand calling for the deportation of all foreigners whether they are born in France or not has been advocated as the most effective solution to the current immigrant situation.

A law passed in 2006 attempted to "regain control over immigration" by adopting a policy of selective admission of foreigners. It allows highly skilled professionals to enter under a program similar to the United States' H-1B program and foreign students receiving degrees to remain and work in France. The situation is quite different for those who do not meet these credentials, however. For them family unification and illegal entry have been the only available options, and the lack of documentation poses the same grim employment situation as it does for women elsewhere. Almost 80 percent of poor workers are women, and the situation is particularly severe for women who are not French citizens (De Silva 2004). As in the United States, undocumented women are largely dependent on informal networks within the ethnic community for employment.

The situation of the undocumented is particularly problematic in France given the recent law regulating legal entrance. It lays down strict conditions for family unification. Only after a minimum of 18 months of residency can an immigrant apply for permission to be joined by family members—a condition that is much more strict than the requirements in either the United States or Britain. The individual must also demonstrate the ability to support family members without any reliance on state social or medical assistance, a requirement that is consistent with policies found in many other countries, including the United States. Given the average length of time needed to process a family unification request, the projected waiting time for family members to enter has become considerably longer than it was previously. Restrictive conditions are also laid down for those entering under the auspices of family unification. Spouses of French citizens must wait three years before applying for their own residency permit and must be married to a French citizen for four years before they are eligible to submit an application for French citizenship.

In addition to these rules the recent law requires all immigrants, including family members, to sign a "welcome and integration" contract. In order to receive

French residency and acquire citizenship, immigrants must take French language and culture courses. All family members must also agree to respect the basic principles of family life in France. This dictates that all entrants recognize France as a secular state, accept the principles of equality between men and women, and be monogamous. Individuals unwilling accept these conditions can be denied entrance. The consequences of these reforms cannot be overstated. Spouses who wish permanent residency and citizenship become entirely dependent on the family member sponsoring their entrance and on maintaining their marital relationship for a period of seven years. At the same time they must accept state principles about family relationships, which, for many, are at odds with accepted family structures. This quintessential paradox of being dependent on family membership while renouncing a traditional family structure leaves many women in a totally untenable position.

Recently North African, sub-Saharan and Muslim immigration has outstripped immigration from other non-EU countries, and in many respects the provisions of the new law, including the principle of a secular state and the formal rejection of the patriarchal structure of the family affect them more seriously than they do other immigrants. In particular, the legislation has posed a fundamental dilemma for Muslim women. The social isolation of undocumented women before the passage of the new law, the new requirements of an extended waiting period before being eligible to receive a residency permit and French citizenship, and the required endorsement of the French concept of gender relationships within the family have left women in an especially vulnerable position. If one's family and social circle endorse traditional values and the tenets of family law laid down in the Qur'an or interpretations of them, it is virtually impossible for a dependent person to comply with government requirements. Returning to the home country, lying, or being undocumented are the only options. Then there is the issue of monogamy, which poses a real conundrum for some families. Polygamy may be relatively rare in the home country for economic reasons. For some families adopting the practice of polygamy demonstrates the economic success that has resulted from immigrating. It shows that the family is now wealthy, and multiple wives enhance the family's social status in much the same way that foreign maids enhance that of Italian and Greek families. Thus the French requirement to renounce polygamy may have a significant impact on the family's standing back home (Wihtol de Wenden, Leveay, and Mohsen-Finan 2001).

Research has suggested that in France, as in the United States, immigrant women's employment has given them some leverage in defining themselves. However, Muslim women have confronted a number of disadvantages in the labor market. These difficulties have been compounded by the fact that there are significant differences among women coming from different countries. For example, Algerian women have been the best integrated into French culture and society, while Turkish women have been the least well integrated. Indeed, level of integration would appear to be related to whether the women came from a more urban or rural society (Wihtol de Wenden, Leveay, and Mohsen-Finan 2001).

Despite differences among Muslim women in France, like women elsewhere, they all have experienced job discrimination and are found primarily in low-wage jobs. It has been estimated that among immigrant women with foreign names the unemployment rate has been roughly three times greater than it has been for nonminority women. Wearing the head scarf has added to their employment problems. A number of studies have found that women who wore the head scarf (*hijab*) were less likely to be hired, and if they were, they were paid less than women who did not. This has constituted a real dilemma for women. Studies have found that wearing the head scarf reassures a woman's family and gives her greater family support for participating in the work force. The tenuous status of women's residency under family unification, especially since the enactment of recent reforms, has meant that family approval for women to work has become more critical than ever. For some women, there is an additional issue. Wearing the head scarf is seen as a moral obligation, an important reflection of religious beliefs, and a demonstration of respect for a promise made to their families "back home" (Salton 2010).

The occupations available to women who are employed are similar to those of immigrant women in the United States: domestic service, hotels, and catering. Many find employment in the informal economy where wages are low and working conditions poor. In general, not only have women been clustered in low-paying jobs, but they have also tended to be more overqualified for the jobs than nonminority women. As in Britain, the situation does not appear to improve over time for second-generation ethnic minority women; while employment opportunities have tended to improve over time, wage convergence has not. Nonminority French women and immigrant men continue to earn more than first- and second-generation women immigrants. For example, although employment rates for second-generation women from North Africa have become about the same as for nonminority French women, the majority of the ethnic minority women have remained more poorly paid. In short, while more second-generation ethnic minority immigrant women work, pay and advancement remain stagnant. As in Britain, they work longer hours for lower wages than nonminority French women and continue to be overrepresented in low-paying jobs regardless of their skill level or language proficiency.

As in the United States, French authorities define immigrant women within the context of family. That means that official policies reflect the assumption of a male breadwinner and dependent women whose wages are supplemental to the family income. There are no direct governmental prohibitions on women's employment, but by the same token government policies do not facilitate it. Language and culture courses are given—indeed they are now compulsory for the newly arrived and for those wishing to become citizens—but programs that teach women marketable skills are virtually nonexistent. Moreover the language and culture courses that are available are located in government buildings or schools where women are officially forbidden to wear the head scarf. If anything, the new policies leave women in a situation of economic and social dependency on their families and ethnic community, while at the same time expecting them to renounce the traditional core values of the family and community on which they are dependent. The contradictory notions entrenched in official policies leave women in an extremely vulnerable position. Defining them as dependent and extending the waiting period for a residency permit and citizenship has subjected them to greater family scrutiny and control and placed in jeopardy the goals of acculturation that the new legislation has sought to accomplish. If anything, the new policies leave women in a situation of economic and social dependency on their families and ethnic communities.

The pattern of women's immigration to Germany was somewhat different from that of women coming to the United States, Britain, and France. In the 1960s and 1970s the Federal Republic of Germany actively recruited foreign women to work in the plastics, chemical, metal working, electronics, paper production, food processing, fishery, and canning industries rather than in the domestic or caregiving areas as was the case elsewhere. As a result, about a quarter of all the women immigrants worked in these industries. By 1973 a third of the official foreign labor force were women. A substantial number of these women were Turkish. Some of the women followed their husbands who came to work in heavy industry and construction, but many came first and were subsequently joined by their husband. This pattern of immigrant female labor persisted into the decade of the 1970s. Indeed, there was a 63 percent employment rate for immigrant women during this period, and they had a higher labor force participation rate than native-born German women (Munscher 1984). In 1974 changes in immigration policy altered the employment pattern significantly. Work permits were no longer granted automatically. Women entering under the new policy for family unification, many of whom were Turkish, were either denied a work permit or confronted with a waiting period. These changes had a chilling effect on their employment and moved many into the informal economy, where the majority now work.

Several factors contributed to the movement of immigrant women into the informal economy. First, there were the policies regarding work permits. Starting in the 1970s, women entering under the auspices of family unification were no longer assured of getting a work permit. During periods when the domestic unemployment level rose or feelings of xenophobia prevailed, regional and local jurisdiction cut back on the size of the foreign labor pool and denied work permits to women admitted under the auspices of family unification. Without the necessary authorization, employment in the informal economy became the only viable option available to them. Then there was the policy that made German language courses available only to those who were legally employed. Unless a woman worked, she was ineligible to take such courses. Needless to say without language fluency women faced serious obstacles to obtaining employment in the formal economy. Moreover, since language courses also facilitated cultural integration, they were helpful in allowing individuals to master the cultural cues necessary for obtaining better-paying jobs with upward mobility. Lacking these skills, immigrant women found themselves at a disadvantage in the job market. Then there was the issue of child care for women with children. Limited space in kindergartens has meant that immigrant children are less likely to get accepted. This has clearly hampered immigrant women wishing to find full-time employment. Even employment in electronics and manufacturing where Turkish women had been easily able to find jobs was affected. In addition, pay in "female occupations" has been notoriously low, and trade unions have never mounted a serious campaign against the practice. As a result women who need to increase their income have been forced to work overtime or increase piece work. The informal economy has provided just such an opportunity.

Both before the changes in German immigration policy and afterward women have been clustered in the lower end of the occupation ladder in much the same way as women have been in other countries. They have been almost twice as likely to be employed in low-level, unskilled, or semiskilled jobs as native-born women. They have also been more likely to be employed in fields where there is a high level of job fluctuation and where the work is piecemeal. Their waning employment in manufacturing in the mid-1980s, coupled with their failure to be absorbed into the newly emerging service sector, resulted in soaring unemployment. As a result many have turned to jobs in the informal economy. Those women who have continued to be employed in the industrial sector have held jobs in the least desirable and most hazardous industries, such as chemical and electronic production. Although recently some women have found employment in the service sector, they have been largely relegated to manual labor, especially janitorial and cleaning services in hospitals, hotels, restaurants, and schools. This has meant that, like women immigrants elsewhere, many work under insecure and precarious conditions and for substandard wages (Munscher 1984).

The position of ethnic minority immigrant women was further eroded at the end of the 1980s by the wave of immigration of ethnic Germans from the old Soviet Empire. The arrival of foreign ethnic Germans in combination with unification with East Germany (the former German Democratic Republic) and a downswing in the economy have resulted in increasing unemployment among foreign workers in general and in particular those of Turkish origin. In 2007 the unemployment rate for foreign-born women was slightly over 15 percent. This was the second-worst employment rate, with only the 17 percent unemployment rate for immigrant women in France being higher (Liebig 2007). Even ethnic German women immigrants have not fared particularly well during the current economic downswing. Although initially the rate of employment among them approximated that of native-born Germans, their unemployment rate has recently risen significantly. Nevertheless it is the nonethnic German women immigrants who have experienced the highest level of unemployment. In sharp contrast with earlier patterns, Turkish women's employment rate has dropped to about 4 percent.

In 2005, in an effort to address the variety of immigration problems facing the country, Germany enacted a new law creating the equivalent of the US "green card." Women admitted under family unification now have the same right to work as the principal immigrant. While this has removed some of the barriers to women's employment, it has not improved the financial situation of those who fall into the category of low-wage, flexible labor. Moreover, employment opportunities for nonethnic German women immigrants have not improved over time. This has certainly been true for second-generation nonethnic German women. A recent study has credited the wage and employment gap for Turkish women to lower levels of educational achievement and higher fertility rates. This seems a somewhat dubious conclusion given the previously high employment levels for ethnic minority immigrant women, especially Turkish women who arrived in the 1960s and 1970s. A more reasonable explanation would seem to be that ethnic minority women in Germany, as elsewhere, are simply considered a part of a surplus low-wage flexible work force that can be called on when the labor market needs their services. In any event government policy does little to address the inequities and possible discrimination.

Women's Employment and Attitudes in Ethnic Communities

Government policies are not the only forces shaping the employment of immigrant women. Ethnic communities have also played a role. Their influence has been exerted in a number of ways. First, as mentioned earlier, the ethnic community often acts as a job exchange or informal employment agency. Nonprofessional and low-skilled immigrants need help and advice about what jobs are available. Until they have established suitable employment references, they require someone to vouch for them as reliable, willing workers. For undocumented workers recommendations and job tips are especially crucial in finding employment. Although this is true for both men and women, it is especially important for women, who are particularly likely to search for jobs in the informal economy first. For them, tips about available jobs and character references are a prerequisite for getting hired. Members of their ethnic community give advice to newcomers about where jobs can be found, put in a good word for them with a potential employer, and help them fit into a new work environment. In some cases the members of the community who provide such information and assistance are paid directly or indirectly by having the newcomer work as subcontractor for them. In short, the ethnic community acting as an employment agency can be vital to the immigrant's employment and can influence the kind of jobs that are available.

The ethnic community also shapes the kind of jobs that women take by setting standards for appropriate gender rules. Prominent members of the ethnic community—usually the male leadership—set and enforce norms for acceptable personal behavior and patterns of family life within the community. Using a variety of techniques, including shunning, they lay down the ground rules for the roles that men and women ought to play within the context of family life, including the distribution of household chores. When an ethnic community emphasizes women's responsibility for all the household tasks and child care, serious limitations are imposed on her employment opportunities. The time-consuming tasks of caring for children, cooking, cleaning, shopping, and so on make it difficult if not impossible to accept any work other than part-time jobs. The situation for women is exacerbated by the fact that official governmental policies have defined them as dependent and tied their admission to remaining part of the family. This puts women in the tenuous position of accepting the norms of their ethnic community or facing possible deportation if they are no longer accepted as part of the family.

Ethnic communities often facilitate the creation and development of small businesses as a means by which their members may achieve upward mobility. Often small "ma and pa" stores provide the income for families to improve their financial situation and acquire the resources to educate their children. This is certainly true in Britain, for example, where ethnic businesses in the Indian, Pakistani, and Bangladeshi neighborhoods have proved to be an important route to acquiring middle-class status. However, small ethnic businesses have tended to compound rather than help women's employment problems. The scarcity of funding available to women wishing to start businesses combined with their limited experience in running them places them at a disadvantage in obtaining the necessary capital to cover start-up costs. Thus they often find themselves working as employees rather than co-owners or owners in these ethnic enterprises. As employees in small family businesses they are likely to work long hours for little or no pay—a condition roughly resembling indentured servitude. Few alternative options are available to women, however, since their employment opportunities are limited and their connection to family and the ethnic community is usually essential.

While there are certain similarities in the role ethnic communities play in the employment situation of women, there are also important variations among them in terms of providing information about jobs and of assistance afforded in gaining better pay and working conditions and promoting advancement. The United States offers several telling illustrations of this. For example, in a study of Latina workers in Los Angeles, Hondagneu-Sotelo (1994) found that ethnic networks were critical in finding employment as domestics. In some cases men in the community who worked as gardeners or repairmen passed word along to the women about job openings. In other cases women learned of openings at social events such as parties, or in the waiting rooms of medical clinics where they met other women from their community who told them about available jobs. Women in the community who already had domestic work often hired recent arrivals as helpers. This strategy included subcontracting enabled women who were already working to take on more cleaning jobs and thus increase their own income. At the same time it has meant low wages for newly arrived women working as helpers. Clearly in cases such as those described by Hondagneu-Sotelo, the ethnic community has played a pivotal role in helping newer women immigrants find employment and in improving the position of those who were already settled.

At the same time there are practices in ethnic communities that are less benign and more exploitative than those reported in the Hondagneu-Sotelo study. For example, although Foner's study of immigrant women's employment in New York pointed to the pivotal role of the ethnic community in locating employment opportunities, it also reported that it could foster exploitation (1999). Chinese,

Dominican, and Columbian women working in businesses owned by coethnics have been found to earn low wages, enjoy minimal benefits, and have few opportunities to improve their situation. This is not unique to Caribbean and South American women. Studies, for example, have shown that Korean women working in family-owned businesses are also poorly paid, if they are paid at all, and receive few if any benefits (Kang 2003; Min 1999). The women's treatment has been defended on the grounds that as family members, relatives, or friends of the family pay would be inappropriate; yet without any independent source of income these women are highly vulnerable to exploitation and abuse. The same has been true for Asian women living in Britain who work in small family-owned shops and businesses.

There are exceptions, of course, to the pattern of women working for others. Some ethnic businesses are owned and operated by women. Probably nail salons are the best known of these female enterprises. Asian women, mostly Korean on the East Coast of the United States and Vietnamese on the West Coast, own and operate these businesses, although some Eastern European women immigrants have also opened nail salons and day spas. In 2000 there were over ten thousand licensed Korean women manicurists working in nail salons in the New York metropolitan area, and if one takes into account those who are unlicensed, the number would be much larger than that. The equipment and start-up costs for these salons are relatively low, which make them feasible to be owned and operated by women. Since service is the key factor in developing a steady cliental, which is essential to the success of the business, a manicurist's limited language skills is not a necessary drawback in either attaching clients or finding workers. Studies of these nail salons indicate that in contrast to the pattern of women's employment in some male owned-ethnic businesses, there are fewer issues over nonpayment of wages. Either manicurists are hired and paid by the salon owner who depends on them to maintain an ongoing client base or they work as independent contractors. As independent contractors, the women pay the owner a fee for their station in the salon. Although the owner sets the fees for a manicure and the manicurists pay the owner for the right to work there as independent contractors, manicurists' salaries depend on the number of clients they service and the tips they receive. Under these arrangements the women have some assurances that they will receive income. They have, in other words, some control over how much money they make. There is also an opportunity for social interaction among the women working in these salons in that they provide an opportunity for ongoing, regular networking among fellow ethnic women. This interaction has allowed the women to support each other in the new environment in which they find themselves, and the nature of the services the women provide allow for the acquisition of at least some rudimentary language proficiency (Kang 2003).

The role of employment in facilitating networking among immigrant women appears to be dependent on shared ethnicity, however. In the Korean and Vietnamese nail salons the manicurists are almost exclusively members of the same ethnic group. This is usually the case in day spas owned and operated by Eastern European women as well. In these shops there are not only networking opportunities for women, but the women owners also often serve as mentors for those who have recently arrived in the country. This is not always the case when women belong to different ethnic communities, though. Case studies of women who come from different Latin American and Caribbean countries but are employed in the same place have reported tensions among them. For example, in a study of attempts to unionize maids from different countries of Central America working in a San Francisco hotel little networking took place. Instead there was considerable rivalry among the women. Competition over evaluations and promotions was intense with each of the groups seeking to benefit itself at the expense of the other groups, and claims of favoritism when the supervisor belonged to a different ethnic community were common (Hondagneu-Sotelo 1994).

The significance of the ethnic community's role in women's employment is by no means unique to the United States. Several studies of ethnic minority women in Germany have reported similar findings. For example, in the Turkish communities in Germany, women are expected to assume full responsibility for child care and the household. The lack of available child care for Turks has meant that the women with young children are forced to accept part-time or piecemeal work for low wages and no benefits. Household chores and child care often mean that even after children have reached school age piece work is the only viable option available since full-time jobs involve putting in long hours and doing shift work. Even when they work long hours, the women remain responsible for all domestic chores. They must prepare the meals for their children the night before or prior to leaving in the morning depending on the hours they work or the shifts they are assigned. If their lunch break is long enough they use the time to shop for groceries or do house-related errands. Although among second-generation or later Turkish families there is some effort to have children—boys as well as girls—do household chores, the bulk of the work continues to fall on women, and men rarely participate on an equal basis. In interviews reported in one study, one woman responded that "her husband never helps," another that "Turkish men don't help their wives, perhaps one percent," and still another that her husband claimed he was too tired to do chores at home after working all day. A similar study found that Turkish women in Denmark face the same situation (Mirdal 1984). Like Turkish women in Germany, they work in hard, dirty, and dangerous jobs, rarely complaining for fear of being fired. Their work load, however, is no excuse for justifying a more equitable distribution of household tasks with their husbands. The ethnic community in which they live, like the Turkish ethnic communities in Germany, exerts a strong control over the behavior of their members, leaving the women in the position of having to hold two full-time jobs: that of wife and worker (Munschen 1984).

In Britain, too, women often experience serious stress from meeting both the norms of their ethnic community and working. This is especially the case for recently arrived immigrant communities like the Somalis. The difficulties Somali men experience in finding work has resulted in their feeling that they are disposable. Unable to fill the role of breadwinner, they see their manhood jeopardized. The employment of Somali women while contributing to a feeling of greater independence on their part has intensified male insecurities and feelings of inadequacy. When the women suggest that men should assume a larger role in child care and housework, the men become deeply resentful. Their resistance to any redistribution of household responsibilities is supported and enforced by their ethnic community.

In France, ethnic communities, particularly from North Africa, play an important role in the area of women's employment. As is the case in Germany, Denmark, and Britain, they reinforce gender roles regarding family responsibilities: household tasks and child care are the exclusive responsibility of women. Given the time commitments involved in these activities, women's job opportunities tend to be limited to poorer-paying part-time work. An additional issue in France, however, is women's dress. For the Muslim community as well as for the French, the use of the head scarf is pivotal. As was discussed earlier, women experience significant discrimination both in finding employment and in improving their position in the labor market when they wear it. At the same time, there is considerable pressure on the part of the ethnic community and within the family for women to cover their heads. Indeed, family permission and community approval to leave the house and go to work is often dependent on women's agreeing to cover their heads. Thus the ethnic communities affect women's employment not only by underscoring clearly defined gender roles but also by calling for the use of the head scarf.

These examples of the role of ethnic communities in the United States and Western Europe indicate the importance of these communities to women's employment. Although both more indirect and mixed than government policies, they influence the kind of work women may do, especially in the case of women who fall into the category of low-wage, flexible labor. Furthermore, their impact does not appear to fully dissipate over time. Indeed, when a community perceives itself as under threat from the broader society, as is sometimes the case for Muslim immigrant communities in Europe and particularly in France, its insistence on traditional values, including gender roles, may actually increase. Its control is exercised by setting and enforcing norms that place restrictions on the kinds of employment that women may take and its insistence that household and child-care duties fall exclusively within the domain of women. At the same time the ethnic community has also played a positive role in the lives of women. It often serves as an employment service, allowing women to find work. It has provided the opportunity to network with other women and has allowed them to overcome the isolation they often feel. It has also facilitated their adjustment to the world of work through informal mentoring by women who are more familiar with life in the receiving country.

Women's Voice and Employment

Women's visions of themselves, their aspirations, and their reactions to their new life, like government policies and ethnic community norms and expectations, also shape employment opportunities. These reflect two contradictory assessments: one is negative, and the other, optimistic. The first focuses on the high levels of stress stemming from attempts to balance the demands of work and the norms of their ethnic community concerning gender roles. In one study after another the women have complained about the problems they face in combining employment with the pressures of fulfilling the traditional gender roles of managing a household and child-care responsibilities. This is as true for immigrant women in the United States as it is for those in Western Europe. These grievances are not without basis. For example, one study found that between household duties and employment outside the home, Korean women immigrants worked on average 76 hours a week (Min 1994). Some Dominican women in New York reported working on average 18 hours a day when time spent performing household tasks and jobs outside the home were combined. To achieve a balance between employment and family and child-care responsibilities, many women have been forced to accept part-time work at low wages with few if any benefits and with little chance for advancement. Nor have length of hours a week worked and salary been their only concern. Poor working conditions have also been cited. With virtually no government inspections of the workplace and the extreme vulnerability of many of the workers, especially the undocumented, the women have often been forced to work in unhealthy and unsanitary conditions. Even women with professional backgrounds have spoken about stress. They have been upset about the fact that their opportunities for advancement are more limited than they expected and that they are employed in positions below their level of skill and expertise.

Although the relationship of mothers and daughters will be discussed in detail in the following chapter, it should be pointed out that in a number of studies of immigrant families where the mother worked, there was a tendency by the mother to excuse daughters from doing household chores. Many mothers were adamant about daughters studying and performing well at school. This is quite significant, since mothers are usually held responsible by their ethnic community for ensuring that the next generation of women absorb and respect traditional ethnic values. It is also noteworthy since the mothers are clearly overstretched by their employment and household duties.

The second theme is more positive. Studies of immigrant women in both the United States and Western Europe have found that wage earning is transformative to their lives in two respects. The women claim that contributing to the family income has given them more authority in the house. They have repeatedly said that when both husband and wife add to the family income the dynamic in the relationship between husband and wife changes. Women feel that they have a right to co–decision making and that they should rule equally. As Foner puts it in her study of Dominican women in New York, the women believe that they should be "co-heads" in the family.

Wage earning has also fostered a higher level of self-esteem among the women, enhancing their confidence in their ability to cope successfully with a new environment. Many of the women in various studies have spoken of their satisfaction in doing their job well and take pride in meeting the demands of their workplace. This sentiment has been expressed not only by women in professional fields such as nursing but also by women working in the low-wage, flexible labor market such as the garment trade and domestic service. Women working as maids, nannies, or caregivers have talked with pride about their contribution to the children or people they cared for. They have seen themselves as able to manage complex situations with skill and a level of professionalism. Their increased self-esteem and self-confidence have spilled over into their activities in the broader society as well and given them increasing ease in their interaction with schools their children attend, social service agencies, and government institutions.

Immigrant women have also mentioned another advantage of working: learning about alternative ways to structure family life. Women both in professional positions and in low-wage, flexible jobs come in contact with women from other ethnic backgrounds as well as with those who are native born. These interactions have provided immigrant women with alternative models for their own lives and those of their family members. They have seen a different way of doing things, which has broadened their perceptions and aspirations. In a number of interviews women mentioned the fact that among other groups the distribution of home and child-care duties was more equitably shared, and they aspired to achieving this in their own family.

Immigrant women in Western Europe have expressed similar sentiments. Studies of Turkish women working in Germany and Denmark have reported that the women have seen working and earning money as very important. Many of them specifically mentioned that working conferred on them a sense of independence made them feel good about themselves. Despite feelings of stress and exhaustion, they were proud of themselves and their ability to cope in such a difficult environment. Whereas they had previously thought themselves incapable, they now saw themselves as competent and able to manage.

The benefits of being employed and earning an income seem, however, to be a mixed blessing in some ways. While employment was a source of both stress and satisfaction in their lives, it also created marital tensions. The government's initial definition of women as dependent family members has often been interpreted by the husband as supporting the authority of the male family head, and that, along with the gender role norms of the ethnic community, has been taken as a justification for abusing women who do not conform to these expectations. Many women mentioned the fact that their husbands and male family members were often upset by the fact that they earned money and in some cases were the principal breadwinners of the family. Social workers have often attributed the level of physical abuse in immigrant families to the change in power relations within the family that have accompanied income differences. Frustrated and distressed by their inability to fill the role of provider for the family, the men have resorted to physical violence.

Conclusion

Although to some extent the importance of government policies dissipate as time passes and residency issues are no longer critical, they nonetheless have had a critical impact on immigrant women's employment. By initially defining women as dependent and channeling them into gender-stereotypic and mostly low-paying jobs these policies have limited their initial opportunities. As a result women's earnings have started out lower than those of similarly situated men, and their chances for advancement have been delayed. Immigrant women never fully recover from this initial disadvantage, and the possibility for convergence of their wages with both male immigrants and native-born women is reduced. Based on studies of second-generation ethnic minority women in Britain, France, and Germany, earnings continue to remain somewhat lower, although the negative effects on employment of gender typing does begin to improve somewhat.

The effect of ethnic communities on employment has been both more indirect and mixed. Control has been exercised by setting and enforcing norms that have placed restrictions on the kinds of employment that women may take and by making them the custodian and enforcer of traditional values within the family. The full responsibility of household and child care along with employment has made part time the only viable option for many women. This has meant low wages, long hours, and high levels of stress. Furthermore, women's economic contribution to the family often leads to marital tensions and in some cases physical abuse. Government policies tying women's admission to the country and subsequent residency to their continuing family membership and an ethnic community's backing of traditional gender roles has left women with few, if any, choices for dealing with abuse. At the same time the ethnic community often plays a positive role in the lives of women. Their employment opportunities and adjustment to the world of work in the receiving country has been tied to their community, and especially to the women in it.

The sentiments expressed by women are also mixed. Although many worked prior to immigration, their subsequent jobs and working conditions have been different. Their common employment in menial jobs or ones for which they are overqualified coupled with full responsibility for child care and maintaining the house have led women to complain about high levels of stress. Long hours of work and low wages have been the rule. Aspirations for a better future for themselves and their families, especially for their daughters, appear elusive. The results have often been poor health and a sense of hopelessness. Balanced against these negative feelings, however, was the confidence and increased sense of self-esteem that came from working. Women's economic contribution to the family has allowed them the opportunity to renegotiate the work load in the family and given them at least limited independence. Beyond that the nature of women's employment even in the informal economy has exposed them to different life-styles. Unlike male immigrants who were more likely to interact with fellow ethnics in the labor market, women's employers often belonged to different ethnic groups. Their jobs as maids or nannies, or caregivers afforded women exposure to alternative patterns of behavior. This exposure has provided women with some hope for optimism. Perhaps more important, working has built in the women a sense of self-confidence and pride. The conflicting sentiments uttered by immigrant women give a special poignancy to their voice, which is lacking in government policies and in the leadership in ethnic communities, which attempt to define them and their role in the labor market.

SECTION 3

Immigrant Women Speaking for Themselves

I love people, I love my family, my children . . . but inside myself is a place where I live all alone and that's where you renew your springs that never dry up.
—Pearl Buck

CHAPTER 7

Listening to Immigrant Women (Re)Creating Their Own Social Identity

As we have seen, government laws and policies assign a social and economic identity to women immigrants. Ethnic immigrant communities also often do something similar when they allocate particular domestic and social roles and responsibilities to them. What role, if any, do immigrant women play in this process? Are they simply objects defined by others? Is a new social identity imposed on them? What say do they have in (re)creating their social identity? If they do have a role, is it tangential or do they possess some real degree of agency?

Some research suggests that immigrant women have little input in (re)creating a social identity. It portrays them as victims trapped in oppressive familial and governmental patriarchal structures from which they have little chance of escape. Depicted as vulnerable to abuse and overworked, they are viewed as trapped in a web of family, community, and government rules and regulations in which they can barely survive and which offers little opportunity for improvement. In short, their situation is pretty much hopeless and their oppression unrelenting.

Sometimes these descriptions reflect negative attitudes held by mainstream society in the receiving state that associate immigrant women with outmoded values, backwardness, and dependence on public funds. Sometimes, however, they stem from concern and sympathy: immigrant women are seen as victims who require outside intervention if they are to thrive or even survive. In either case immigrant women are defined as "other" and require extensive support in their new environment. Considered helpless, they are seen either as deserving assistance or as a burden and permanent fiscal liability. Such assessments exclude the idea of agency: immigrant women are not seen as possessing the wherewithal to (re)create a social identity on their own.

Other research posits an altogether different interpretation, and, in contrast to the view that immigrant women are victims, it sees them as having agency.

The claim is that immigration provides a transformative experience that allows women to grow and develop a new, positive sense of self. The contention is that a dramatic change in environment and new responsibilities provide immigrant women with an opportunity to realize their potential and exert agency. Employment is thought to be a vital part of a process that furnishes the necessary space to alter the dynamics of family relationships, gain self-confidence, and develop feelings of self-worth. In short women have the option of (re)creating their own social identity.

Some scholarship stressing agency has equated contemporary women immigrants with an idealized notion of previous generations of immigrants who are pictured as conquering the challenges of living and succeeding in a new environment. While acknowledging the struggles and setbacks experienced by earlier generations, this research has concluded that ultimately contemporary women are able to assert themselves as strong, liberated individuals capable of flourishing in new surroundings. Regardless, though, of whether or not today's immigrant women are associated with previous generations, this interpretation has seen women as able of overcoming the obstacles that confront them. Far from seeing them as victims, it argues that they possess the agency to (re)create their own social identity.

These appraisals of immigrant women as either victims or individuals who possess agency are clearly contradictory. Is either an accurate description? What is the reality of women's experiences? Do they see themselves as victims or as possessing agency? What do they say about (re)creating their social identity? Before attempting to tackle these questions it is necessary to step back a moment and take note of some fundamental limitations in the existing research. In the first place, much of our knowledge of women's experiences is based either on small-scale case studies of women from specific countries or geographical regions or on the autobiographical or semiautobiographical/fictional writings of individual women. Moreover, this work deals with immigration occurring at a specific period of time. Each of these studies offers a snapshot of a small group immigrating at a particular moment in time. Individual studies look at specific national groups arriving at a specific period of time. For example, American research looks at Irish or Italian immigrants arriving in the late nineteenth or early twentieth centuries and Mexican women arriving in the twenty-first century. The problem is that their experiences are different. European women arriving in the United States a hundred or more years ago did not confront the same environment as Latina women coming in the twenty-first century. Moreover, the experiences of each of these groups have differed from those of women coming from the Indian subcontinent to Great Britain or North African women coming to France in the second half of the twentieth century. All these women were or are immigrants, but conditions affecting their settlement and integration were not the same. The liberating effects of immigration for Irish women coming to England or the United States at the end of the nineteenth or early twentieth centuries have not existed for Turkish women arriving in Germany or rural Bangladeshi women arriving in Britain during the second half of the twentieth century. These differences need to be recognized before any explicit or implicit conclusions can be drawn about the impact of immigration on women's lives and their efforts to (re)create a social identity. In short, generalizing about the efforts of women from disparate geographic backgrounds who immigrated at very different points of time to (re)create a social identity is, to say the least, risky.

A second and equally important problem involves the acceptance of the idea of *the* immigrant woman. Despite a common assumption that all immigrant women are basically alike, the truth is that there is no single prototype. As we have seen in previous chapters, women immigrating on their own do not face the same problems as women immigrating as part of a family unit, and neither group confronts the same situation as women immigrating as refugees and asylum seekers. Furthermore, although little research deals with the immigration of racially and ethnically privileged women, data seem to suggest that race, ethnicity, social class, level of education, geographical origin, and religion privilege some and disadvantage others.

Unfortunately comparing the impact of privilege is complicated by the fact that little research has focused on women immigrants who might be considered privileged in terms of race, religion, ethnicity, and education in the receiving country. With few exceptions research has not looked at women immigrants, refugees, and asylum seekers coming from privileged backgrounds. There is one study of economically privileged Chilean women immigrating to Britain following the military coup in their home country in the early 1970s, and some work has looked at women in allied health fields and at women doctors, scientists, and engineers from the former Soviet Union who resettled in Israel. Beyond that, little scholarly attention has been paid to professional women immigrants and their efforts to (re)create a social identity. Indeed, some scholars have explicitly stated that they have little interest in looking at highly educated, professional women immigrants (Phizlackea 2000). The absence of such research is unfortunate for two reasons. Globalization has contributed to an increase in the immigration of highly educated women to fill professional and executive positions in banking, IT, and international business. Since their numbers are likely to increase, it is important to understand how they have adapted and changed. A second reason has to do with our understanding of the importance of privilege. Without that understanding it is difficult to comprehend the range of immigrant experiences and to identify the diversity of reactions and adaptations to it. Work that looks at Irish, Italian, Northern European, and Eastern European women immigrating to the United States at the end of the nineteenth and beginning of the twentieth century is insufficient, since these women were not particularly privileged at the time of their arrival. Few had any advanced formal education, and in some cases their religion was a liability. Thus, although we have data about how various groups of less privileged women have coped with the pressures of immigration, we know little about how privileged professional women have maneuvered conflicting pressures and demands and the extent to which their reactions and responses are typical.

The marginal position of less privileged women, particularly those who are likely to be found in the informal labor market, does suggest, however, the importance of privilege in areas such as level of education, ethnicity, race, geographical origin, and religion. Employment opportunities for these women have been clearly restricted. Evidence shows that they have certainly been clustered in the informal labor market in comparison to native women or immigrant men. When they have sought to improve their economic situation, they have had less access to loans to start small businesses, and their opportunity to pursue entrepreneurial activities except at the lowest and least financially rewarding level has been virtually nonexistent. Limited employment opportunities have also hindered their access to the broader society. In short, privilege along with government policies and the expectations of ethnic communities have affected the immigrant experience.

Despite important differences among women immigrants there are nevertheless some similarities. All contemporary immigrant women have confronted problems adjusting to a new environment, and they have all faced some level of anti-immigrant sentiment. Furthermore, all have been affected by government policies and regulations. As we have seen, laws and policies have defined and reinforced the roles that women should fill and shaped both their opportunities and societal attitudes toward them. The priority given to family unification, the pattern of granting temporary work visas for employment in stereotypic female occupations, and a reticence in granting asylum or refugee status to women with children who are unaccompanied by a male family member have influenced women's employment opportunities, reinforced their association with the concept of the patriarchal family, and contributed to a mind-set that has equated immigrant women with welfare dependency. To escape stereotypes and be accepted in mainstream society women have had to demonstrate that they were different. They have had to prove that they were "modern" in their outlook and beliefs if they wished to achieve upward economic mobility.

Despite these liabilities, adjustment has been less traumatic for some women than for others. Some have been able to "fit in" more easily. Women who were physically, culturally, or religiously distinctive have tended to face more serious obstacles in being employed or even incorporated into their new country than those who were physically, culturally, or religiously similar. White Canadian women immigrating to the United States, for example, have had a different experience than West African women. Similarly Irish or Australian women have had fewer problems adjusting in Britain than South Asian or African women. Thus, while immigration has been unsettling and even painful for all women, there have been significant variations.

Another problem in assessing women's role in (re)creating their social identity has been the virtual absence of longitudinal studies that have looked at the integration of immigrant women over time. At present we do not have any standard for examining how women have adjusted to a new environment over time or the costs it has imposed on them. We do not know what role privilege has played for second- or third-generation women. Equally important, we cannot evaluate the long term impact of intersectionality on immigrant women and the (re)creation of social identity outside the fact that the less privileged have tended to remain so.

Bearing in mind these deficiencies, this chapter examines women's own reactions and responses to the various factors that are attempting to define them. Using the framework of intersectionality and stressing the critical role that immigration status—family unification, temporary work visa, refugee, asylum seeker, and so on—has played, this chapter considers several areas women have pinpointed as important to the development of their social identity. In the first section, motives for immigration and the repercussions for adjustment are discussed. Also included are employment and its physical and psychological effects on social identity within the family, the community, and the broader society. The second section deals with gender roles and relationships within the family, particularly with husbands and children. Women have continually mentioned their relationships with their daughters. Many place a high priority on their daughters' social and educational development. Interactions within the family and their role in family decision making, as well as attempts to expand the options for daughters, provide important insights into women's efforts to adjust and (re)create a social identity. The third section focuses on feelings about the new environment, attitudes about "homeland," and nostalgia. By examining the significance of these factors for women's efforts to maneuver the conflicting pressures of immigration, government regulations, and their ethnic community, it is hoped that the voices of immigrant women can be added to the current discourse.

Motives for Migrating

Although the literature has long suggested a variety of reasons for immigrating, the most widely mentioned have been civil unrest and economic improvement. In some instances these two have overlapped. In the case of civil unrest, for example, it may be difficult or impossible to earn a living in an area experiencing civil disturbances or fighting. Although civil unrest and financial necessity have been as valid for women as they are for men, different motives have usually been attributed to them: a husband or his family's decision to immigrate or a desire for personal growth. In the first case the assumption has been that the husband decides and his wife dutifully complies. Given the fact that the earlier pattern of male immigration has now largely disappeared and that increasingly women immigrating outside the context of family have increased, this explanation is no longer valid. Furthermore, since there has been little empirical evidence to support the hypothesis that women played little or no role in the decision to immigrate, one wonders if this was ever a compelling explanation. Indeed, one is tempted to think that this description simply reflected gendered assumptions about patriarchal family decision making.

More recently the motives assigned to women have stressed personal growth. These have included a desire to improve professional credentials, a need to escape from a difficult family or romantic relationship, a wish to find a husband, a quest for adventure, or a yearning for more personal freedom. The evidence has seemed to suggest a more practical reason. Like earlier generations of male immigrants, escape from the chaos of war, financial need, and a desire to improve their financial situation have been crucial to a woman's decision to immigrate. Personal growth might be a long-term objective, but it has been secondary to the traditional economic reasons that encouraged immigrants in the past.

Recent work, including extensive personal interviews, biographies, and autobiographies, which has concentrated on women immigrating outside the context of family unification, has clearly underscored the point that the desire to earn money and send it to their families back home has been the primary motivation. Personal growth was secondary to the economic motive. This appears to be the case for all women regardless of social class, race, or ethnicity. Although, as mentioned earlier, there has been virtually no research dealing with highly educated, professional women immigrants employed in areas such as financial services and IT, it is reasonable to assume that salary and a promotion have been important incentives for them. Among other women the evidence has been clear and consistent. In the area of allied health the majority have reported that their decision was based on a demand for their services, the amount of money they could make abroad compared with what they could earn at home, and the ability to acquire work experience that would enhance their credentials if they returned home. This was certainly the case for many Filipina nurses, who frequently referred to the economic pressures to go abroad to work and the need to send money back home to their families. Similar reasons have been cited by women seeking employment in other fields. Mexican women, for example, have mentioned the need to support a family back home and their aspirations for upward economic mobility as critical factors in their decision to come to the United States. For the Filipina women immigration meant a better job and more pay. For Mexican women it has meant moving from a job as a domestic to becoming a nurse's aide (Monsen 1999; Chell 1997). In both cases the expected result was higher wages.

While earning money has been consistently mentioned as the most important reason for immigrating, employment and wages have been dependent on a variety of factors ranging from length of stay, landed immigrant status as opposed to a temporary work permit, and admission under a family unification program. It must be acknowledged, of course, that among all women level of education and skills, such as language proficiency, affected compensation. The ability to speak the language has certainly been an important component of employability. Race, ethnicity, and religion have also often been mitigating factors. Intersectionality, too, has shaped compensation. Regardless of qualifications, privileged women like white Canadians and Australian women immigrating to the United States or the United Kingdom have been more likely to receive a higher level of compensation than for Asian or African women. However, for both privileged and less privileged women, economic considerations have been primary.

In some case studies and interviews, unmarried women mentioned the possibility of enhancing their chances of finding a suitable husband, but earning money was always mentioned first. A study of Moroccan women mentioned in an earlier chapter is a good example of this (Salih 2003). Married women with families at home, on the other hand, have emphasized sending money home so that their children would be able to complete their schooling and improve their life chances. In some instances financial considerations have even been a factor in arranged marriages. It has been claimed that in cases of women immigrating as brides under the auspices of family unification, the marriage was based on the need to discharge its financial obligations to another family. In Germany and Great Britain it has been reported that family debts are paid off through arranged marriages with young women from the home country (Glennie 2010). In all these instances economics has been the strongest underlying reason for immigrating in the case of both married and unmarried women.

If the quest for economic improvement has been an important component, what has been its impact for the (re)creation of social identity? For some, financial expectations have been met. Money has been saved and sent home. As a result the woman's standing in her home community has been boosted and feelings of self-esteem have been strengthened. However, the picture has not been a universally rosy one. Monetary expectations have not always been met. For some women there has been a good deal of disillusionment over the amount of money they could actually save. Earnings have often proved to be much smaller than expected, and the cost of living much higher. Furthermore, earnings have not always compensated for the costs of immigrating. For example, women recruited to come and work in the fields of allied health or as domestics or nannies have often had to pay large fees to recruiters. Five years ago, for example, Filipina nurses coming to the United States claimed that they had to pay upward of five thousand dollars to employment agencies. That sum has increased dramatically over the past five years. For those entering illegally the costs have been even higher. Women smuggled into the United States from Mexico and Central America have had to pay anywhere from five to ten thousand dollars (King and Black 1997). Covering these costs has made saving difficult and decreased the possibility of setting aside money to send home.

The cost of immigrating, along with living expenses, has meant that many women have been unable to amass sufficient savings to return home permanently or to meet the monetary expectations of their families. As a consequence, the possibility of returning home as a success story has been undermined. The implications have been serious on both a personal and structural level. As pointed out in earlier chapters, significant financial pressures such as agency fees have meant that, unable to accumulate enough savings, some women have attempted to compensate by passing on their jobs to younger family members when their work visa has expired; and a new form of indenture has been the legacy (Chell 1997). For other women the answer has been to avoid returning home by dropping back into the informal economy by becoming "illegal." For those women with family back home, a decision to remain illegally not only has been monetarily and personally costly but also has provided an additional incentive for their family members to immigrate illegally.

Earnings have been only one aspect of unmet economic expectations. The desire to upgrade credentials has also been disappointing. There have been numerous complaints about job discrimination, even by women who were privileged in terms of education and training. Women in the health fields have frequently charged that they were relegated to low-level positions beneath what their training and experience warranted. This accusation was mentioned by women in other fields as well. For example, South Asian women in Canada believed that even when they were more qualified than Canadian women, there was a real resistance to acknowledging their accreditation and work credentials (George and Ramkissoon 1998). Similar claims have been made by other women health professionals. Some have maintained that although they were well-qualified health professionals in their own country, they found themselves employed as glorified nannies and caregivers. Few believed that their talents and abilities were adequately recognized and used. Similarly in a study of immigrant women professionals in the European Union the feeling was that competencies were ideologically constructed and reflected cultural values rather than particular skills (Zulauf 2001). Even those who were employed in their profession insisted that they were passed over in terms of promotion and salary increases. With very few exceptions expectations of advanced training went unfulfilled.

Disillusionment with immigration has been unsettling on many levels. Regardless of whether or not a decision to immigrate is based on financial considerations, it is, to say the least, a major undertaking. It requires courage, a willingness to be flexible and open to new things, a level of organization, an ability to plan, and a sense of adventure. Women who immigrate have been special. They have been different from women who remained behind. Research has shown that they were likely to be better educated than the average woman in their home country and were likely to have worked outside the home before immigrating (Andrall 2000). Furthermore, women who have immigrated on their own have demonstrated a sense of empowerment (Griffith 2002). In short, all women immigrating outside the context of family have had to display a relatively high level of competency and self-confidence. Perceptions of job discrimination and poor working conditions coupled with the difficulties of establishing adequate savings to support their families back home have constituted threats to these feelings. Furthermore, if their visas are temporary work permits, there is no possibility of improvement over time. If personal growth is the primary objective, the job situation they have encountered certainly has done little to promote a sense of personal growth and self-confidence. Employment has rarely fulfilled their economic expectations. Reinforcement of feelings of competency and self-esteem has had to come from other sources.

For women immigrating outside the context of family there are other pressures in addition to financial ones. Unlike those in earlier generations, many women are married and have children whom they have left in the care of others back home. Ironically their employment often entails domestic caregiving. The women have often mentioned the paradox of caring for the children or families of others, but not their own. Guilt about leaving their families, family problems that have emerged in their absences, their children's resentment at their mothers' absence, and strains in their marital relations resulting from separation have been consistent themes in their writing and in interviews (Doty 2003). These family concerns compounded by financial worries have intensified the cultural conflicts endemic to immigration and influenced the (re)creation of their social identity.

For women immigrating under the auspices of family unification or as refugees and asylum seekers the situation has been somewhat different. Employment has often proved to be a positive experience. Married women living in a family setting have consistently recounted with pride their economic contribution to the family. Employment has meant more authority in family decision making and greater independence. As several studies of Turkish women in Germany mentioned in earlier chapters reported, the women felt that their earnings allowed them to have a greater say in family decision making and that this was particularly true when they pooled their money with that of their husband (Munschen 1984). For women with college degrees, however, the tendency has been for them to have their own bank account. This, they claimed, allowed them to enjoy more power in family decision making (Bhopal 1997). Caribbean and East Asian women who immigrated to the United States have also asserted that employment increased their role in family decision making. Interestingly enough, though, while women who immigrated before their husbands were more likely to be employed, women who immigrated with their husbands were likely to enjoy higher wages but were also less likely to participate in the labor force. Perhaps this difference can be explained by the comments made by a number of women that it was necessary to preserve and acknowledge the husband's primacy within the family. Often this entailed showing deference to him as the wage earner. As mentioned in an earlier chapter, this has been especially a problem in Somali immigrant families where husbands have tended to resent any erosion of their role as breadwinner, and it has also been mentioned by East Asian women (Berns and McGown 1999; Griffiths 2002).

Although there are a number of barriers that hinder the employment of refugee women, including government regulations, the absence of adequate training programs, and the emotional and physical costs involved in escaping persecution, they too have found employment to be empowering. Like women who immigrated under family unification, they have expressed pride in their accomplishments. At the same time, some have faced conditions that have physically precluded them from working. For example, as many as a third of the East Asian women refugees were physically disabled as a result of the Indo-Chinese wars and thus were unable to work.

Employment in a new environment, like immigration itself, requires adaptation. An important component of the (re)creation of a social identity is the development of day-to-day mechanisms for dealing with the momentous changes in the routines of daily life. Some have described it as a lived experience that encompasses practical and domestic activities (George and Ramkissoon 1998). Social networks and support systems have been a critical component of this lived experience and have had a significant effect on the (re)creation of a social identity.

Women immigrants, like immigrants in general, have talked about feelings of loneliness. However, women have consistently mentioned other subjects as well. One has been climate. In many cases the climate is much colder than the women were used to, and in some cases traditional clothing has offered them little protection against the cold, rain, or snow. Language has also posed a problem. An inability to communicate effectively with government agencies, schools, and a whole host of community services has created serious isolation for women and contributed to a feeling among them that they don't exist (De Silva 2004). This has especially been the case for women entering as part of a family or as refugees and asylum seekers, for the opportunity for them to get out and interact with others outside the context of work has often been restricted to a small group in their ethnic community. Women's groups and social networks have served an important function by expanding their circle by providing women with information about jobs, negotiating conditions of employment, and standards for adequate compensation. Feedback on working conditions has been extremely useful, for often the standards are different from those that existed in the home country. Moreover businesses run by members of their own ethnic community have often been exploitative. Women's groups and social networks have sometimes been in a position to offer solutions for dealing with such employers or to refer the woman to another available job.

Employment advice is only one function performed by women's social networks. There are numerous areas where women need advice—for example, recommendations of doctors who will be sensitive to cultural traditions. Social networks have offered guidance on a variety of issues of concern ranging from how to deal with children growing up in a transnational setting to where to buy food, clothes, and other necessary items. Intimate partner violence, which has not been uncommon in some immigrant families, is another area where advice and support have been provided. Legal remedies to domestic abuse have often not been useful since the end result could be deportation. In such instances women's groups have acted as intermediaries and in some instances have provided economic as well as social support to abused, abandoned, or widowed women (Kibria 1990). In short, women's social networks have played an important and positive role in the (re)creation of viable functional social identity.

At the same time informal social networks have not always been beneficial to the process of adjusting to a new environment. While they have often provided a sheltering environment in an otherwise alien setting, social networks have often reinforced an ethnic group's expectations about "appropriate" gender behavior and the concept of the "imagined community." Clustering policies imposed by government settlement programs have increased the importance of ethnic neighborhoods and strengthened social networks within them. In turn, this has compounded problems of adjustment. As discussed in earlier chapters, the expectations of some ethnic communities have tended to limit the range of acceptable employment opportunities for women and compromised their upward economic mobility. Extensive interaction within an ethnic social network has often buttressed community norms and decreased the opportunities to become more familiar with the new society and perhaps even the possibility of becoming proficient in speaking and understanding its language.

Adjusting to Change

Adjustment is a complex social process. Immigration opens up a cultural space where negotiation of difference creates a tension particular to borderline existence (Bhabha and Shutter 1994). As a number of studies and interviews have pointed out, the immigrant woman is not a tabula rasa. Immigrant women bring with them "cultural and ideological baggage" (Hondagneu-Sotelo 2001). (Re)creating a social identity that integrates the old and the new is at the core of adjusting to immigration. Adjusting entails a number of quite difference components. At the most basic level it involves adapting to a new set of living conditions: climate, including cold, rain, snow, and the like; a different type of accommodation, often an urban as opposed to a village or more rural setting; different types of food; and changes in clothing necessitated by the weather. These practical domestic activities require changes in routines and behavior. Old ways of cooking, dressing, and behaving are no longer as appropriate as they once were. Changes in life-style must be made. Such adjustments, which are perhaps best described in terms of "lived experiences," are required.

Personal interactions in both the home and the world outside also necessitate changes in behavior. Transportation, shopping, dealing with government agencies, and registering and supervising school-age children all demand modifications of previous expectations, routines, and behavior. Among other things they require some level of proficiency in speaking the language and in negotiating transactions in a new currency. Aside from these more impersonal changes and adaptations, adjustments in personal interaction are required. As discussed in earlier chapters, the dynamics of family decision making are changed when women contribute to the family income. With a husband no longer the sole support of the family, or with a family economically dependent on social services, patriarchal authority is weakened, and family relationships altered. In dealing with these changes women have often developed hybrid patterns of interacting to ease tensions and avoid conflicts. For example, Turkish women in Germany have reported that they do not bring home friends from work because their husbands would not like it. They felt that if they did so their husbands would interpret it as a put-down in terms of their authority and that it would create strains in their marriages (White 1999). A similar strategy was reported in a study of a Vietnamese community on the West Coast in the United States where women accepted the husband's role as patriarch because it preserved parental authority and promised some measure of economic security (Kibria 1999).

Social services agencies also impact family relationships, particularly with daughters. Different values regarding gender roles imbedded in social service programs for girls and young women, especially those involving birth control, abortion counseling, and advice on arranged marriages, have posed serious threats to parental value systems. In some instances these differences have been reconciled, but in others conflicts have persisted. These challenges to a family's traditional expectations about behavior have often resulted in deterioration in communication both within the family and between the family and the social service agency. Several studies of North African immigrant families in France, for example, have referred to the problems posed within the family over the head scarf. Job discrimination has prompted many employed daughters to give up wearing the head scarf to the dismay of their families. In some cases the family has modified its objections, but in many other cases the controversy has created serious riffs in the fabric of family life and triggered not only a breakdown in communication between generations but also estrangement. Mothers immigrating within the context of family, either under family unification programs or as refugees accompanied by children, have spoken extensively and with deep emotion in interviews about the anguish of trying to merge conflicting values and enforce "appropriate" behavior for their children. The evidence suggests that relationships within the family have continued to be haunted by these clashes. For the girls the result has often been an alienation from both their families and their ethnic community, which has left them isolated and adrift. For parents and children, and particularly for mothers and daughters, the psychic costs have been very high (Scott and Scott 1998).

Problems of adjusting have been further complicated by attitudes toward and treatment of immigrants in the receiving country. For example a women's group in France, Ni Putes, Ni Sournises, expressed concern that complaints about violence against women in working-class immigrant neighborhoods was used to reinforce damaging stereotypes of foreigners (De Silva 2004). Negative opinions about foreigners and discrimination have in turn undermined immigrants' feelings of self-worth and generated feelings of being threatened and under attack. One response has been to curtail further efforts to integrate, to withdraw into one's ethnic community and to become defensive of it. Often a special space—a "third space"—that provides both sustenance and resistance to the unwelcoming environment started has been created (Chatterjee 1989). This third space might be a community center, a church, or even a public park. The only requirement is that it provides a private, supportive location.

There are both pluses and minuses to a "third space." Although it has met important needs in an environment that questions the immigrant's sense of self-worth, it has also tended to reinforce ethnic differences. In the workplace this has sometimes meant that immigrant women belonging to different ethnic communities have been pitted against each other. For example, in a study of hotel chambermaids in California, feelings of discrimination surfaced and charges of favoritism emerged when the ethnicity of a woman worker was different from that of her supervisor (Hondagneu-Sotelo 2001). For lower-status women, kinship has been an important source of support and reinforcement of feelings of self-worth, although it, too, has tended to slow adjustment to their new environment. At the same time some have argued that, although difference has seemed to make coalitions impossible, alliances are nonetheless built. Even under difficult circumstances immigrant women of different ethnicities who have appeared powerless have mobilized resources and secured for themselves areas of control (Abraham 1995).

It would be incorrect to assume that any one pressure or situation shapes adjustment and the (re)creation of social identity. The creation of a third space has certainly offered a refuge that can and has strengthened an ethnic identity, sometimes at the expense adjustment to a new society. At the same time, the challenges of making new friends, interacting with new people in the workplace, attending classes, and living in a new environment have all challenged and encouraged women to make those adjustments (Brown 1988). Multiple forces and pressures, then, have led to women to live on multiple levels, which have been perhaps most accurately described as multilocal and binational (Guarnizo 1998). As a consequence women have developed a hybrid personality and a marginal identity, which is quite different from being marginalized.

This marginal identity has positioned women on the cusp of two worlds. In some instances it has meant that they have become uniquely qualified to be a mediator between modernity and tradition and enabled them to act as intermediaries between the family and social agencies. This role of mediator or intermediary perhaps explains why some researchers have concluded that women have tended to be more affected by community-level factors than men, who have been more affected by household and family concerns (Akhtar 1999). Women's orientation toward the community perhaps also accounts for the finding that women have tended to gravitate to the new society and identify with its political life, while immigrant men have tended to be more concerned with the old world and its politics (Jones-Correa 1998). Perhaps this explains why men have been more likely than women to express a desire to return home.

A marginal identity carries with it some important benefits. It conveys an ability to bridge the gap between two groups—two worlds. The gift of being able to "speak the language" of more than one group allows the marginal person to be an effective communicator. At the same time a social personhood that encompasses boundaries and territorialized difference leaves an individual with deep anxieties about who one really is and where home is (Salih 2003). These anxieties have taken a toll on women's health. Research has indicated that high blood pressure is common among immigrant women. The same is also true for depression (Tang, Oatley, and Toner 2007; Pumariega, Rothe, and Pumariega 2005; Hiott et al. 2006). For younger women with children back home the pressures of (re)creating a functional social identity have been especially daunting since they must constantly alternate not only between multilocal and binational identities but also between being an absent mother to their own children back home and a worker in another country. Indeed, given the scrambled codes involved it may not be possible for them to (re)create any meaningful social identity (Doty 2003). Some research on the adjustment of immigrant women has emphasized the need to have "grit" (Scott and Scott 1998). While grit might help, it alone will not resolve all the problems of conflicting identities.

For immigrant children, too, the situation has been problematic. As discussed in an earlier chapter, children have found it particularly hard to live in two worlds. Although some research has found that children adjusted to immigration more readily than older people in terms of language skills, dress, and the like, there tends to be high levels of antisocial behavior and higher suicide rates among them (Hovey and King 2008). Adjustment and the development of a coherent social identity have been shaped on the one hand by parents' efforts to transmit traditional cultural values and, on the other hand, by the mainstream culture and values they are exposed to in school and by the media. The difficulties in reconciling these values are exacerbated by government policies that restrict travel to their country of ethnic origin (Menjivar 2002).

Where Is Home?

Some scholars have referred to immigrant adjustment as a process consisting of several stages. The first stage is characterized by a sense of wonderment. It is a period when things are explored. Everything is new—different. Contrasts are made between what one has known and been familiar with and what one now sees, but at some point the newness is no longer exciting or exhilarating. Instead it becomes baffling, strange. Old rules—norms—are no longer useful, and new rules unclear. Culture shock often accompanies this recognition of differences, and the realization that things are not the same may give way to feelings of depression. For some, depression can be temporary, but for others it can be severe and lead to a mental breakdown. Culture shock, depression, and the stress of being unclear about expectations produce a yearning for certainty and with it a mythologizing of one's former life where things were familiar. This yearning has typically been associated with nostalgia, which is usually defined as a sensation of sadness resulting from a desire to go back to the past—to what one knew or remembers.

All immigrants experience some degree of nostalgia, at least temporarily. The wish to be free from the discomfort of conflicting cultural values and norms takes the form of a desire to go back to an idealized homeland constructed from collective memories, shared meanings, and interpretations. However, almost invariably, this imagined homeland includes notions about an appropriate social order for home, family, and community (Bellelli and Amatulli 2000). For women nostalgia for the homeland has been a double-edged sword. It provides a kind of psychological relief from conflict brought on by discontinuity in roles and expectations. However, although old routines have been disrupted and fears about what immigration means for their lives and for their relationships have been awakened, the imagined homeland is not all that reassuring. As discussed in earlier chapters, in many ethnic immigrant communities memories of this imagined homeland entail rigid gender roles and restrictive norms for women's behavior. Thus, while it affords a sense of continuity in face of present fears and conflicting cultural pressures, it also emphasizes roles and duties that are at odds with those women must now fulfill. As a consequence, instead of reducing anxieties, the imagined homeland can generate additional ones or intensify existing ones.

Some research has suggested that women are more likely than men to experience nostalgia. The basis for this conclusion has been that, since men go off to work, they are distracted and therefore less likely to feel depressed. Women, the other hand, were described as more likely to be at home and therefore more liable to experience nostalgia and bouts of depression. As we have seen, however, even in the heyday of male immigration a majority of the women worked. Furthermore interviews and published research by social scientists and mental health professionals have reported that depression is common among contemporary women immigrants regardless of whether they enter under programs of family unification, as employed women with temporary work visas, or as refugees or asylum seekers. While these findings are based on relatively small-scale studies of specific ethnic groups, especially those coming from the Third World, they all point to significant levels of depression and sadness among immigrant women.

Do these feelings of depression and sadness mean that immigrant women suffer from nostalgia? Research published by mental health professionals working with immigrant women would seem to indicate that status as first or second generation has also been a factor. For first-generation immigrant women nostalgia has not been exactly the same as that associated with yearning for an imagined homeland (Elhag 2010). What women have seemed to be yearning for was the comfort and support of a tight-knit family kinship group. They were worried about their job. They were worried about their children. They were worried that they might be going crazy. Moreover, these concerns had a tendency to become more pressing over time. In their home country, mental illness usually carried a serious stigma, so seeking counseling or psychiatric help was out of the question. For many their religion precluded suicide. What the women needed was to share their hopes and their fears with a group of people like themselves whom they could trust. What they were nostalgic for was the strong social network of family they remembered or imagined that they once had (Black, Markides, Miller. 1998). This need has perhaps been best demonstrated by the lower rates of depression, high blood pressure, and illness among women who have recreated these social networks.

For daughters the picture has been somewhat different. They have been torn between two cultures (Tarr 2000). They have not yet established a secure bicultural identity and consequently face more chronic stressors (Pumariega, Rothe, and Pumariega 2005). Pressures at home to maintain the "old traditions" and pressures at school and in mainstream society to assimilate have often produced profound confusion about who they are and where home is. Research has indicated that the greater the discrepancy is between the culture of the country of their parents' origin and the host country, the more difficult the adjustment has been for children. For example, the daughters of Bosnian refugees in the United States adapted much more easily than the daughters of Somali refugees, whose culture was more alien (Rothe et al. 2002).

Much of the recent literature written by immigrant daughters reflects a nostalgia that, unlike that of their mothers, tends to reflect the more traditional yearning associated with an imagined homeland. Like the nostalgia of their mothers, it seeks to escape the conflicts emanating from a clash of the old and new worlds. Rather than seeking solace in a network of kindred women with whom one can be oneself, though, it focuses on a utopian vision of a land and people with which the daughter identifies. In this imagined homeland, which is usually depicted as rural, the marginalized female ethnic can find a voice (Talahite 2000). It provides an escape from conflict and tension in much the same way as nostalgia associated with the imagined community by constructing a heritage that comes to terms with a hybrid personality.

Conclusion

Just as there has been no single prototype of *the* woman immigrant, there is no single voice that speaks for immigrant women. Rather there has been a variety of voices that have echoed their diversity. A woman's status as a worker, part of a family group, a refugee or asylum seeker, or documented or undocumented has affected her attempts to (re)create a social identity. So, too, have educational achievement, language proficiency, and ethnicity. Their acceptance in the receiving country government policies and pressures in some ethnic communities all play a part in the (re)creation of social identities. At the same time, within the context of family, women have articulated a particular leitmotif revolving around the questions "Who am I?" and "Where is my home?" Strong social networks have been critical in coming to grips with these concerns and have provided women with an oasis from conflicting value systems and cultural pressures. In some instances these networks have encouraged women in their attempts to (re)create their social identity and facilitated their adjustment; in others they have not. Women who have managed successfully to reconcile contradictory values and pressures have done so by constructing a hybrid personality. This has permitted them to operate in two worlds and has positioned them to exert a leadership that we associate with the concept of marginality.

Selected Bibliography

Abay v. Ashcroft, et al. 368. F 3d 634.
Abraham, M. 1995. *Ethnicity, Gender, and Marital Violence: South Asian Women's Hants.* Aldershot: Johns Hopkins University Press.
———. 1995. "Ethnicity, Gender and Marital Violence: South Asian Women's Organizations in the United States." *Gender and Society* 9: 450–68.
———. 2000. *Speaking the Unspeakable.* New Brunswick, NJ: Rutgers University Press.
Agger, I. 1994. "Abused Refugee Women: Trauma and Testimony." *Refugee* 14: 19–22.
Akhtar, S. 1999. *Immigration and Identity: Turmoil, Treatment and Transformation.* New York: Jason Aronson.
Albor, R. 2006. "Abused Immigrant Women to Get Help and Hope." *Daily News. Suburban*, 2.
Anderson, B. 1993. *Britain's Secret Slaves: An Investigation into the Plight of Overseas Domestic Workers in the United Kingdom.* London: Anti-Slavery International.
———.2000. *Doing the Dirty Work?: The Global Politics of Domestic Labour.* New York: Zed Books.
Anderson, M. 1993 "A License to Abuse: the Impact of Conditional Status on Female Immigrants." *The Yale Law Journal* 102: 1401–30.
Andrall, J. 2000. *Gender, Migration and Domestic Service.* Burlington, VT: Aldershot.
Andrall, J. 2000. *Gender, Migration and Domestic Service.* Aldershot: Ashgate.
Anthias, F. 1992. *Ethnicity, Class, Gender, and Migration: Greek Cypriots in Britain.* Hants: Aldershot.
Anthias, F., and G. Lazaridis. 2000. *Gender and Migration in Southern Europe.* London: Berg Publishers.
Aronowitz, M. 1984. "The Social and Emotional Adjustment of Immigrant Children: A Review of the Literature." *International Migration Review* 18: 237–57.
Bagley, C. 1972. "Deviant Behaviour in English and West Indian School Children." *Research in Education* 8: 47–55.
Bakan, A., and D. Stasiulis, eds. 1997. *Not One of the Family: Foreign Domestic Workers in Canada.* Toronto: University of Toronto Press.
Beach, C., and C. Worswich. 1993. "Is There a Double-Negative Effect on the Earnings of Immigrant Women?" *Canadian Public Policy* 19: 36–53.
Bellelli, G. and M. Amatulli. 2000. *Nostalgia, Immigration and Collective Memory.* In *Collective Memory of Political Events*, edited by J. Pennebaker. New York: Taylor Francis.
Berger, P., and T. Luckmann. 1966. *The Social Construction of Reality: A Treatise on the Sociology of Knowledge.* Garden City, NY: Anchor Books.

Bernstein, N. 2007. "Special Visas for Victims Remain Elusive Despite a Law." *The New York Times*, B1.
———. 2010. "Do You Take This Immigrant?" *The New York Times*. June 13, 31
Bertrand, D. 1998. "Refugees and Migrants, Migrants and Refugees. An Ethnological Approach." *International Migration* 36, no. 1: 107–11.
Bhabha, J., and S. Shutter. 1994. *Women's Movement: Women under Immigration, National and Refugee Law*. Staffordshire, UK: Trentham Books.
Bhopal, K. 1997. *Gender, Race and Patriarchy: A Study of South Asian Women*. Aldershot: Ashgate.
Black, S. A., K. S. Markides, and T. Q. Miller. 1990. "Correlates of Depressive Symptomatology among Older Community Dwelling Mexican Americans." *The Journals of Gerontology: Series B, Psychological Sciences and Social Sciences* 53: 198–208.
Bloch, A., T. Galvin, and B. Harrell-Bond. 2000. "Refugee Women in Europe: Some Aspects of the Legal and Policy Dimension." *International Migration* 38, no. 2: 169–90.
Boeri, T., G. Hanson, B. McCormick, and H. Brucker. 2002. *Immigration Policy and the Welfare System*. Oxford: Oxford University Press.
Boyd, Monica. 1985. *Ascription and Achievement: Studies in Mobility and Status Attainment in Canada*. Ottawa, Canada: Carleton University Press.
———. 1999. "Gender, Refugee Status and Permanent Settlement." *Gender Issues* 17: 5–24.
Buchanan, Patrick J. 2006. *State of Emergency*. New York: St Martin's Press.
———. www.commonwealthclub.org/achieve/0202-01 Buchanan-Speech.html.
Brown, T. A. 1988. *Migration and Politics*. Chapel Hill: University of North Carolina Press.
Camino, L. 1994. "Refugee Adolescents and Their Changing Identities." In *Reconstructing Lives, Recapturing Meaning: Refugee Identity, Gender and Culture Change*, edited by L. Camino and R. Kruelfeld. Australia: Gordon and Breach.
Camino, L., and R. Kruelfeld, eds. 1994. *Reconstructing Lives, Recapturing Meaning: Refugee Identity, Gender and Culture Change*. Australia: Gordon and Breach.
Campbell, B. 1995. *Welfare Law and Immigration*. Bristol: Jordans.
Cerulo, K. 1997. "Identity Construction: New Issues, New Directions." *Annual Review of Sociology* 23: 385–409.
Chatterjee, P. 1989. "Colonialism, Nationalism, and Colonized Women: The Contest in India." *American Ethnologist* 16: 622–33.
Chell, V. 1997. "Gender-Selective Migration: Somalian and Filipina Women in Rome." In *Southern Europe and the New Migration*, edited by R. King and R. Black. Brighton, UK: Sussex Academic Press.
Equality and Human Rights Commission. 2006. "Factfile 1 Employment and Ethnicity." http://www.cre.gov.uk.
Condero-Guzman, H., R. Smith, and R. Grosfoguel, eds. 2001. *Migration, Transnationalization and Race in a Changing New York*. Philadelphia, PA: Temple University Press.
Dasgupta, S. 2000. "Charting the Course: an Overview of Domestic Violence in the South Asian Community in the United States." *Journal of Social Distress and the Homeless* 9: 173–85.
De Silva, M. 2004. *Le Monde diplomatique*.
Dominguez, V. 1975. *From Neighbor to Stranger: The Dilemma of Caribbean People in the United States*. New Haven, CT: Antilles Research Program, Yale University.
Doty, R. 2003. *Anti-Immigration in Western Democracies: Statecraft, Desire and the Politics of Exclusion*. London: Routledge.

Dugger, C. 1996. "Woman's Pleas for Asylum Puts Tribal Ritual on Trial." *The New York Times*, April 15.

Duleep, H. O., and M. Regets. 1996. "Earnings Convergence: Does It Matter Where Immigrants Come from or Why?" *Canadian Journal of Economic* 29: 130–34.

Espenshade, T., and G. Huber. 1999. "Fiscal Impacts of Immigrants and the Shrinking Welfare State." In *The Handbook of Immigration: the American Experience*, edited by C. Hirschman, Philip Kasinitz, and Joshua Dewind. New York: Russell Sage.

Evans, H. 2007. "Immigrant Wives in Peril. Abuse Follows Them to the U.S." *Daily News*, January 21.

Fawz, C. 1993. "Gender Tensions among Somali Muslims in Britain." *Immigrants and Minorities* 12: 21–46.

Federal Register. Department of Justice. Immigration and Naturalization Service. 8CRF Part 208. 65:236. 76588.

Foner, N. 1999. "Immigrant Women and Work in New York City, Then and Now." *Journal of American Ethnic History* 18: 95–113.

———, ed. 2001. *Islands in the City: West Indians in New York*. Berkeley: University of California Press.

———, ed. 2001. *New Immigrants in New York*. New York: Columbia University Press.

Forst, L., S. Avilia, S. Anozie, and R. Rubin, R. 2009 "Traumatic Occupational Injuries in Hispanic and Foreign Born Workers." *American Journal of Industrial Medicine* 53: 344–51.

Fraeman, A. 2005. "Spain: Immigrant Women Denied Help against Domestic Violence." *IPS—InterPress Service/Global Information Network*.

Gabaccia, Donna. 1994. *From the Other Side: Women, Gender and Immigrant Life in the United States*. Bloomington: Indiana University Press.

George, U., and S. Ramkissoon. 1998. "Race, Gender, and Class: Interlocking Oppressions in the Lives of South Asian Women in Canada." *Affilia* 13: 102–19.

Glennie, A. 2010. "Migration: Development on the Move." http://www.opendemocracy.net/5050/alex-glennie/migration-development-on-the-move.

Goldenberg, A. "The Educational Adjustment of Immigrant Children." *JIAS*. Autumn.

Greenlees, C., and R. Saenz. 1999. "Determinants of Employment of Recently Arrived Mexican Immigrant Wives." *International Migration Review* 33: 354–77.

Griffiths, D. 2002. *Somali and Kurdish Refugees in London*. Aldershot: Ashgate.

Guarnizo, L. 1998. "The Rise of Transnational Social Formations." *Political Power and Social Theory* 12: 45–94.

Hajdukowski-Ahmed, M. 2008. "A Dialogical Approach to Identity: Implications for Refugee Women." In *Not Born a Refugee Woman: Contesting Identities, Rethinking Practices*, by M. Hajdukowski-Ahmed, N. Khanlou, and H. Moussa. New York: Berghahn Books.

Hajdukowski-Ahmend, M., N. Khanlou, and H. Moussa. 2008. *Not Born a Refugee Woman: Contesting Identities, Rethinking Practices*. New York: Berghahn Books.

Hao, L., and M. Bonstead-Burns. 1998. "Parent-Child Differences in Educational Expectations and the Academic Achievement of Immigrant Students." *Sociology of Education* 71: 175–98.

Harzig, Christiane. 2009. *What Is Migration History*. Cambridge: Polity Press.

Hiott, A., J. Grzywacz, T. Arcury, and S. Quandt. 2006. "Gender Differences in Anxiety and Depression among Immigrant Latinos." *Families, Systems and Health* 24: 137–46.

Hirschman, C., P. Kosinitz, and J. DeWaid, eds. *The Handbook of International Migration*. New York: Russell Sage Foundation.

Hondagneu-Sotelo, P. 1995. *Gendered Transitions: Mexican Experiences of Immigration.* Berkeley: University of California Press.

———. 1994. "Regulating the Unregulated? Domestic Workers' Social Networks." *Social Problems* 41: 50–64.

———. 2001. *Domestica: Immigrant Workers Cleaning and Caring in the Shadows of Affluence.* Berkeley: University of California Press.

Hovey, J., and C. King. 1996. "Acculturative Stress, Depression and Suicidal Ideation among Immigrant and Second Generation Latino Adolescents." *Journal of the American Academy of Child and Adolescent Psychiatry* 35: 1183–92.

Howard, J. 2000. "Social Psychology of Identities." *Annual Review of Sociology* 26: 367–93.

Huang, Fung-Yea. 1997. *Asian and Hispanic Immigrant Women in the Work Force: Implications of the United States Immigration Policies since 1965.* New York: Garland.

Jacobson, M. F. 1995. *Special Sorrows: The Diasporic Imagination.* Cambridge, MA: Harvard University Press.

Human Rights Watch. 2001. *Hidden in the Home: Abuse of Domestic Workers with Special Visas in the United States.* Washington, DC: Institute for Policy Studies.

Joly, Daniele, Lynette Kelly, and Clive Nettleson. 1997. London: Minority Rights Group.

Jones, Mary. 1988. *These Obstreperous Lassies: A History of the IWWU.* Dublin: McGill and Macmillan.

Jones-Correa, M. 1998. "Different Paths: Gender, Immigration and Political Participation." *International Migration Review* 23: 326–49.

Jordan, B., and F. Duvell. 2002. *Irregular Immigration: The Dilemmas of Transnational Mobility.* Cheltenham, UK: Edward Elgar.

Kang, M. 2003. "The Managed Hand: The Commercialization of Bodies and Emotion in Korean Nail Salons." *Gender and Society* 18: 820–39.

Kay, Diana. 1989. "The Politics of Gender in Exile Chilean Glasgow." In *Reluctant Hosts: Europe and Its Refugees*, by D. Joly and R. Cohen. Hants, UK: Aldershot.

Kelson, G., and D. Delaet. 1999. *Gender and Immigration.* New York: New York University Press.

Kibria, N. 1990. "Power, Patriarchy, and Gender Conflict in the Vietnamese Immigrant Community." *Gender and Society* 4: 9–24.

Kim, Y. 2008. "Asylum Law and Female Genital Mutilation." *CRS Report for Congress*, February 15.

King, R., and R. Black. 1997. *Southern Europe and the New Immigrations.* Brighton, UK: Sussex University Press.

Kleinberg, O. 1979. "An Interdisciplinary and International Perspective." In *A Quarter Century of International Social Science*, edited by R. Stein. New Delhi: Concept Publishing.

Kleiner, J. 1977. "On Nostalgia." In *The World of Emotions*, by C. W. Socarides. New York: International University Press.

Koslowski, R. 2000. *Migrants and Citizens: Demographic Change in the European State System.* Ithaca, NY: Cornell University Press.

Kotlowitz, A. 2007. "Asylum for the World's Battered Women." *The New York Times Magazine.* February 11.

Lawyers Committee for Human Rights. 2004. *Refugee Women at Risk: Unfair US Laws Hurt Asylum Seekers.* New York: Women's Commission for Refugee Women and Children.

Liebig, T. 2007. "The Labour Market Integration of Immigrants in Germany." *OECD Social, Employment and Migration Working Papers.*

Loescher, Gil. 1993. *Beyond Charity: International Cooperation and the Global Refugee Crisis.* New York: Oxford University Press.
Luibheid, Eithne. 2002. *Entry Denied.* Minneapolis: University of Minnesota Press.
Marcelli, E. A. 1999. "Undocumented Latino Immigrant Workers: The Los Angeles Experience." In *Illegal Immigration in America: A Reference Handbook*, edited by D. W. Haines and K. E. Rosenblum. Westport, CT: Greenwood Press.
Martin, P. 2000. Smuggling and Trafficking: A Conference Report. *International Migration Review* 34, no. 3: 969–975.
Massey, D. 2004. *Crossing the Border.* New York: Russell Sage.
Mattingly, D. 2001. "The Home and the World: Domestic Service and International Networks of Caring Labor." *Annals of the Association of American Geographers* 91: 370–86.
McGown, R. Berns. 1999. *Muslims in the Diaspora: The Somali Communities of London and Toronto.* Toronto: Toronto University Press.
McVeigh, T., and T. Sutton. 2010. "British Girls Undergo Horror of Genital Mutilation Despite Touch Laws." *The Observer*, July 25.
Mehta, C., N. Theodore, I. Mora, and J. Wade. 2002. "Chicago's Undocumented Immigrants: An Analysis of Wages, Working Conditions and Economic Contributions." Chicago: Center for Urban Development.
Menjivar, C. 1999. "The Intersection of Work and Gender: Central American Immigrant Women and Employment in California." *American Behavioral Scientist* 42: 601–27.
———. 2002. "Living in Two Worlds? Guatemalan Origin Children in the United States and Emerging Transnationalism." *Journal of Ethnic and Migration Studies* 28, no. 3: 531–52.
Menjivar, C., and O. Salcido. 2002. "Immigrant Women and Domestic Violence: Common Experiences in Different Countries." *Gender and Society* 16: 898–920.
Meyers, D. 2006. "Immigration in France." http://www.migrationpolicy.org.
Min, P. G. 2001. "Changes in Korean Immigrants' Gender Roles and Social Status and Their Marital Conflicts." *Sociological Forum* 16: 301–18.
Minde, K., and R. Minde. 1976. "Children of Immigrants: The Adjustment of Ugandan Asian Primary School Children in Canada." *Canadian Psychiatric Journal* 21: 371–81.
Mirdal, G. M. 1984. "Stress and Distress in Migration: Problems and Resources of Turkish Women in Denmark." *International Migration Review* 18: 984–1003.
Monahan, J. 2006. "Plan for Immigrants Call Threat to Abuse Victims." *Telegram and Gazette* (Boston).
———. 2006. "Romney Plan for Immigrants Called Threat to Abuse Victims: Critic Says Battered Women Won't Ask Police for Help." *Telegram and Gazette* (Worcester), A3.
Monsen, J. H. 1999. *Gender, Migration and Domestic Service.* London: Routledge.
Moore, J., K. Musalo, and R. Boswell. 1997. *Refugee Law and Policy: Cases and Materials.* Durham, NC: Carolina Academic Press.
Munscher, Alice. 1984. "The Working Routines of Turkish Women in the Federal Republic of Germany: Results of a Pilot Study." *International Migration Review* 18, no. 4: 1230–45.
OECD (Organisation for Economic Co-operation and Development). 2006. "Employment and Labour Market Statistics." Paris: OECD.
O'Sullivan, Patrick, ed. 1995. *Irish Women and Irish Immigration.* London: Leicester University Press.
Pearce, S. 2006. *Immigrant Women in the United States: A Demographic Portrait.* Washington, DC: American Immigration Law Foundation.

Permits Foundation. www.permitsfoundation.com
Phillips, Caryl. 2007. *Foreigners*. New York: Knopf.
Pessar, P. 1999. "The Role of Gender, Households and Social Networks in the Migration Process: A Review and Appraisal." In *The Handbook of International Migration: The American Experience*, by C. Hirschman, P. Kasinitz, and J. DeWind. New York: Russell Sage Foundation.
Pessar, P., and P. Graham. 2001. "Dominicans: Transnational Identities and Local Politics." In *New Immigrants in New York*, edited by N. Foner. New York: Columbia University Press.
Phizacklea, A. 2009. *Gender and Migration: West Indians in Comparative Perspective*. London: Routledge and Kegan Paul.
———. *Migration and Mobilization: A Feminist Perspective*.
Portes, A. 1999. "Immigration Theory of a New Century." In *The Handbook of Immigration: the American Experience*, edited by C. Hirschman, Philip Kasinitz, and Joshua Dewind. New York: Russell Sage.
Powell, Enoch. 1968. "Rivers of Blood." Speech given at the General Meeting of Midlands Area Conservative Political Center. April 20.
Powers, M., and W. Seltzer. 1998. "Occupational Status and Mobility among Undocumented Immigrants by Gender." *International Migration Review* 32: 21–55.
Pumariega, A., E. Rothe, and J. Pumariega. 2005. "Mental Health of Immigrants and Refugees." *Community Mental Health Journal*. 41: 581–97.
Plyler v Doe 457 US 202 (1982).
Quack, S. 1995. *Between Sorrow and Pity*. Cambridge, UK: Cambridge University Press. http://Cabinetoffice.gov.uk /reaching out:think family (June 2007)
Raghuram, Parvati. 2004. "Migration, Gender, and the IT Sector: Intersecting Debates." *Women's Studies International Forum* 27: 163–75.
Raijman, Rebecca, and Moshe Semyonov. 1997. "Gender, Ethnicity, and Immigration: Double Disadvantage among Recent Immigrant Women in the Israeli Labor Market." *Gender and Society* 11: 108–25.
Ramos, E. R. 2000. *The Legal Construction of Identity: The Judicial and Social Legacy of American Colonialism in Puerto Rico*. Washington, DC: American Psychological Association.
Rassool, N. 1999. "Flexible Identities: Exploring Race and Gender Issues among a Group of Immigrant Pupils in an Inner-City Comprehensive School." *British Journal of Sociology of Education* 20: 23–36.
Repak, T. 1995. *Waiting on Washington: Central American Workers in the Nation's Capital*. Philadelphia, PA: Temple University Press.
Rimote, N. 1991. "A Quest of Culture and Cultural Approval of Violence against Women in Pacific-Asian Communities and Cultural Defense." *Stanford Law Review* 43: 1311–26.
Robertson, C. L., L. Halcon, K. Savik, D. Johnson, and M. Spring 2006. "Somali and Orono Refugees Women: Trauma and Associated Factors." *Advanced Journal of Nursing* 56: 577–87.
Ryan, L. 2003. "Moving Spaces and Changing Places: Irish Women's Memories of Emigration to Britain in the 1930s." *Journal of Ethnic and Migration Studies* 29, no. 1: 67–82.
Summers, D. 2009, January 3. "White Working-Class Fears on Immigration Exposed in Report." *The Guardian*, 9.
Salih, R. 2001. "Moroccan Migrant Women: Transnationalist, Nation-State and Gender." *Journal of Ethnic and Migration Studies* 27, no. 4: 655–71.

———. 2003. *Gender in Transnationalism: Home, Longing and Belonging among Moroccan Women*. London: Routledge.
Schaeter, T. 1998. *Race, Class, Women and the State: The Case of Domestic Labour in Canada*. Toronto: Black Rose Books.
Schoeni, R. 1998. "Labor Market Outcomes of Immigrant Women in the United States: 1970 to 1990." *International Migration Review* 32: 57–77.
Scott, R., and W. Scott. 1991. "Children's Personality as a Function of Family Relations within and between Cultures." *Journal of Cross Cultural Psychology* 22: 182–208.
———. 1998. *Adjustment of Adolescents*. New York: Routledge.
Shukla, S. 1997. "Building Diaspora and the Nation: The 1991 'Cultural Festival of India.'" *Cultural Studies* 11: 296–315.
Simcox, D. 1988. *U.S. Immigration in the 1980's: Reappraisal and Reform*. Boulder, CO: Westview Press.
Stier, H., and M. Tienda. 1992. "Family Work and Women: The Labor Supply of Hispanic Immigrant Wives." *Intternational Migration Review* 26: 1291–1311.
Tajfel, H., and J. Turner. 1986. "The Social Identity Theory of Intergroup Behavior." In *Psychology of Intergroup Relations*, by S. Worchel and W. G. Austin. Chicago: Nelson.
Takac, M. 1976. *Problems of Immigrant Children*. Gothenburg: City Council.
Talahite, A. 2000. "Constructing Spaces of Transition: 'Beur' Women Writers and the Question of Representation." In *Women, Immigration and Identities in France*, by J. Freedman and C. Tarr. Oxford: Berg.
Tang, T., K. Oatley, and B. Toner. 2007. "Impact of Life Events and Difficulties on the Mental Health of Chinese Immigrant Women." *Journal of Immigrant and Minority Mental Health* 9: 281–90.
Tapinos, Georges. 2000. *Combatting the Illegal Employment of Foreign Workers*. Paris: OECD.
Tarr, C. 2000. "Where Women Tread." In *Women, Immigration and Identities in France*, by J. Freedman and C. Tarr. Oxford: Berg.
Tuan Anh Nguyen et al. v INS. 533 U.S. (2001).
UNHCR. March 18, 2008. "Asylum Levels and Trends in Industrialized Countries, 2007 Statistical Overview of Asylum Applications in Europe and Selected Non- European Countries." New York: United Nations.
UNHCR. *Statistical Yearbook 2006 Trends in Displacement, Protection and Solutions*. New York: United Nations.
UN Statistical Yearbook. 2001. Vol. 56. New York: United Nations..
US Census Bureau. "US Census Bureau Statistical Abstracts of the United States." Washington, DC: US Census Bureau.
Vernez, Georges. 1999. *Immigrant Women in the US Workforce: Who Struggles? Who Succeeds?* Lanham, MD: Lexington Books.
White, J. 1999. "Turks in the New Germany: Images of Self and Images of Self against Other." *American Anthropologist* 99, no. 4: 754–69.
Wihtol de Wenden, C., R. Leveay, and K. Mohsen-Finan. 2001. *L'Islam en France et en Allemagne: identites et citoyennetes*. Paris: La documentation Francaise.
Wilke, I. 1975. "Schooling of Immigrant Children in Germany, Sweden, England: The Educationally Disadvantaged." *International Review of Education* 21, no. 3: 357–82.
Women's Commission for Refugee Women and Children. 2009. "Refugees Defined as Terrorists: Human Rights First Report featured in Washington Post." http://www.humanrightsfirst.org/refugees.

Young, W. 1997. "U.S. Detention of Women Asylum Seekers: Failing to Practice What We Preach." http://www.refugees.org/world/articles.detention_women_wrs97.

Yuval-Davis, N. 1997. *Gender and Nation*. London: Sage.

———. 2005. "Gender and Nationalist Imagining: War and Peace." In *Gender and Conflict Zones*, edited by W. Giles and J. Hyndman, 170–93. Berkeley: University of California Press.

Zetter, R., D. Griffiths, S. Feretti, and M. Pearl. 2003. "An Assessment of the Impact of Asylum Policies in Europe 1990–2000." *Home Office Research Study 259*. London: Home Office Research Development and Statistics Directorate.

Zinn, M. B., P. Hondagneu-Sotelo, and M. Messner. 2005. *Gender through the Prism of Difference*. New York: Oxford University Press.

Zhou, Min, and R. Nordquist. 1994. "Work and Its Place in the Lives of Immigrant Women: Garment Workers in New York City's Chinatown." *Applied Behavioral Science Review* 2: 201.

Zulauf, M. 2001. *Migrant Women Professionals in the European Union*. Basingstoke: Palgrave Macmillan.

Index

Abay v. Ashcroft (2004), 71
Abraham, M., 93, 153
Adams, John Quincy, 52
Addams, Jane, 87
Afghanistan, 1, 33, 66, 71, 74
Agger, I., 105
Akhtar, S., 153
Albor, R., 95
alcoholism, 95, 101
Aliens Act (1905), 24–25, 27
amnesty, 33, 40, 59, 61, 119, 124
Amnesty International, 96
Andrall, J., 8, 12, 117, 148
Anthias, F., 117
anti-immigration sentiment
   Europe and, 4, 59, 81, 83, 125
   family unification and, 51
   government policy and, 25, 29, 75, 144
   stereotypes and, 4, 52, 111–12
   United States and, 4, 59
   violence and, 4–5
Aronowitz, M., 100
arranged marriages, 50, 99, 147, 152
assimilation, 9–10, 23, 34–35, 58, 102, 156
asylum seekers
   applications, 30, 63–66
   categorization of, 37
   criteria for, 66–75
   humanitarian grounds for, 63–64, 75–77

   illegal aliens and, 57
   increase in number of, 31–34, 124–25
   men as, 45
   persecution and, 71–74
   policies regarding, 14–15, 39–40, 63–66
   social identity and, 89, 92, 100
   stereotypes of, 1, 3–4, 111
   studies on, 31
   temporary asylum, 82–84
   United Kingdom and, 24, 63
   United States and, 23, 30, 63, 77–79
   Western Europe and, 79–82
   women as, 7, 12, 105–7, 122, 143–45, 149–50, 155–56

Bagley, C., 100
Bakan, A., 56, 118
Bangladesh, 70, 90, 93, 120–24, 131, 143
Beach, C., 120
Bellelli, G., 155
Berger, P., 14
Bernstein, N., 46, 96
Bertrand, D., 37
Bhabha, J., 44, 151
bias, gender and, 45, 54, 75
Black, S. A., 156
Bloch, A., 69, 75
Boeri, T., 58

Bosnia, 64, 70, 156
Boyd, Monica, 40, 44, 60, 66, 69, 77
British Alien Act (1905), 24–25
British National Party (BNP), 4
Brown, T. A., 153
Buchanan, Patrick, 3
Buck, Pearl, 139
Bureau of Border Security (BBS), 30
Bureau of Citizenship and Immigration Services (BCIS), 30

Camino, L., 93, 95, 98, 100
Campbell, B., 53
Canada
   asylum seekers and, 31–33, 63, 66, 69, 72–74, 76
   caregivers and, 56
   family unification and, 40, 43–44
   illegal aliens and, 57
   immigrant children and, 100–101
   immigration and, 1, 3, 6
   immigration policies, 22–24
   solo immigration and, 52
   United States and, 6, 144, 147
   women immigrants and, 7, 12–13, 113–14, 117, 119–20, 123, 148
Cerulo, K., 14
Chatterjee, Partha, 97, 102, 153
Chell, V., 36, 91, 146, 148
China, 1–2, 21, 23–24, 33–34, 38, 90, 94, 131, 150
Chinese Exclusion Act (1882), 24
Commonwealth Immigration Act (1962), 29
Condero-Guzman, H., 116

Darfur, 1, 70
Dasgupta, S., 94Deferred Enforced Departure (DED), 82–83
Denmark, 5, 66, 83, 90, 94, 120–21, 133–34, 136
dependent status, 6, 15–16, 23, 25–27, 30, 39, 40–45, 48–50, 53–55, 61, 67, 85

deportation, 22, 25, 39–40, 43–45, 48, 58–61, 67, 72–73, 76, 78, 81, 93, 95–96, 114, 116, 121–22, 124–25, 131, 150
De Silva, M., 125, 150, 152
Diner, Hasia, 12
disease, 3, 7, 52
domestic abuse, 43, 45, 73, 95–96, 150
Dominguez, V., 117
Doty, R., 8, 149, 154
dowry murder, 69, 73, 84. *See also* honor killing; murder
drug trade, 2–3, 5–6
Dugger, C., 78
Duleep, H. O., 51

education
   anti-immigrant sentiment and, 4, 60
   asylum seekers and, 83, 85
   children and, 4–5, 48–49, 57, 59, 100–103
   effect on immigrant experience, 12–13, 100, 107, 143
   ethnic communities and, 89, 92, 98
   family unification and, 43
   gender persecution and, 71
   identity and, 92, 95–96, 143–48, 150–51, 154, 156
   immigrant work force and, 6, 53–54
   immigration policy and, 60–61, 75
   UN protocols and, 39
   women and, 35, 50, 61, 109–11, 113–14, 116, 118–24, 127, 129–36
employment gap, 115, 130
English Defense League (EDL), 4
Erin's Daughter in America (Diner), 12
Espenshade, T., 4
ethnic communities, identity and
   asylum seekers, 105–6
   domestic violence, 93–97

education for children, 100–103
gender norms, 97–100
gender relationships, 91–93
overview, 89–90
women immigrating solo, 103–4
ethnic profiling, 6
European Human Dignity and Social Exclusion Project (HDSE), 49
European Union (EU), 31, 33, 57, 63, 76, 120–21, 126
Evans, H., 93, 95
Exceptional Leave to Remain (ELR), 82–83

family unification programs
asylum seekers and, 66–67, 79, 83, 85, 105
creation of, 25
dependents and, 61
Europe and, 29–30, 124–25, 127–29
Exceptional Leave to Remain (ELR) and, 83
gender and, 66–67
H-1B and, 53–54
immigrant community and, 103–4
predominance of, 40–51
solo immigration and, 52–53, 55
United Kingdom and, 41, 44–46, 49–50, 52, 59, 121
United States, 7, 25, 30
women and, 10, 26, 61–62, 79, 90, 92–93, 95, 106–7, 113, 143–52, 155
Fawz, C., 94
female genital mutilation (FGM), 69, 71–74, 77–78, 81, 84, 99
Foner, N., 99, 103, 112, 131, 135
Fraeman, A., 96
France, 4–5, 12, 22, 24, 26, 28–29, 31, 45, 48–50, 52–53, 55, 57–60, 66, 76, 80–81, 83, 90, 124–29, 134, 137, 142, 152
From Sicily to Elizabeth Street (Gabaccia), 12

Gabaccia, Donna, 12, 26
gender persecution, 69–74, 77
genital mutilation. *See* female genital mutilation
George, U., 93, 148, 150
Germany, 3–4, 22, 24, 26, 28–29, 31, 44, 47–48, 50–53, 55, 59, 63, 66–67, 70, 73, 76, 80–82, 90, 94, 98, 101, 112, 120–21, 128–30, 133–34, 136–37, 142, 147, 149, 152
Glennie, A., 35, 147
Goldenberg, A., 100
government policies, women immigrants and
family unification, 40–51
illegal aliens, 57–60
overview, 39–40
solo immigration, 52–55
temporary work visas, 55–57
Great Britain
anti-immigrant sentiment, 2, 4–5, 60
asylum seekers and, 31, 63, 67, 70, 73–74, 76–77, 79, 82–83
family unification and, 41, 44–46, 49–50, 52, 59, 121
historical immigration, 21–23
immigrant identity and, 91–93, 97, 99, 101, 147
immigration policy, 24–25, 27–29, 41
increase in immigrant population, 31, 33, 90
temporary work visas, 55
women immigrants and, 12–13, 103–4, 106, 113, 117, 120–25, 127–28, 131–34, 142–44
Greenlees, C., 111
Griffiths, D., 149
Guarnizo, L., 153

Haiti, 1–2, 57
Hajdukowski-Ahmed, M., 4, 12, 14, 50, 67, 74
Hao, L., 101

Harzig, Christiane, 12
health care, access to, 5, 59–60, 98, 111
health care workers, 10, 35, 54–57, 61, 90, 103, 113–14, 120
Hiott, A., 154
Homeland Security, 30, 49, 57, 59, 72, 78–79, 82, 96, 116
Hondagneu-Sotelo, P., 11, 92, 115–16, 131, 133, 151, 153
honor killing, 73, 84, 92. *See also* dowry murder; murder
Hovey, J., 154
Howard, J., 14
Huang, Fung-Yea, 35
Human Rights Watch, 77, 115

illegal aliens, 1, 15, 37, 43, 57–60, 81, 83, 96, 116
Illegal Immigration Reform and Immigrant Responsibility Act (1996), 72, 78
Immigrant Victims of Violence Protection Act (2005), 96
Immigration Acts (1917, 1921, 1924, 1952, 1965), 25, 26, 30, 53, 59
Immigration and Naturalization Service (INS), 30, 52, 78
Immigration and Refugee Protection Act (2002), 43
Immigration Marriage Fraud Amendment (1986), 43
Immigration Nursing Relief Act (1989), 56
Immigration Reform and Control Act (1986), 30
Italy, 4–5, 28, 31–33, 35–36, 48, 52, 55, 66, 80–82, 90, 112, 117, 121
IT workers, 53–54, 143, 146

Jacobson, M. F., 91
Johnson-Reed Act (1924), 25
Joly, Danielle, 69
Jones, Mary, 26
Jones-Correa, M., 91–92, 153
Jordan, B., 3
"jus sanguinis," 31

Kang, M., 132
Kay, Diana, 91
Kelson, G., 93
Kibria, N., 92, 95, 151–52
Kim, Y., 72
King, R., 147
kinship, 35, 153, 155
Kleinberg, O., 100
Kleiner, J., 89
Koslowski, R., 31
Kosovo, 82
Kotlowitz, A., 72

Legal Construction of Identity, The (Ramos), 13
Le Pen, Jean-Marie, 125
Lewis v. Gross (1986), 43
Liberia, 70, 82
Liebig, T., 47, 51, 129
Loescher, Gil, 65
Luckman, T., 14
Luibheid, Eithne, 25

maids, 2, 10, 115, 117, 126, 133, 136–37, 153
Marcelli, E. A., 57
Martin, P., 52, 68
Massey, D., 11
Mattingly, D., 114
McCarran Walter Immigration and Naturalization Act (1952), 25
McGown, R. Berns, 106, 149
McVeigh, T., 77
Mehta, C., 115, 119
Menjivar, C., 93, 100, 116, 154
Meyers, D., 50
Min, P. G., 94, 111, 117, 132, 135
Minde, K., 101
minimum wage, 115, 119
Mirdal, G. M., 133
Monahan, J., 95–96

Monsen, J. H., 146
Morrison-Lautenberg Amendment, 65–66
Munscher, Alice, 128–29, 133, 149
murder, 4, 69, 96. *See also* dowry murder; honor killing

NAFTA Implementation Act (1993), 55
nannies, 2, 10, 136–37, 147–48
Naredo, Maria, 96
needle trades, 117–18
Netherlands, 2, 4–5, 28, 31, 49, 67, 83, 112, 121

Organisation for Economic Co-operation and Development (OECD), 112–14, 120–21
O'Sullivan, Patrick, 26

Page Act (1875), 23
Pakistan, 1, 33, 90, 93, 120–24, 131
passports, confiscation of, 116
Pearce, S., 119
permanent alien status, 9
permanent residency, 6, 23, 25, 30, 39–53, 56–57, 64, 77, 82, 96, 121–22, 126
Pessar, P., 12, 35, 104
Phillips, Caryl, 101
Phizlackea, A., 117, 143
Plyer v. Doe (1982), 59
Portes, A., 8
Powell, Enoch, 29
Powers, M., 119
prostitution, 2, 7, 23, 26, 52, 69–70, 73, 104, 116
Pumariega, A., 154, 156

Quack, S., 92

Raghuram, Parvati, 54
Raijman, Rebecca, 54
Ramos, Rivera, 13–14

rape, 67, 69–70, 72–73, 78–79, 84, 96
Rassool, N., 101
Refugee Act (1980), 65, 77
refugee policy, women and
 asylum based on humanitarian concerns, 75–77
 forms of gendered persecution, 69–71
 gender and, 66–69
 overview, 63–66
 patterns of generalized gender persecution, 71–74
 refugee status, 74–75
 temporary asylum, 82–84
 US asylum policy, 77–79
 Western Europe and, 79–82
regulation, immigration and
 immigrants at end of twentieth century, 30–36
 immigration status, 37
 introduction of immigration controls, 24–27
 overview, 21–23
 twentieth century immigration policy, 27–30
remittances, 35
Repak, T., 119
Rimote, N., 94
Robertson, C. L., 105
Roosevelt, Theodore, 25
Rothe, E. M., 154, 156
Ryan, L., 103–4

Salih, R., 36, 147, 154
Sarkozy, Nicolas, 50, 53
Schaeter, T., 118
Schoeni, R., 112–13
school. *See* education
Scott, R., 152, 154
sex trafficking, 2
sexual harassment, 34, 59, 116–17
sexually transmitted diseases, 7, 52
Sharia law, 5
Shukla, S., 89

Simcox, D., 43, 58, 66
social identity
  adjusting to change, 151–54
  motives for migrating, 145–51
  nostalgia and, 154–56
  overview, 141–45
social identity theory, 14
Somalia, 33, 36, 82, 90–91, 93, 106, 121, 133–34, 149, 156
Stier, H., 110, 118
Summers, D., 4
Switzerland, 5, 28

"tagalongs," 8
Tajfel, H., 14
Takac, M., 101
Talahite, A., 156
Taliban, 1, 71
Tarr, C., 156
temporary asylum, 40, 77, 82–84
temporary work visas
  domestic workers and, 36, 61, 90
  ethnic community and, 15–16, 92–93
  family and, 40–42, 47, 51, 61, 63
  government policies and, 53, 55–57
  H-1B visas, 53–55, 114
  highly skilled workers and, 49, 53
  illegal aliens and, 57–58
  overstaying of, 57–58
  women immigrants and, 7, 10, 40, 61, 90, 92–93, 103, 144–46, 149
torture, 64, 69–71, 84
Tuan Anh Nguyen et al. v. INS (2001), 52
Turkey
  earthquake in, 1
  emigrant women in Germany, 28, 44, 47, 94, 98, 128–30, 136, 142, 149, 152
  Europe and, 21, 90, 136
  France and, 126
  Germany and, 28, 44, 90, 133

undocumented workers. *See also* illegal aliens
  ethnic community and, 9
  identity and, 93, 96, 104, 106, 156
  immigration and, 33
  immigration law and, 6, 61, 124–26
  immigration status and, 37, 40
  increase in number of, 31
  job tips and, 130
  wages and, 36
  women and, 111–19, 122, 130, 135
United Nations (UN), 37, 64–65, 68–71, 73, 75–77, 84–85
United Nations High Commission for Refugees (UNHCR), 7, 27, 31–33, 63, 74–75, 78–79, 81
United States
  anti-immigrant sentiment in, 3–6, 59
  asylum seekers and, 23, 30, 63, 77–79
  Canada and, 6, 144, 147
  family unification and, 7, 25, 30
  illegal immigration and, 2
  immigrant heritage, 2–3, 22–23
  immigration policy, 6–7, 9, 15, 28–35
  introduction of immigration controls, 24–27
  sex trafficking and, 2
  slavery and, 22

violence
  anti-immigrant sentiment and, 4–5
  as cause for immigration, 8, 35, 69–70, 81, 105
  domestic violence, 45, 59, 67, 72–73, 90, 92–96, 106–7, 117, 136, 150
  women and, 69–70, 152
visas
  administration of, 30, 52–53, 84
  confiscation of, 116

domestic workers and, 117, 122, 148
European Union and, 76
gender and, 113–14
H-1B visas, 53–55, 114
illegal immigration and, 57–58
preference visas, 30
U Visas, 96

wage gap, 54, 113–15, 119–20, 130
Walmart, 2
welfare
  asylum and, 75–77
  cost of, 5
  dependence on, 6, 77, 83, 85, 107, 144
  illegal aliens and, 59–60
  immigrants and, 4–5
  legislation and, 50, 75
  stereotypes of, 4, 52, 60, 107, 111–12, 144
White, J., 94, 98, 152
Wihtol de Wenden, C., 59, 126
Wilke, I., 101
work force, immigrants and
  anti-immigrant sentiment and, 3, 5, 125
  attitudes toward women in, 130–34
  discrimination and, 12, 16, 127
  ethnic community and, 15, 130–34
  H-1B program and, 53–54
  identity and, 94, 103
  illegal aliens and, 58
  overview, 109–12
  quality of jobs, 23, 28, 34–36, 47, 51, 91, 94, 97, 113–14
  temporary work permits and, 55–57
  training for, 85
  women and, 109–10, 114–24, 127–29, 130–36
World War I, 3, 21, 25, 27, 70
World War II, 3, 27–28, 31, 37, 41–42, 44, 51, 70, 118, 125

xenophobia, 4, 48, 51, 81, 83, 111–12, 128

Young, W., 78
Yuval-Davis, N., 9, 91, 97

Zetter, R., 76
Zulauf, M., 114

Printed in the United States of America